Charles Seale-Hayne Library

University of Plymouth

(01752) 588 588

LibraryandITenquiries@plymouth.ac.uk

Bringing the World to Early Modern Europe

Bringing the World to Early Modern Europe

Travel Accounts and Their Audiences

Edited by

Peter Mancall

BRILL

LEIDEN · BOSTON
2007

This book is printed on acid-free paper.

Library of Congress Cataloging-in-Publication Data

A C.I.P. record for this book is available from the Library of Congress.

ISBN-13: 978 90 04 15403 2
ISBN-10: 90 04 15403 5

PRINTED IN THE NETHERLANDS

CONTENTS

The content of this volume is a reprint of Volume 10, Nos. 1–2 (2006) of
Journal of Early Modern History

INTRODUCTION:
WHAT FYNES MORYSON KNEW

PETER C. MANCALL

Fynes Moryson, the son of a member of the English Parliament, saw much of early modern Europe. Born in 1566, he studied law at Cambridge but found his true calling, as many others did, when he went to see the world. He first left England on May 1, 1591 and during the next four years he traipsed through northern Europe, making stops in Germany, Denmark, Austria, and Poland before he reached Italy in October 1593. After returning briefly to England in 1595, he set out again, this time to the Adriatic and the Mediterranean. He visited the greatest capitals of the ancient world, including Jerusalem, Constantinople, Antioch, and Tripoli before he went back to London in 1597. He spent the next twenty years, as far as can be learned from the extant sources, either in England or Ireland. During that time he wrote a long account of his travels. And then he burned it. Fortunately, his dissatisfaction with his initial attempt did not turn him from the idea of writing about his travels. Instead, he produced a journal that is among the most remarkable of the early modern age. It was published in London in 1617. Moryson apparently died soon after.

Moryson's *Itinerary . . . Containing His Ten Yeeres Travell through the Twelve Dominions of Germany, Bohmerland, Sweitzerland, Netherland, Denmarke, Poland, Italy, Turky, France, England, Scotland and Ireland* presented his observations about much of Europe and the Mediterranean world during the closing decades of the sixteenth century. But it is more than a typical traveler's account. Whatever might be said about Moryson's judgment about the peoples and civilizations he encountered—he was, after all, caught up in the predictable biases of his age—he left something valuable to posterity: a set of recommendations for how travelers should behave when they were abroad and when they returned home again. He called this part of his book "Precepts for Travellers, which may instruct the unexperienced." In it he offered perhaps the most sustained early modern European analysis of the nature of travel as an act to be both undertaken and then systematically analyzed.[1]

Moryson's "Precepts" consisted of a list of 27 items that all travelers needed to know. He aimed the vast majority of his comments at the inexperienced, though he also made suggestions for those who had already made journeys. He began by telling travelers to pray daily, and then offered a series of highly practical recommendations. He instructed them to make sure they had a trustworthy associate in their home town who could maintain good relations with a local merchant, who could provide credit for the traveler. Such associates were especially important since it was often dangerous to carry money abroad. But travelers needed to make other preparations too. They should be skilled in cosmography, prepare a will, make amends with any enemies before departure, and study local languages, preferably in selected cities known for the purity of the residents' command of their native language. Some of the precepts were precise. An English traveler, for example, should go first to Germany, where he would eat poorly and sleep in an uncomfortable bed, and in the process learn "to moderate our aptness to quarrel." Entering a city, the traveler should quickly climb to the top of a high steeple to get an accurate sense of the layout of the community. In Germany he should also be certain to ask the town's doctor for information. Such a gesture would appeal to the native's inflated sense of himself. "For as Weomen easily beleeve such as tell them that they are faire, though indeed they bee deformed," Moryson noted, "so men of best quality will easily beleeve, that their name is knowne among strangers, and they take these visitations for honours done unto them." Travelers should not be accompanied by a friend from home, but it did make sense to bring "some good Booke." Of course, a companion could offer useful protection, but a lone traveler would have to make do by locking the door wherever he slept at night, hiding money under the pillow, and sleeping with a sword by the side of the bed. Travelers could prepare themselves for further hardships by avoiding wine and by fasting, but it was not necessary to learn how to swim.[2]

Moryson was concerned about the internal effects of travel too, including the relation between mind and body. "I will onely say," he wrote, "that mirth is a great preserver of health, and sadnesse a very plague

---

[1] Fynes Moryson, *An Itinerary . . . Containing His Ten Yeeres Travel* (London, 1617), part III, Book 1, 11-37.
[2] Moryson, *Itinerary*, 9-19, quotations at 17, 19.

thereunto. The bodie followes the temper of the mind, as the temper of the mind followes that of the body." He spoke from experience, having twice been on the verge of death. He also offered tips for those suffering from sea sickness and the base unpleasantness of being on a long journey. "To avoid the ill smelles of the ship" it would be best to carry red roses or their dried leaves, or at least oranges, lemons, or herbs.[3]

Moryson understood that the sum of travel was equal to more than accumulated experiences. There was a psychology to the journey that every traveler needed to understand. A traveler should not condemn unfamiliar acts: "Let him reprove nothing in another mans house, much lesse in a strange Common wealth[.]" Similarly a traveler should dress to blend with the locals, and act humbly too. Those venturing into new lands needed to contain their curiosity, the trait that killed Pliny when he went to see the eruption of Mount Aetna, and many needed to conceal their religion lest they arouse the hostility of their hosts.[4] Travelers should also be wary about making quick judgments about other societies. Perceptions of women's behavior, for example, could be misleading. Italians in England took the women "for Harlots, who are much chaster then their Women would be, having liberty as ours have." Virgins in Holland skated far from home in the company of young men, but that did not mean they were having sex.[5]

For all of his own hard-won wisdom, Moryson knew that it was crucial to encourage others to tell their tales too. He recognized that travelers had much to offer because they had seen distant places with their own eyes. As a result, they gained authority. But that standing came with certain responsibilities, such as observing "the underwritten things," including the natural resources of a distant land. Moryson offered specific guidelines for producing an authoritative account. Because "the memory is weake," it was important for travelers to take notes "for hee lesse offends that writes many toyes, then he that omits one serious thing." A traveler should "write these notes each day, at morne and even in his Inne, within writing Tables carried about him, and after at leasure into a paper booke, that many years after he may looke over them at his pleasure." Writers needed to preserve these papers, especially in dangerous locales. If the traveler could follow all of Moryson's

---

[3] Moryson, *Itinerary*, 22-23.
[4] Moryson, *Itinerary*, 23-25, 30.
[5] Moryson, *Itinerary*, 34.

precepts and return home, he should share what he learned. "I advise him, that after his returne, he sparingly & not without intreaty, relate his journeys and observations." He should do so "eloquently and judicially." If "stale Harlots" could "make their putrified wares saleable" by telling tales, "how much more shall Travellers, whose discourse more pleaseth in the stomack then in the mouth, make the very stones and insensible creatures to daunce and hang upon their mouthes, as they are said to have been moved by the eloquence and musick of *Ulysses* and *Orpheus*."[6]

Moryson's "Precepts" carried authority because they accompanied his lengthy report about his years on the road. By including these suggestions, he provided a service to others who ventured out and enriched the minds of those who stayed at home. Every traveler wanted to be believed. Every writer and publisher of travel accounts sought to shape tales of adventure and exotica for eager readers.

*

The publication of Moryson's *Itinerary* in 1617 came at a decisive moment in a larger European intellectual project. Narratives of journeys had been popular in Europe at least since manuscripts describing Mandeville's fabulous account spread across the continent in the fifteenth century. The return of Christopher Columbus in 1493 encouraged the publication of many more accounts, especially those that described aspects of the Western Hemisphere.[7] By the middle of the sixteenth century so many travel stories were circulating in Europe that publishers and editors produced not single narratives but instead collections of reports.

The essays here focus on accounts that span the period from the late sixteenth century through the era of Moryson to the late eighteenth century. As these articles and much other modern scholarship reveal, a small number of individuals propelled the rising popularity of travel accounts in Europe. Among these literati was Giovanni Battista Ramusio (1485-1557), a Venetian geographer and secretary to the Council of Ten, who collected and published three volumes of travel accounts published as *Navigationi e Viaggi* (Venice, 1550-1559). Within a generation of Ramusio's death a young Englishman known as Richard Hakluyt the

---

    [6] Moryson, *Itinerary* [12; misnumbered as 10], 36-37.
    [7] See Peter C. Mancall, "The Age of Discovery," *Reviews in American History* 26 (1998), 26-53.

younger (1552?-1616) consciously mimicked his Venetian predecessor and produced a major edition of travel narratives published with the title *Principall Navigations, Voiages, and Discoveries of the English Nation*, which appeared in London in 1589. Hakluyt, who trained for the ministry but studied geography while at Christ Church, Oxford, became the most famous producer of travel accounts in Elizabethan England. After the appearance of his book (he had published a much smaller collection in 1582 entitled *Divers Voyages touching upon America and the Ilands adjacent*), Hakluyt continued to collect additional accounts. By the end of the century he felt compelled to offer a far more substantial edition, now entitled *The Principal Navigations, Voyages, Traffiques and Discoveries of the English Nation*, which appeared in three volumes (London, 1598-1600). Ramusio and Hakluyt provided minimal editorial intervention in their volumes; each preferred to allow travelers to speak for themselves, or at least that was the message their volumes sent.

By the time of Hakluyt's death another Englishman trained for the ministry, Samuel Purchas (1575?-1626), had begun to publish more reports of journeys, though his methods differed radically from those of Ramusio and Hakluyt.[8] The first three editions of Purchas's collection, each entitled *Purchas his Pilgrimage* (published in London in 1613, 1614, and 1617), contained Purchas's rewritings and interpretations of travel accounts. Sometime in the 1610s Hakluyt either gave or sold previously unpublished manuscripts to Purchas. When he published his next edition in 1625, a work typically called *Hakluytus Posthumus*, Purchas followed the lead of his predecessors by printing accounts without obvious editorial interference. His debt to Hakluyt was obvious, but rumors spread that he never managed to publish all of the works he obtained. The French writer Melchisédech Thévenot wrote in 1680 to John Locke asking for information about the missing manuscripts. Nicholas Dew opens his fascinating study of Thévenot, published here, with that very request. The Frenchman's effort was in many ways an apt metaphor for the publication of travel narratives in the early modern age. No matter what one had collected the possibility of learning more remained.

---

[8] For the crucial biographical details of Ramusio's life see Antonio del Piero, "Della vita e degli studi di Gio. Battista Ramusio," *Nuovo Archivo Veneto*, n.s. IV (1902), 5-112; for Hakluyt's life see David B. Quinn and Alison Quinn, "A Hakluyt Chronology," in David B. Quinn, ed., *The Hakluyt Handbook*, 2 vols., Hak. Soc. 2nd Ser. 144-45 (London, 1974), I: 263-331; for Purchas see Loren E. Pennington, ed., *The Purchas Handbook: Studies of the Life, Times and Writings of Samuel Purchas, 1577-1626*, Hak. Soc. 2nd Ser., 185-86 (London, 1997). I treat Hakluyt's life and especially his efforts to publish travel narratives at length in *Hakluyt's Promise* (New Haven, forthcoming).

Three of the contributions to the set of essays here relate specifically to the production of travel narratives by European masters of the genre. Mary Fuller engagingly demonstrates the contrasting purposes of Richard Hakluyt and his English predecessor Richard Eden, and sees in their respective narratives a shift in English conceptions of travel accounts. Nicholas Dew treats the larger intellectual agenda of the French scientist-author Thévenot, while Anne Good's sparkling essay focuses on the German traveler Peter Kolb, who was eager to write the definitive account of southern Africa and the Khoikhoi, whom Europeans then called Hottentots. As each of these authors' essays reveals, these early modern writers and editors strove to produce truthful, and hence authoritative, accounts.

Hakluyt and Thévenot shared a passion for the publication of travel accounts composed by others. For Hakluyt, as Fuller proves, the publication of such reports became by 1589 part of an effort to promote the English nation. As a result, Hakluyt sought narratives for his collections from authors who were either English themselves or whose writings and actions promoted English international efforts. Thévenot, by contrast, saw travel narratives as providing crucial evidence necessary for his universal "history of nature." With that goal in mind, Thévenot had no obvious motive for promoting exclusively French contributions. Instead, he spent much of his time corresponding with a circle of scholars around Europe who provided texts in other languages (such as English or Dutch), which he felt needed to be translated into French. Fuller's and Dew's close attention to detail also reveals differences in the style of production from one editor to another. The size of Hakluyt's massive book declared its authority. Across the water, Thévenot published fifty-five independent fascicles, which meant that readers needed to impose their own order on the material. Fuller and Dew each recognize that the form of the narrative was in many ways as significant as the message itself. Thévenot might have wanted to follow the path established by Ramusio and Hakluyt, but his *Relations de divers voyages curieux*, published between 1663 and 1672, was a different creature entirely.

By comparison, Peter Kolb probably harbored no illusion of being either the next Hakluyt or Thévenot. Judging by Good's account of him, he had little patience for scholars who spent their life collecting other peoples' experiences but having few of their own. Neither Hakluyt nor Thévenot was known as a traveler, though each made journeys; Hakluyt spent the period from 1583 to 1588 shuttling back and forth between Paris and London. Kolb, however, was a true adventurer. His great work, *Caput Bonae Spei Hodiernum*, first published in Nuremberg in 1719, was a lengthy first-hand account of his own time among the Khoikhoi.

Unlike the earlier monuments of travel literature, Kolb's book appeared in an already crowded field. As Good reports here, two hundred and fifty printed accounts of southern Africa appeared in Europe before 1719. Yet despite the abundance of information, Kolb believed that his account had much to offer since he, unlike many of the authors of other accounts, had actually spent much time in Africa. He was convinced, like Thévenot (and even Hakluyt, who had more on his mind than promoting English expansion), that his book could advance European knowledge. He was especially keen to help solve the problem of longitude, which remained difficult to determine when at sea, but his readers might have been more attracted by his ethnography of the Khoikhoi and a description of the African environment based on his eight years living at the Cape of Good Hope. The posthumous spread of Kolb's account across Europe testifies to the wide appeal of his work.

Hakluyt, Thévenot, and Kolb treated travel accounts—their own or others'—as evidence for what life was like beyond Europe. For Hakluyt and Thévenot, that meant relying on earlier reports, some of which came to seem dubious. Hakluyt, for example, in 1589 included the testimony of an English sailor named David Ingram, who claimed that he had walked from the Gulf of Mexico to modern-day Canada; but when he published his expanded material on the Western Hemisphere eleven years later Ingram was nowhere to be found. The decision was in all likelihood based on a shift in Hakluyt's opinion about trustworthiness. He kept accounts that seemed truthful but dismissed Ingram's which had come to seem unlikely.[9] The logic that Hakluyt employed, like that of Thévenot (who was more explicit in his goal), was straightforward: travel narratives were useful to the extent that they provided accurate information about a place that most readers would either never see or would need to know about before they arrived.

The American abolitionist Anthony Benezet (1713-1784) had a different goal in mind when he picked up travel narratives. As Jonathan Sassi points out in his essay, when Benezet read works like the slave trader William Snelgrave's *A New Account of Some Parts of Guinea and the Slave-Trade* (first

---

[9] Hakluyt, *Principall Navigations, Voiages, and Discoveries of the English Nation* (London, 1589), 557-62.

published in 1734), he did so with the goal of extracting information that could benefit his political agenda. As Sassi reveals, Benezet ignored evidence that did not support this agenda. He even played down reports of African intellectual abilities and cultural prowess because he feared that such information, if widely known, would help slavers who argued that many Africans willingly participated in the noxious commerce. As a result, Benezet's *Some Historical Account of Guinea*, published in 1771, was at times a brazen manipulation of existing travelers' accounts. But the contents were nonetheless remarkable. Using books available at places like the Library Company of Philadelphia, an institution founded by Benjamin Franklin, Benezet managed to construct an intellectual profile of West Africans that transformed them into what Sassi calls "proto-Quakers" embodying that religion's core values. Among the sources that Benezet harvested was none other than Peter Kolb's account, providing further proof of Kolb's authority. The legacy of Benezet's book, evident in the writings of his contemporaries and those who later commented on his work, revealed the power of his argument and the success of his exploitation of travel accounts. It revealed too that the European use of travel accounts had transferred easily across the Atlantic.

To supplement the case studies of Hakluyt, Thévenot, Kolb, and Benezet offered in this volume, Joan-Pau Rubiés steps back from the particular and looks at larger trends. His essay treats the role of travel narratives in the evolution of humanist thinking in Europe between the sixteenth and eighteenth centuries. Rubiés recognizes that Enlightenment luminaries such as Jean-Jacques Rousseau were wrong in their belief that the publication of travel narratives had little effect on the ways that Europeans understood the wider world. Instead, early modern editors, including some who became travelers themselves, made a valuable contribution to the development of European culture. Specifically, those involved with the collection and presentation of travel accounts organized their texts to address crucial European concerns about the nature of civilization. Information about non-Europeans found in works by travelers such as Kolb functioned as pieces of evidence that, when put together in print, promoted the European Enlightenment.

Fynes Moryson could not have known how later generations of Europeans would read first-hand accounts of travel such as those that he or Peter Kolb produced. But as someone who undoubtedly knew the work of Hakluyt, and hence Ramusio, he understood the inherent value of producing trustworthy, knowledgeable reports about distant places and peoples. He recognized too the power of print to spread such accounts to a wide audience. That realization gave him the confidence to generate his "Precepts." That section, tucked near the end of his *Itinerary*, had none of the ruminations about the nature of civilizations to be found in the works of some later Enlightenment writers. It lacked too the kind of specific political agenda to be found in Benezet's work. But the "Precepts" nonetheless spoke to the timeless pursuit of knowledge, the scientific value of learning about other places, and the urgency of spreading accurate information brought home by travelers.

*

The essays in this volume were developed for the first annual conference of the USC-Huntington Early Modern Studies Institute, which met in Los Angeles at Doheny Memorial Library on the campus of the University of Southern California in April 2004. That conference was funded by grants to the Institute from the Mellon Foundation and the USC Center for Religion and Civic Culture, as well as more general support from the USC College of Letters, Arts, and Sciences and the Huntington Library. Each of the papers then went through a rigorous peer-review process with the *Journal of Early Modern History*, so the versions here are substantially revised from the original papers presented at the conference. From the moment of the original presentation through revision and now publication the authors and I benefited from the careful support of the *Journal*'s editorial staff, and the Institute has continued to benefit from the generous support of its funders. Like Fynes Moryson, we too recognize the importance of patronage in the publication of scholarship.

MAKING SOMETHING OF IT:
QUESTIONS OF VALUE IN THE EARLY ENGLISH TRAVEL COLLECTION

MARY C. FULLER
MIT

ABSTRACT

In the second half of the sixteenth century, experiences and narratives of English travel to distant places first began to matter enough to be collected and published. Tracing early accounts of West Africa and Muscovy through the several collections of Richard Eden (1553, 1555) and Richard Hakluyt (1589, 1600) allows for comparison of how different editors handled the same materials at different moments. The evidence suggests that both editors differentiated between the African and Russian materials according to perceptions of these materials' value, or meaning, for their own collecting and publishing projects. Looking at how this was so, and considering *why* it was so, provides a closer and more detailed look at how travel writing acquired value in the context of print; it also offers an an approach to the larger question of how Englishmen "read" the places and cultures they encountered, actually or virtually, outside of Europe.

1.

I begin with a massive material object: the second edition of Richard Hakluyt's great collection of travel documents, commonly known as *The Principal Navigations of the English Nation*. Roughly 2000 closely-printed folio pages, it was issued as two or three large volumes in the successive years 1598-1600. In imagination, set next to this book its earliest English predecessor. Richard Eden's collection, *A Treatyse of the newe India* (1553), was a poorly printed octavo of 204 pages.[1] These are books which take up quite different amounts of space, and have enjoyed quite different reputations. Eden's has remained relatively obscure; Hakluyt's has become known as the "great prose epic of the English nation". Apart from their contents, the sheer difference in size has surely played some role in the physical survival of both books, and consequently in their present value— as distinct from their reputation. Hakluyt's three volumes are a common possession of rare book libraries: a recent census has located some two

---

[1] The copy of Eden at the John Carter Brown library, trimmed in the 19th century, is 13.5 × 9.5 cm in its current state.

© Koninklijke Brill NV, Leiden, 2006
Also available online – www.brill.nl

hundred and forty sets. As this article was being written, a copy priced at $20,000 was for sale online: hardly a casual purchase, but still not outside the reach of a generous research budget, not to mention a reasonably well endowed library.[2] Eden's *Treatyse of the newe India* survives in only six copies;[3] were one to come on the market, it would be almost beyond price.

What changed between 1553 and 1598? While the pace of English travel and exploration certainly increased during these 50-odd years, Eden and others were simply not interested in many of the existing materials which Hakluyt sought out for his larger collection.[4] Many of Hakluyt's documents had never been printed before, and some of the voyages they recorded were forgotten by the time Hakluyt began his work; in some cases, the records themselves had already vanished, and testimony was solicited from elderly survivors. The idea of getting voyage narratives into print and disseminating them was evidently not as obvious in the middle of the sixteenth century as it may now seem in the wake of Hakluyt, Purchas, and the last century or so of publications by the Hakluyt Society and others. During the 45 years which separated Eden's first book and the second edition of *Principal Navigations*, the materials which Hakluyt collected had acquired a value which they did not seem to have earlier.

In this essay, I will examine how value is assigned both to, and in, two particular sets of materials present in both Eden's and Hakluyt's collections: English accounts of West Africa and Muscovy from the 1550's. As compared to other parts of the Hakluyt anthology, these materials have received relatively little attention from modern scholars; yet they have a particular importance for a history of the travel book. Documents on both regions appeared in Eden's second collection (1555), were reprinted by Richard Willes in his 1577 revision of Eden, and

---

[2] Abebooks listing, 11/14/05, offered by D. and E. Lake, Toronto, Ontario.

[3] As listed by ESTC, 11/18/05; with thanks to Richard Ring.

[4] Edward Arber prefaced his edition of the first three English books on America with a long list of all the voyages *not* represented in Eden's first and second collections (Arber 1885, xii-xx). In addition to Eden 1553 and 1555, Arber includes a short, earlier pamphlet translated from German, *Of the newe lãdes of ye people founde by the messengers of the kynge of Port~ygale named Emanuel: being the description of the voyage of D. Francisco de Almeida from Lisbon to India in 1505 / by Balthazar Springer. Together with Of the .X. dyuers nacyons crystened. & Of Pope Johñ and his landes and of the costely kepes and wonders molodyes that in that lande his* (Antwerp, ca. 1515). John Parker gives a more detailed account of Eden's first two books in *Books to Build an empire: a Bibliographical History of English Overseas Interests to 1620* (Amsterdam, 1965).

again reprinted with changes and additions by Hakluyt in 1589 and 1599. They represent an early stage in the collection of first-person narratives, while also allowing us to compare the treatment given them by editors and editions over several decades; Eden's and Hakluyt's framing comments and organizational schemes give some sense of the ways these two editors understood both the documents and the places the documents described.

What kinds of enterprises led the English to the coast of West Africa and to Muscovy? In the early years of the decade, overlapping groups of English investors set in motion a series of voyages in two directions. The first trading voyage to West Africa took place in 1553, the same year that a newly constituted company sent three ships to the northeast in search of a passage to Cathay.[5] Both voyages combined a kind of disaster with a kind of success.

From the West African coast, two of three ships returned, but with only forty out of the initial complement of one hundred and forty men; the rest died of disease or were abandoned in Benin, and more died soon after the return to England (*PN* VI, 151). Nonetheless, the voyage turned a considerable profit, and in 1554 a second voyage was captained by John Lok—whose brother Michael would become London Agent for the Muscovy Company. Two of the three ships which sailed northeast likewise came to grief, delayed and finally wintering in Lapland, where the crews froze to death. The remaining ship, the *Edward Bonaventure*, managed to round the Kola Peninsula and anchor in the White Sea, at the mouth of the Dvina River (roughly, present day Arkhangel'sk). From there, its captain—Richard Chancellor—proceeded south to Moscow at the Tsar's invitation and delivered a letter from Edward IV intended for "the Kynges, Princes, & other potentates inhabytynge the Northeast partes of the worlde towarde the myghtye Empire of Cathay" (Eden 1555, 308).[6] Chancellor returned with information about the country and its goods which encouraged the promoters to seek a charter from the crown, which they received from Philip and Mary in 1555. Later that year, Chancellor returned to Muscovy with two ships, bringing

---

[5] An earlier voyage was planned in 1481 and "may have taken place" despite Portuguese objections (Timothy F. Garrard, *Akan Weights and the Gold Trade* [London and New York, 1980], 72). Garrard cites an anonymous seventeenth century source on the outcome of the voyage (96, n. 6).

[6] This is Eden's heading; the body of the letter addresses "all Kynges, Princes, Rulers, Judges, and the gouernours of the earthe, and all other hauynge any excellent dignitie on the same in all places under the universall heauen" (Eden 1555, 308 recto).

agents of the newly incorporated Muscovy company who were duly granted privileges by the Tsar. Goods traded included cordage and hemp, flax, train-oil (oil made from the rendered fat of whales or seals), furs, hides, tallows (candles made from animal fat), and wax. The Muscovy Company retained a monopoly of the White Sea trade into the 1570s, as well as an exclusive right to trade in the interior without duties or tolls.[7]

This northern route to Muscovy was not unknown, and had been described in print by the Hapsburg emissary Sigismund von Herberstein, whose account both Eden and Hakluyt made use of in their collections.[8] The White Sea route was "not commonly frequented" before 1555, much less was it a corridor for regular trade, and Muscovy itself remained poorly known to western Europeans.[9] More broadly, the English shared with some other Europeans both intense interest in the northern parts of Asia and a general ignorance about them. When members of what would become the Muscovy company met to consider setting forth a voyage in this direction, they could do no better than to interview two Tartar grooms:

> ... two Tartarians, which were then of the king's Stable, were sent for, & an interpreter was gotten to be present, by whom they were demaunded touching their Countrey and the maners of their nation. But they were able to answere nothing to the purpose: being in deede more acquainted (as one there merily and openly said) to tosse pottes, then to learne the states and dispositions of people.

The scene suggests both the cosmopolitan nature of London's population, and the paucity of its geographical knowledge.

So if the "discovery" of a trade to Muscovy was new more in regard to English trading patterns than in respect of actual knowledge, it was nonetheless undertaken within the context of very long-distance exploration, and the company would continue (albeit sporadically) to pursue the grail of a Northern passage to Cathay and the Indies even as it undertook regular and settled trade along the route Chancellor pioneered. The voyages to West Africa, by contrast, were not a discovery at all, since Portugal had an established trade along the coast dating

---

[7] For details, see T.S. Willan, *The Early History of the Russia Company* (New York, 1968), chapter 1.

[8] Sigismund von Herberstein, *Rerum moscoviticarum commentarii* (Vienna, 1549). Marshall Poe locates Herberstein in the context of sixteenth century European accounts of Russia in *"A People Born to Slavery": Russia in Early Modern European Ethnography, 1476-1748* (Ithaca, 2000).

[9] See Poe, *"A People"*, chapters 1-3.

from the 1440's; by the mid-sixteenth century, there were permanent trading bases and a significant Afro-Portuguese population, some settled on the previously uninhabited Cape Verde Islands off present-day Senegal.[10] The French had preceded the English as interlopers in this trade, which at the time primarily exchanged cloth and metal goods for ivory, gold, and malaguetta pepper ("grains of paradise"). As the results of the first voyage and others made clear, the coast was not without its dangers, but these came primarily from the disease environment rather than from a population which, generally speaking, had been involved in long-distance, cross-cultural commerce well before the advent of Europeans and saw certain advantages in adding new trading partners to compete with the old.[11]

For Hakluyt, both sets of materials like many other documents in the collection—were valuable in general terms because they described the extension of English presence, and commerce, into areas that were at least new to them. Hakluyt wrote in the preface to the first edition of *Principal Navigations* (1589) that

> during my five years abroad [in Paris, 1583-88] . . ., I both heard in speech, and read in books other nations miraculously extolled for their discoveries and notable enterprises by sea, but the English of all others for their sluggish security, and continual neglect of the like attempts . . . either ignominiously reported, or exceedingly condemned.[12]

His collection sought to remedy the sense that, outside Europe, most areas were still new to the English. For Eden in the 1550's, the situation was quite different, both rhetorically and historically: there, the secondary, imitative, or dependent quality of English endeavor was simply a fact, with consequences visible both in the work of the editor, and in the experiences which his collection records.

---

[10] See (*inter alia*) George Brooks, *Landlords and Strangers: Ecology, Society, and Trade in Western Africa, 1000-1630* (Boulder, CO, 1993), chapter eight.

[11] At least for the fifteenth and sixteenth centuries, Brooks sees West African traders as advantageously situated between the various European traders on the coast, and Mande traders linking them to trans-Saharan and other interior markets (*Landlords*, 135). Fernand Braudel provides a broad overview of the Atlantic and trans-Saharan gold trade in "The Mediterranean and the Gold of the Sudan" (*The Mediterranean and the Mediterranean World in the Age of Philip II*, trans. Siân Reynolds (New York, 1976), vol. I, 463-76). Volumes IV and V of the UNESCO *General History of Africa* provide more fine-grained information on both markets.

[12] Hakluyt, "Epistle dedicatorie," *The principall navigations: voiages and discoveries of the English nation*. London, 1589; Cambridge, 1965, *2r-v. A note on primary sources: for the second edition of *Principal Navigations* (Hakluyt, 1598-1600) I have used the Glasgow reprint edition of 1903-05 for ease of reference.

2.

A well-connected translator and sometime employee of the treasury, Eden assembled his *Treatise of the New India* in the last year of Edward VI's reign. It was followed in 1555 by a second collection, *Decades of the new world*. Eden's collections both ostensibly translated other books. The first both translated parts of Sebastian Münster's cosmography, and followed it in dividing its material between Spanish voyages to the West, and Portuguese ones to the East. Eden's prefatory matter mentions two English initiatives—both the Cabot discoveries of the late 1400's and the voyage then under way to find a Northeast passage to China—but neither was documented in the collection.[13] The second Eden anthology translated part of Pietro Martire de Anghiera's *De orbe novo* (1516-30). Eden added to this translation not only additional Spanish material but two accounts of English voyages to West Africa, and a rather larger assortment of items related (somewhat loosely) to English voyages in the North.

Decades opens with an encomium to the almost divine achievements of the Spanish in discovering and conquering America and an effusive description of marriage celebrations between Philip of Spain and Mary Tudor, proceeding to an insistent demand that England acknowledge the authority of Spain. The contrast between this moment and the patriotic prefaces of Hakluyt's Elizabethan collections is nothing short of breathtaking: "stoop, England, stoop and learne to know thy lord and master, as horses and other brute beasts are taught to do" (Eden 1555, bi verso).[14] Nonetheless, the deference of *Decades* was complicated. John Parker suggests that England's northern voyages (begun in the reign of Edward VI, continued after the accession of Mary) lay behind the appearance of Eden's collections, devoted even as they were largely to the accomplishments of other nations.[15]

---

[13] Eden's *Treatyse* translated and excerpted a Paris edition of Munster's *Cosmographia* from 1550, which in turn translated a Basel edition of 1544 (Alden, *European Americana*). Where possible, I have given page references both to Eden's 1553 original and to the reprint in Arber, *The first three English books on America* (Birmingham, 1885).

[14] The dedicatee of Eden's earlier volume—John Dudley, Duke of Northumberland—had in 1555 only just been executed for treason under the new regime; no doubt Eden felt he needed to make a point.

[15] "... [T]he fact that *A treatyse of the newe India* appeared just at the time Eden's friend Sebastian Cabot was promoting the first northern voyage of his company of merchants, and that Eden praised this venture, suggests strongly that this little book was no publisher's venture, but a subsidized publication, designed to praise and advertise this voyage which was only the first of many to the northeast" (Parker, *Books*, 40). This occa-

The first of Eden's two original narratives of travel to West Africa was thematically concerned precisely with the issue of how to place oneself in relation to a foreign expertise which had to be acknowledged, because it could not be duplicated at home. It is a story with a moral, and a surprisingly pointed one: the disastrous consequences of an English captain's bad behavior towards his Portuguese second-in-command.[16] Failing to respect foreign knowledge, as this story goes, was a sure pathway to disaster. "The first voyage to Guinea and Benin" describes an expedition which left London in August 1553 with the *Primrose*, *Lion*, and *Moon* pinnace under the command of Captain Thomas Wyndham. After briefly trading for malagueta pepper at the River Sess (Liberia), and for gold in the country surrounding the Portuguese installation at Mina (Ghana), the three ships proceeded on to Benin and sent a party upriver to trade for pepper. Trading was interrupted by illness and Wyndham's death; the the *Lion* was abandoned at Benin with a group of English merchants and seamen while the *Primrose* and *Moon* returned to England in late June or early July of the following year.[17]

For an English mariner at this early date, Thomas Wyndham must have passed for being both well-travelled and well-informed. He had

---

sional linkage between maritime books and the promotion of particular maritime enterprises would persist at least for another few decades, through Hakluyt's first collection, the quarto *Divers Voyages* of 1582. An expanded version of the 1555 *Decades* was completed after Eden's death by Richard Willes; this volume, which appeared in 1577 as *The history of travail*, included some primary sources on English travel to Russia and Persia, perhaps as a form of promotion for the Frobisher voyages to the Northwest with which its appearance coincided. Similarly, Hakluyt's first collection, *Divers Voyages* (1582), has been persuasively identified by David Quinn as part of a promotional effort accompanying Humphrey Gilbert's westward enterprises in the early 1580's (*Richard Hakluyt, editor. A Study Introductory of the Facsimile Edition of Richard Hakluyt's* Divers voyages *(1582)* [Amsterdam, 1968], 9).

[16] The personal animus of the narrative is noted by in P.E.H. Hair and James Alsop, *English Seamen and Traders in Guinea 1553-1565: The New Evidence of Their Wills* (Lewiston/ Queenston/Lampeter, 1992), 9. The introduction to this volume provides a detailed study of the texts and their history. The early voyages are also discussed by Garrard (*Akan weights*, passim). For Benin, see A.F.C. Ryder, *Benin and the Europeans: 1485-1897* (London, 1969), 76-79. Some details on the itineraries of these voyages can be found in Garrard, *Akan Weights* (passim) and in the introduction to section III of Blake, *Europeans in West Africa* (London, 1942), II: 249-94. Blake prints some supplementary documents on the voyages in Hakluyt, and also comments on Hakluyt's omission of voyages to Barbary which we know now only through court proceedings (ibid., 273). Hakluyt's account is found at VI, 145-52.

[17] Among those abandoned in Benin was "a relative and probably a brother" of one of the voyage's major investors; Hair and Alsop comment that this "no doubt helps to explain the bitter tone of the Eden narrative" (*English Seamen*, 9).

made two voyages to Morocco in 1551 and '52, and invested in the northeast passage search of 1553, one instance of the numerous overlaps between these undertakings.[18] Nonetheless, the backers of the voyage instructed him to share command with someone familiar with the West African coast: Wyndham was to rely on the expert knowledge of António Anes Pinteado, an "expert Pilote as well as a politike captaine" who had held a position of authority in the King of Portugal's service at sea until, the "politike" side failing him, he fell out of favor and took refuge in England.[19]

Having previously been charged with patrolling the coasts of Brazil and Guinea, Pinteado was well and recently informed; but Wyndham did not take well to this recruitment of foreign expertise. Once the small fleet had passed Madeira, Wyndham became "a terrible Hydra," removing Pinteado from command, stripping him of subordinates and "leaving him as a common mariner, which is the greatest despite and grief that can be to a Portugale or Spaniard, to be diminished of their honor, which they esteem above all riches." Once they reached the coast of Guinea, the men were persuaded by "this tragicall captaine" to ignore Pinteado's advice to lade grains of paradise, and instead to press further south in search of gold. Near Mina, they took a hundred and fifty pounds of gold in trade, and again Wyndham overbore the "counsell and experience" of Pinteado, commanding that they continue south to Benin rather than remaining in place to sell the remainder of their goods as Pinteado suggested. Meanwhile, Pinteado provided not only knowledge of the coast and its commodities, but also translation: the king (or Oba) of Benin, for instance, spoke Portuguese but, unsurprisingly, no English.

Wyndham remained dependent on Pinteado for information, but refused to defer even minimally to his experience and recommendations: for instance, he overbore Pinteado's view that it would be unwise to venture south so late in the year. In Benin, the English began to die,

---

[18] He was also associated with William Hawkins, who had on an earlier voyage to Brazil "touched at the river of Sestos upon the coast of Guinea, where hee traffiqued with the Negros, and tooke of them Elephants teeth, and other commodities" (*PN* XI, 23-24).

[19] A second Portuguese refugee, the pilot Francisco Rodrigues, also went on this voyage (see Hair and Alsop, 54 n. 21); he is mentioned only briefly as one of those who went upriver to Benin with Pinteado. E.G.R. Taylor cites references to Pinteado's involvement with English voyages from two manuscript sources" (*Tudor Geography 1485-1583* [London, 1930], 94.

partly through the extremity of the climate, "partly having no rule of themselves, but eating without measure of the fruits of the countrey, and drinking the wine of the Palme trees" (*PN* VI, 150). Wyndham was unwilling to stay until the trade initiated under his orders was concluded; he commanded Pinteado back to the ship, but in the interval sickened and died himself. On Pinteado's return, the mariners abused and mistreated him, and insisted on leaving forthwith, thus abandoning in Benin the remaining merchants who had accompanied Pinteado to the king's court. Within a few days' sail, Pinteado died "for very pensiveness & thought."

Between calling for Pinteado's return, and his own descent into illness and death, Wyndham broke up and destroyed Pinteado's chests containing his personal possessions, including "such provision of cold stilled waters and suckets as he had provided for his health," and leaving him nothing: "neither of his instruments to saile by, nor yet of his apparel" (VI, 151). The contents of the chest were not only valuable to Pinteado, but represent what made him *of* value: his knowledge of the climate and ability to regulate or temper his body in it, by use of the quasi-medical provisions, and the specialized skills as a navigator represented by his instruments. It hardly needs saying how self-destructive was this rage of Wyndham's, which *spoiled* what it lacked rather than seeking (if nothing else) to make use of it. That Wyndham sickened and died immediately afterwards suggests (in the narrative) a deep connection between the emotional intemperance of destroying Pinteado's possessions, and the intemperate lack of self-care which a contemporary observer might indeed have understood to cause fatal illness.

Against Pinteado's admirable knowledge and self-control, English *in*temperance—greed for gold, immoderate diet, unrestrained rage, impatience—looks especially problematic. That narrative itself was the product not of a single disaffected pen, but both instigated and informed by persons additional to the author: Eden was asked to write it by "certaine of [his] friends," and based the story on "the information of such credible persons, as made diligent inquisition to know the trueth thereof." The impression of a kind of corporate authorship makes even more striking this narrative's commitment to championing the Portuguese Pinteado against the English Wyndham and his crew; indeed, Eden appends (and Hakluyt reproduces) a series of letters from the Portuguese court in order to demonstrate Pinteado's virtue and value. It might be said that Eden's early account of English achievement pillories English failure to recognize, defer to, and make use of the superior wisdom of a foreigner.[20]

Particularly given the shifting sympathies displayed in Eden's prefaces, one might read this account as a castigation of English unruliness and insubordination (as in the 1555 preface), or (more positively) as a warning that the English are failing to take advantage of foreign knowledge when it is put at their service—as in the 1553 dedication, when Eden regrets the decision not to give further employment to his friend, the navigator Sebastian Cabot.[21] In Eden's narrative, national conflict coincides with a conflict between knowledges or authorities: it is a tragedy of [English] captains asserting authority over [foreign] pilots who know better.[22] John Parker suggests that the second of Eden's two Africa narratives made the point of English incapacity from another direction, simply by way of its form:

> The 1554 voyage was . . . little more than a journal of distances, rivers, soundings, and other matters of navigational interest. Eden implied that a want of navigational information made this approach necessary (fo. 343r-360v) (Parker, 48).

Eden's treatment of the northeast voyages was rather different. *Decades* offers virtually no primary sources on Muscovy. Eden does print the letter from Edward VI sent with Chancellor and Willoughby in 1553, and and some copies include the reply from Ivan IV; irregular pagination and a break in running headers suggest that these were added late in the process of printing.[23] Most of the material which Eden's collection

---

[20] Eden's original contains additional criticism of Wyndham; the cuts were made not by Hakluyt himself, but are in his source text, Richard Willes' *The history of travayle* (1577), which enlarges and tries to improve on Eden 1555 (see Willes' preface). For what Willes left out, see in particular Eden 345v.

[21] Eden wrote in 1553 that if the English hadn't been lacking in manly courage to pursue voyages under Cabot in the time of Henry the 8th, from which they turned because of Thomas Pert's faint heart, the Peruvian treasure might now belong to them (Eden 1553, aa.4 recto; Arber 1885, 6). Hakluyt prints later documents on African trade in which English participation is an act of charity to destitute Portuguese emigrants, followers of Dom Antonio; merchants organizing a voyage in 1588 "have bene perswaded and earnestly moved by certaine Portugals resident within our Dominions, to undertake and set forward a voyage to certaine places on the coast of Guinea . . ."—which will not only provide a trade beneficial for England, but "also be a great succour and reliefe unto the present distressed estate of those Portugals, who by our princely favour live and continue here under our protection" (*PN* VI, 443).

[22] The number of foreign pilots found in Hakluyt's documents suggests that this narrative's overlay of professional and national friction was probably not unique.

[23] Copies of Eden's *Decades* survive as produced by four different printers: E. Sutton, R. Jugge, W. Seres, and R. Toye. According to Alden, *European America*, the unpaginated letter from the Tsar does not appear in the copies printed by Sutton.

adds to Martyr's *Decades*, however, concerns the northern parts of Europe and Asia, and Muscovy in particular: these materials include a wide array of hearsay testimonials to "the vyage to Cathay and East India by the north sea," a history of Muscovy written for Pope Clement VII, descriptions of Greenland, Iceland, and Scandinavia, as well as a discussion of climate in "the North Regions," necessary to argue that these cold climates were habitable, "contrary to thoppinion of the owlde writers" (Eden 1555, 249 recto, 263 verso).

The two accounts of Africa in *Decades* lacked the penumbra of royal letters and accompanying geography and theory associated with Russia.[24] Following a description of the lands and peoples from Muscovy east to Cathay, Eden appended a treatise on metals, because "it seemeth to me a thynge undecent to reade so much of golde and syluer, and to knowe lyttle or nothynge of the naturall generation thereof" (Eden 1555, 325 verso). The African narratives follow the treatise, as if in illustration of its arguments about where metals would be found. Otherwise, the voyage narratives of 1553-54 stand alone.

3.

If Eden's accounts even of English voyages thematized their dependence on foreign skill, the case was altered with Hakluyt, though not immediately; Hakluyt's first collection was continuous in strategy with its predecessors. By the time *Divers Voyages* appeared in 1582, there *were* more English voyages to talk about than was the case in 1550's; these included the multiply-documented Frobisher voyages of the 1570's. Yet as with Eden's first two collections, although the preface to *Divers Voyages* mentions both Frobisher and the Northeast voyages of the 1550's, neither is represented by a document in the collection. *Divers Voyages* was a miscellaneous and spotty assembly of sources covering the coast from Newfoundland south to Florida, with information drawn from Italian, French, and English voyages—perhaps to promote further voyages under Humphrey Gilbert's patent for North America. If the scope was smaller than Eden's, the intention was consistent—to provide a foundation of evidence regarding the regions to which English voyages were intended— evidence which would necessarily come chiefly from foreign sources.

---

[24] His remarks do indicate that the West African trading coast, only a few degrees above the equator, was considered an equally extreme climate, torrid as Muscovy was frigid; Eden 1553 Miii verso, or Arber 41.

The first edition of *Principall Navigations* in 1589 was already a very different animal. Hakluyt took as a model *Navigationi e Viaggi*, the more systematic collection of G.B. Ramusio which had appeared in the 1550's, and a copy of which he owned; while Hakluyt used some of Ramusio's material in translation, by far the most important borrowing was a structure of systematic global coverage. Hakluyt would follow Ramusio in organizing his materials into volumes on the South and Southeast, North, and West, covering the known globe. Reflecting this expanded geographical range, *Principall Navigations* was *larger* than *Divers Voyages*, 825 pages versus 120 (*Divers Voyages* was for the most part limited to coastal North America). In another dimension, *Principall Navigations* was more limited than its predecessor. Hakluyt wrote in the 1589 preface that "I meddle in this work with the navigations only of *our own nation*: and albeit I allege in a few places ... some strangers as witnesses of the things done, yet are they none but such as either faithfully remember, or sufficiently confirm the travels of *our own people*" (*PN* I, xxiii; emphasis added).[25] Unlike *Divers Voyages*, which printed narratives by Ribault and Verrazano, *Principal Navigations* was to include only *English* navigations, the globe known to Englishmen. Hakluyt managed this combination of expanded size and restricted provenance in part by printing materials like price lists, logs, and oral narratives which had been or had felt to be without value as printed texts. Hakluyt's turn to primary materials on *English* voyages, many never before in print, contrasts sharply with Eden's practice; Eden's *Treatyse* had translated and excerpted in English a French translation of a German account of Spanish and Portuguese voyages. Even in a wider context, however, Hakluyt's national focus was distinctive: Anthony Payne comments that the collection was "unique in ... the period in being devoted to but one particular nation."[26]

When the second edition appeared in 1598-1600, it was again considerably larger than its predecessor, not only because there were more voyages (and more documents) but because the parameters of the collection had again changed.[27] The second edition included a vastly

---

[25] In fact, both editions of *PN* continued to use some foreign sources. For discussion, see Fuller, "Richard Hakluyt's Foreign Relations", forthcoming.

[26] Anthony Payne, "'Strange, remote, and farre distant countreys': the travel books of Richard Hakluyt", in *Journeys Through the Market: Travel, Travellers, and the Book Ttrade*, ed. Robin Myers and Michael Harris (Newcastle, DE, 1999), 18.

[27] Parks gives a useful breakdown of materials for the two editions, by region and period; he estimates the total word count for *PN* 1589 at 699,250, and for *PN* 1600 at 1,699,850 (*Richard Hakluyt and the English Voyages* (New York, 1961), 175 n. 4).

increased proportion of medieval material, "that no man should imagine that our foreign trades of merchandise has been comprised within some few years, or at least wise have not been of any long continuance" (*PN* I, xlvii). The second edition also begins with the north rather than the south, and this shift marks one of the global differences between the first and second editions of *Principal Navigations*.

The first edition had followed both chronological order and Ramusio's precedent in beginning with travel to the South and Southeast: "For . . . the oldest travels . . . were ordinarie to Judea which is in Asia, termed by them the Holy land" (*PN* I, xxv).[28] *Principal Navigations* 1589 opened with a journey toward Jerusalem, the center of medieval cosmographies and maps, by Helena, "daughter of Coelus King of Britaine" and mother of the Emperor Constantine.[29] The second edition begins instead with King Arthur's legendary conquest and conversion of the North (*PN* I, 6). While the two accounts share the linkage of imperial and Christian projects, to begin with Arthur is to begin considerably closer to home— both in geographical location, and in choosing a figure of more specifically British fame.[30] The anthology's initial focus thus moves away from a universalizing, Christian perspective on historical geography towards something more local and, especially, more national.

Indeed, *PN* 1600 groups English material *under* the heading of the North—along with information supporting the viability of northern passages, both east and west, to the regions of spice and gold located by Spain and Portugal. Hakluyt sought to counter the division of the globe into East and West, Portuguese and Spanish spheres of influence, by

---

[28] G.B. Parks points to Hakluyt's previous reliance on Ramusio: "The plan of the *Voyages* was still Ramusio's with modifications. That standard synthesis of the age of discovery had formed three sections of voyages: those to the South, those to the East and Northeast, those to the West. Hakluyt retained this grouping in the first edition of the voyages, and it was not until the final edition that he altered it for patriotic reasons" (*Richard Hakluyt and the English voyages*, 2nd ed. [New York, 1961], 125).

[29] *Principal Navigations* 1600 kept this account, taken from John Bale's *Scriptorum illustrium maioris Brytanniaie . . . catalogus* (Basle, 1557-9), along with its successor, an account of Constantine the Great, but placed them at the beginning of the *second* volume.

[30] These conquests were quite legendary and known to be so in Hakluyt's time. C.R. Beazley remarks, "It is curious that Hak.[luyt] should have begun his great collection with Geoffrey's and Lambarde's collections, when we remember that he attempted rigorously to exclude from the final edition of the *Principal Navigations* anything that seemed . . . to be even in part untrustworthy and exaggerated. From the first Geoffrey's fabrications had been denounced (as by William of Newbury), but Hak [luyt] swallows the whole" (*The Texts and Version of John De Plano Carpini and William De Rubriquis* (London, 1903), 235, note 3).

promoting the North as a region yet unclaimed which gave unfettered access to both the others. England's search for these passages was, he argued, in itself at least as heroic and world-historical as the western and eastern voyages of Columbus and Vasco de Gama, despite or even because it had not as yet yielded the rewards of the latter two (*PN* I, xl-xliv). Accounts of the Muscovy trade and its associated enterprises filled out this narrative—and perhaps also stood as a placeholder for the discovery yet to be made. Repositioning these materials in a first volume which also treated England's past linked them closely to an argument for national achievement.

4.

The organization and contents of both collections provide one kind of information; both editors also commented directly on their materials. Eden's comments are especially informative. He writes that "concernynge Moscouia and Cathay, I was mynded to haue added hereunto dyuers other thynges, but that for certayne considerations I was persuaded to proceade no further" (Eden 1555, 303 recto). Those considerations follow. One was financial: "the parteners at whose charge this booke is prynted . . . doo not . . . cease dayly to caule vppon me to make an end and proceade no further". The other was political: "as touchynge these trades and vyages, . . . there are certeyne secreates not to bee publysshed and made common to all men." Nonetheless, Eden insists that

> if euer sence the begynnynge of the worlde any enterpryse haue deserued greate
> prayse as a thynge atchyued by men of heroicall vertue, doubtlesse there was neuer
> any more woorthy commendation and admiration then is that whiche owre nation
> haue attempted by the north seas to discouer the mightie and riche empire of
> Cathay, by which vyage not only golde, syluer, precious stones, and spices, may
> be browght hether by a safer and shorter way, but also much greater matters may
> herof ensewe in tyme if it shall please God to gyue vnto Christian men such pas-
> sage into those regions (Eden 1555, diii recto).

By contrast, Eden writes that he included first-hand accounts of the voyages to West Africa (with full details of Wyndham's shameful conduct) not on his own initiative but at the request of friends. He praised the African voyages in qualified terms as an important challenge to Portugal: they were

> so much the greatlyer to bee estemed as before neuer enterrpysed by Englysshe
> men, or at the leaste so frequented as at this present they are and may bee to the
> greate commoditie of owre marchauntes, if the same be not hyndered by tham-
> bision of such as for the conquestynge of fortie or fyftie myles here and there, and

erectynge of certeyne fortresses or rather blockhuses amonge naked people, thinke themselues woorthy to bee lordes of halfe the worlde (Eden 1555, 343 recto).

Eden also tells us this material was added as an afterthought, after the bulk of the manuscript preceding it had been delivered to the printers. The point is reiterated at the narratives' close.

> I had not thought to haue wrytten any thynge of these vyages but that the liber-alitie of master Toy [the printer] encoraged me to attempt the same. Whiche I speake not to the reproche of other in whome I thynke there lacked no good wyll, but that they thought the booke wolde be to chargeable (Eden 1555, 360 recto).

As Eden's comments suggest, the inclusion and extent of both sets of materials in the 1555 anthology was the result of negotiations between the editor, his friends and sources, his investors, and the printer Master Toy, balancing the national interest involved in publishing or concealing given pieces of information with more material considerations of time, size, and cost—and, presumably, with the editor's own preferences and priorities. The net effect is to position the Muscovy narratives as valuable intellectual property, while the Africa narratives plead for the value of actions otherwise forgotten, even by the editor himself. In Hakluyt, a disparity of editorial treatment was equally evident.

Hakluyt followed Eden in framing materials on the north as heroic national endeavours. His preface compares the voyages of Chancellor and his successors favorably with those of Columbus and Vasco de Gama:

> True it is, that our successe hath not bene correspondent unto theirs: yet in this our attempt the uncertaintie of finding was farre greater, and the difficultie and danger of searching no whit lesse (*PN* I, xl-xli).

Accordingly, materials on Muscovy are among the most complete for any region covered in the anthology. They draw not only on the papers of Hakluyt's acquaintances, but also on both government papers such as royal correspondence and ambassadors' reports and on the Muscovy Company archive.[31] While Hakluyt moved these materials to the first volume of the 1600 anthology, materials on Africa were grouped in part 2 of the second volume, following materials on the Near East and the Ottoman Empire. In a preface of eleven pages (in the modern edition), they take up less than two sentences, and unlike the Ottoman

---

[31] On completeness, see Simmons, Quinn and Skelton. Willan supposes the company's records to have been destroyed by fire in 1666. In their introduction to the Hakluyt Society reprint of *Principall Navigations* (1589), Quinn and Skelton regard the existence of such an archive as conjectural but very probable ("Introduction", xxxviii-xxxix).

materials, they are not framed as having any significance beyond the fact that they occurred; editorially, they are almost invisible.[32]

The African materials are introduced near the end of the preface to the second volume in the form of two lists; the following is the more detailed of the two:

> I have here set downe the very originals and infancie of our trades to the Canarian Ilands, to the kingdomes of Barbarie, to the mightie rivers of Senega and Gambra, to those of Madrabumba, and Sierra Leona, and the Isles of Cape Verde, with twelve sundry voyages to the sultry kingdomes of Guinea and Benin, to the Isle of San Thomé, with a late and true report of the weake estate of the Portugales in Angola, as also the whole course of the Portugale Carackas from Lisbon to the barre of Goa in India, with the disposition and qulaitie of the climate neere and under the Equinoctiall line . . . (*PN* I, lxxi).

(The sentence continues for twelve more lines after leaving West Africa). This grouping in the preface does not fully suggest the actual incoherence of the materials printed in the second half of the volume. Materials on Africa are followed with accounts of a voyage to the East Indies, with Portuguese accounts of China and Japan, then resume only to be interrupted repeatedly with accounts of conflict between English and Spanish or Portuguese forces: these include Drake's raid on Cadiz, the sinking of the *Revenge* off Flores, the taking of the *Madre de Deus* carrack. One might hypothesize that Hakluyt's mental map of Africa placed it within the Luso-Iberian sphere of influence, a place where the English would always be latecomers; while Eden characterized this secondariness in terms of the need to defer to foreign experience, Hakluyt suggests by this grouping of materials a more conflictual model of raiding and appropriation. Other materials on Africa—like those on Newfoundland— were distributed throughout Hakluyt's final volume in accounts of travel to the Americas and around the world; both places were way-stations on voyages to and from other destinations.[33]

---

[32] It should be noted, however, that within a few years of publishing his second edition, Hakluyt had a hand in the appearance of two account of Africa in English translation: Duarte Lopes on the Congo (1597), and Leo Africanus on Africa more generally (1600). In both cases, the translators credit him with both with providing the original text and with urging that it be translated and put into print.

[33] It was common for long voyages intended to the Americas or the Pacific, as well as to the East Indies, to call at some point on the West African coast for water and provisions. Examples include the voyages of William Hawkins in 1530-32; the voyage of Sir John Hawkins in 1568 (which also took slaves); the intended circumnavigation by Edward Fenton in 1582. On Newfoundland, see Fuller, "Images of English Origins in Newfoundland and Roanoke," in *Decentering the Renaissance: Canada and Europe in Multi-Disciplinary Perspective*, Germaine Warkentin and Carolyn Podruchny, eds. (Toronto, 2001), 141-58.

But wasn't Muscovy also in a sense a way-station, at least conjecturally, on the way to Persia or Cathay? And didn't Africa have at least some of the spices and precious metals by which the search for a hypothetical Northeast Passage was motivated? Scripture itself indicated that rich goods came from the south, as in the account of Solomon's voyage to Ophir and Tarsus which opens the Eden anthology of 1553 (it figures even more prominently in the Purchas collection of 1625).[34] Classical science concurred. Both the 1553 collection and its successor in 1555 were full of observations about climate, attempting to integrate observation (mostly second hand) with the classical theory of zones (frigid, temperate and torrid) in order to predict the distribution of things like gold. Climate theory predicted there would be gold in Africa—hot and close to the equator—but not in Russia. In 1553, for instance, Eden described it as "a general rule" that gold was mostly engendered near the equator where the sun was strongest—"although it be sometimes found in cold regions . . . yet neither pure of itself nor in great quantity" (Eden 1553, n.p.; Arber 1885, 7).[35] Frobisher's Arctic voyages of the 1570's briefly seemed to dispel the belief that gold was found only in hot climates. But practical experience also underwrote these hypotheses: African trade regularly yielded many of the same rich goods—gold, ivory, spices— said to have been found by Solomon.

---

[34] See Purchas, *Purchas his pilgrimes*, chapter 1. When John Dee's *Famous and Rich Discoveries* (1577) argued that the English should seek "the fabled riches of the East", he meant not only the wealth of China, but also the wealth of Ophir (E.G.R. Taylor, *Tudor Geography*, 114). Dee was well-connected with the Muscovy Company and other promoters of exploration; William Sherman describes Dee's account of Ophir as having influenced "Purchas, Hakluyt, and (most likely) Drake" (*John Dee: The Politics of Reading and Writing in the English Renaissance* [Amherst, 1995], 176-77).

[35] The "Book of Metals" added to the 1555 collection reiterated the point (Eden 1555, 325 verso-343 recto). However, E.G.R. Taylor provides a qualifying view: "It was one of the accepted generalizations of the age that precious metals and spices alike were generated from the sun's heat, so that they were to be looked for only in the torrid zone: this led to the complementary view that lands of the far north were necessarily worthless, and merely to be passed by, in the search for the tropics. Gemma did not hold this view, and his favorable description of Baccalaos was read and approved by Eden among others, and the latter paraphrases it in his Preface to the *Decades*" (Taylor 1930, 83). The passage Taylor mentions refers to America, and reads as follows: "besyde the portion of lande perteynyng to the Spanyardes . . . and beside that which pertineth to the Portugales there yet remayneth an other portion of that mayne land reachyng towarde the northeast yet knowen but only by the sea coastes . . . whereas neverthelesse (as wryteth Gemma Frisius) in this lande there are man fayre and frutefull regions, hygh mountaynes, and fayre ryvers, with *abundaunce of gold* and dyvers kyndes of beastes" (Eden 1555, ci recto; emphasis mine).

Indeed, the Sudan—an Arabic term for the land of black people, south of the Sahara—was famous for its gold.[36] Mali's gold was traded north by caravan across the Sahara, where it arrived in the Mediterranean world; the rulers of Mali and Songhay spoke Arabic, and went on pilgrimage to Mecca.[37] A tenth-century Arab writer, Ibn Hawkal, described the king of Ghana (southwestern Mali) as "the richest sovereign on earth".[38] Gold provided an ingredient for fabulous display around the persons of West African rulers, and this display was also legendary well beyond the region. The early fourteenth century Malian ruler Mansa Musa I went on pilgrimage to Mecca accompanied by sixty thousand porters, with five hundred servants decked in gold and carrying golden staffs—a journey on which he gave away so much gold that the price fell. North African observers described his successor as seated on a throne ornamented with gold and ivory, holding spears of silver and gold, surrounded by nobles decked with gold. A fourteenth century Majorcan atlas represented the ruler of Mali (Mansa Musa) holding nuggets of gold.[39]

Hakluyt and his reporters were familiar with the idea that there were rich and powerful kingdoms in the interior of sub-Saharan Africa. A report from Laurence Madoc in 1591 notes the Moroccan conquest of Timbukto and Gao in 1591, with "an infinite treasure . . . more golde then any other part of the world beside"; he remarks that "this king of Marocco is likely to be the greatest prince in the world for money, if he keepe this countrey" (*PN* VII, 101). In the 1620s, following a trading voyage to the River Gambia, Richard Jobson expressed in a petition to the king the belief that Africa's riches—and indeed, Ophir—could be reached directly by travelling up the Gambia, described by another Hakluyt document as "a river of secret trade and riches" (*PN* VII, 91).[40]

Yet the trajectory of Africa and Russia through Eden's and Hakluyt's collections certainly suggests that Russian materials had a kind of value in their eyes which African materials did not have—that gold, or the hope of it, was not all that mattered. So far, we have largely looked at the hard evidence of the book, within the context of actual enterprises;

---

[36] Gold had long been extracted along the upper Niger and Senegal rivers, as well as in the regions of the Volta and Lower Guinea.

[37] D.T. Niane, *Africa from the Twelfth to the Sixteenth Century* (Berkeley, 1984), 146-47.

[38] Niane, *Africa from the Twelfth to the Sixteenth Century*, 617.

[39] Niane, 148, 152, 117; Garrard, *Akan Weights*, 10.

[40] Jobson's petition (BL Royal MS LS a LVIII, 275, ff.1-5v) is printed in David P. Gamble and P.E.H. Hair eds., *The Discovery of River Gambra by Richard Jobson 1623*, Works issued by the Hakluyt Society, 3rd ser. vol. 2 (London, 1999), 199-204).

in what follows, we will look at the more speculative evidence of the texts these books contained.

5.

It will immediately strike readers of the Muscovy narratives that while gold is absent from the list of commodities regularly imported from Russia in the sixteenth century—hides and furs, cordage and cables, flax, hemp, tallow, train oil, wax—it is very much present in the texts.[41] Richard Chancellor's northern voyage in 1553 produced two narratives, one by Clement Adams (a stay-at-home schoolmaster), another by Chancellor himself; at least the first would have been available to Eden, and both were printed by Hakluyt.[42] Both accounts make a parenthetical comment on the name given to a particular court building, Chancellor more amply. His narrative describes an audience with the Tsar in a "palace which is called the Golden Palace, but I saw no cause why it should be so called; for I have seen many fairer than it in all points."[43] Entering this unprepossessing building, he found the Tsar in a dining room crowded with gold vessels; the dinner service was of "very massie" gold, and the gentlemen waiters wore cloth of gold (II, 227-28). Chancellor's complaint—that the name of the palace did not properly correspond to the thing it designated—occasioned a kind of editorial notice quite uncharacteristic of Hakluyt's usual interests. In the preface to volume I, Hakluyt recommends to the reader's attention the *Libell of English Policie*, a late medieval poem on English foreign trade; he does so by referring to Chancellor. Praising the poem's content but apologizing for its "homely" style, he writes,

> I cannot to any thing more fitly compare [*Libell*] then to the Emperour of Russia his palace called the golden Castle . . . described by Richard Chanceller pag. 238. of this volume: whereof albeit the outward appearance was but homely and no whit correspondent to the name, yet was it within so beautified and adorned with the Emperor his majesticall presence, with the honorable and great assembly of

---

[41] The index of Willan's *Early History* lists the goods which English merchants imported to and exported from Muscovy.

[42] The first Muscovy pilot, Richard Chancellor, was personally known to Eden; the longest account of his voyage, by Clement Adams, appeared as a free-standing text in the 1550's, though no copies are known to be extant. Presumably the availability of this text elsewhere helps to account for its absence from the 1555 collection. Hakluyt also prints a shorter, first-person account apparently by Chancellor himself, which he found as a manuscript in Lord Lumley's library.

[43] Adams writes that the English were "conducted into the golden Court, (for so they call it, although not very faire)" (*PN* II, 256).

his rich-attired Peers and Senators, with an invaluable and huge mass of gold and
silverplate, & with other princely magnificence; that well might the eyes of the
beholders be dazzled, and their consultations astonished thereat (*PN* I, 1).

Chancellor objects that the name of the palace is "golden," while the
thing itself is dull; Hakluyt suggests that the outside of the palace was
"homely" while the inside contained the "majesticall presence" of the
Emperor and a "huge mass of gold," effectively opening up the second
term of Chancellor's name/thing distinction to a further opposition
between superficial appearance and hidden truth. Hakluyt makes
Chancellor's literal description into a simile, both of whose terms share
the structure of allegory; this passage marks an uncharacteristic departure from practical and literal concerns into something like aesthetics
and semiotics.

Hakluyt was not the only one to be struck by the dazzle of Muscovy's
gold. Other reporters followed Chancellor in commenting on the Tsar's
abundant displays of gold plate. Eden quoted the description of a similar scene from a continental history of Muscovy: "The kynge hym selfe
with pryncely magnyfycence and singuler familaritiee . . . is accustomed
to dyne openly . . . in his owne chamber of presence where is seene A
meruelous quantitye of syuluer and gylte place standynge vppon two
great and high cubbardes in the same chamber". He adds in the mar-
gin, "Sigismundus [Herberstein] sayth that much of this is golde" (Eden
1555, 288 verso). On Christmas Day 1557, an English observer wrote
that "for goodly and rich plate, we never saw the like or so much
before"; seven hundred people dined at the Tsar's table, all served "in
vessels of gold . . . as much as could stand one by another upon the
tables," while there were still four cupboards standing full of "goodly
plate both of gold & silver" (*PN* II, 432). Gold also appeared as clothing.
Chancellor writes of the Tsar's ambassadors, whose horses, as well as
their persons, were draped with "velvet, cloth of golde, and clother of
silver set with pearles," that he "never heard of nor saw men so sumptuous" in their attire. George Killingworth, in 1555, describes being
brought into the Tsar's presence through a chamber in which sat "neere
a hundred in cloth of gold," and then finding "more then in the other
chamber also in cloth of gold"; like Chancellor, he dined with a hundred
others at tables covered with gold plate, with "a great number of plat-
ters of golde, standing still on the cupboord, not moved."

Chancellor's description of the Golden Palace which was not golden
echoed in the larger story English reporters told of Muscovite life: com-
moners sold themselves into debt bondage, ate stinking fish, and praised

the merry life of prisoners who "haue meate and drinke without any labour" (*PN* II, 241). Yet Chancellor for one did not view this general lack as altogether bad; his comments on Muscovite poverty alternate with praise for their hardiness, a quality immediately connected to their abilities in war.[44] He correlates the poverty of Muscovites in general with the wealth of the monarch and with their dutiful subjection to his authority.

> [A Muscovite] will say, that he hath nothing, but it is Gods and the Duke's graces. . . . Man may say, that these men are in wonderful great awe, and obedience, that thus one must give and grant his goods which he hath been scraping and scratching for all his life to be at his princes pleasure and commandment. Oh that our sturdy rebels were had in the like subjection to know their duty toward their princes. (*PN* II, 232).

English narrators comment that the sumptuous dress of ambassadors was stunning, but "no daily guise, for when they have not occasion . . . all their doing is but mean"; the golden garments of courtiers were borrowed from royal wardrobe and treasury (II, 332). This alternation of the mean and golden staged both the poverty even of elite Muscovites *and* the magnificence of the Tsar—just as the lavish state dinners English reporters described, at which Ivan IV sent food and drink to guests, dramatized both his generosity and the dependence of those who ate at his golden table. In these accounts, the material and legal poverty of the Tsar's subjects indicated not the failure of his regime but the total assent of his subjects; their occasional sumptuousness indicated not their own power and resources, but his favor.

What English observers described bore some relation to Muscovite reality—with some adjustment—but also reflected very considerable state control over the kind of information they received.[45] It would appear that certain scenes were repeatedly enacted. The Tsar's riches, for one, were clearly displayed as a form of communication: regarding his wealth, his magnificence, his capacity to muster easily forms of stunning excess.

---

[44] Chancellor writes of Muscovite soldiers "I beleeve they be such men for hard living as are not under the sun" (II, 230); of the poor, "in mine opinion there be no such people under the sunne for their hardnesse of living" (II, 236).

[45] Marshall Poe, *"A People Born to Slavery": Russia in Early Modern European Ethnography, 1476-1748* (Ithaca, 2000), 47. Poe remarks that foreign visitors to Muscovy were systematically isolated, and that "the Russian court had a clear and singular purpose" where they were concerned: "to display the dignity and might of its prince"; as a result, the European sources he cites had "a marked tendency to exaggerate the power of the Tsar and the servility of his servants" (201). The final chapter of Poe's book assesses the relation between European accounts and Muscovite realities.

By the same token, evidently this display meant something to the English observers who reported it with such repetitive detail. These narratives in effect represented a collaboration between Muscovites who wished to be seen in a certain way, and English observers who saw and described them thus. If we turn to Africa, the circumstances are very different. There, the English did not spend months at a central court whose monarch was concerned with impressing them. They appear to have stayed for the most part on the coast, and wouldn't have seen the richest cities—Timbuktu, Gao, or Jenne—or their rulers.[46] But they certainly saw gold.

6.

In an expansive moment, the anonymous pilot who provided Eden with his generally terse account of the 1554 voyage to Africa described African princes and noblemen as adorned with characteristic tattoos but also jewelry of "gold, copper, or ivory"; women also wore jewelry, bracelets of copper and ivory, "foresleeves made of the plates of beathen golde" and "rings, made of golden wires, with a knot or wreath" (*PN* VI, 173). "Our men," the pilot wrote, were able to buy "other things of golde . . . for exchange of their wares," including "certaine dogchaines and collers". The account of William Towerson's first voyage to the coast of present-day Ghana in 1555 described trade with a captain who assured the English merchants that his people would "bring great store of gold, which in deed . . . they did"; the captain's panoply was made of bark, iron, and cloth, but the narrator notes in passing that "their golde also they worke very well" (*PN* VI, 196-97). Another reference to material culture in the narrative of his second voyage (1556) associates gold with the ceremonial display of royal power. "All these ceremonies first done, the king tooke a cup of gold, and they put him in wine, and hee dranke of it, and when he dranke, the people cried all with one voice. . . ." (*PN* VI, 228).[47]

---

[46] English merchants did visit Benin. One merchant who visited the court commented on the reverence received there by the king (or Oba): "if we would give as much to our Savior Christ, we should remoove from from our heads many plagues which we daily deserve for our contempt and impietie" (*PN* VI, 149).

[47] I haven't been able to identify the town described here, which Towerson's men estimated to be "as big in circuit as London"; it was apparently between Shamma and Mouree.

These references, however, are the only ones which resemble the Muscovy narratives in the sense of describing the use of gold for personal adornment and royal spectacle: a striking absence for a region where gold was so readily available that such uses were relatively wide-spread.[48] Portuguese traders in 1502 returned 2000 ounces of gold from Elmina, on the coast of present-day Ghana, "all in manillas [armrings] and jewels, which the negroes are accustomed to wear".[49] Portuguese, Dutch, and French observers alike commented that African rulers were richly adorned with gold regalia, and that the art of working in gold had reached a high level of sophistication.[50] The English narrators, visiting the same coasts, seem to have paid little attention.

In the English narratives, gold is ubiquitous; but it appears most frequently as a set of numbers describing by weight the amounts which the English obtained in trade. The account of Towerson's voyage in 1556-57 at times devolves into a simple list of dates, places, and quantities:

> This day we tooke one pound and 10 ounces of gold.
> The 24 day we tooke 3 pound and 7 ounces.
> The 25 we tooke 3 ounces and 3 quarters.
> The 26 we tooke 2 pound and 10 ounces.
> The 27 two pound and five ounces.
> The 28 foure pound, and then seeing that there was no more gold to be had, we weighed and went foorth.
> (*PN* VI, 228).

In turn, African material culture registered most decisively on the narratives in terms of its weights and measures. On the first voyage, Towerson's men encountered "one . . . [who] had his weights and scales, and a chaine of golde aboute his necke, and another about his arme" (208).[51] As Towerson's men worked their way down the coast in the

---

[48] Bethwell Ogot comments that "in metalworking and casting, especially in gold and brass, . . . the peoples of Lower Guinea and the Akan in particular excelled," producing "exquisite gold and silver objects, including sword handles, rings, bangles, chains and headgear" as well as "thousands of geometric and figurative gold or brass weights" (Ogot, *Africa from the Sixteenth to the Eighteenth Century* (Berkeley, 1992), 428-29). Garrard provides more detail in *Akan Weights*.

[49] Garrard, *Akan Weights*, 105, citing João de Barros, *Da Asia*, decade 1, translated in Blake, *Europeans in West Africa* I, 93.

[50] Ruy de Pina describes an Akan chief whose arms, legs and neck were 'covered with chains and trinkets of gold in many shapes, and countless bells and large beads of gold were hanging from the hair of his beard and his head" (Garrard, *Akan Weights*, 104, citing Ruy de Pina, *Chronica del Rey Dom João II*, translated in Blake, *Europeans in West Africa* I, 73). For other references, see Garrard 107-09.

[51] For illustrations of gold weights, see Angela Fisher, *Africa Adorned* (London, 1987), 86.

winter of 1557, groups were differentiated by the elaboration of their apparatus for the trade in gold. "We went into the River and found no village, but certaine wild Negros not accustomed to trade" (215); "we tooke but one halfe angel weight . . . which we tooke by hand, for the people of this place had no weight" (216). Finally (in the passage briefly cited above) they reached a place where the captain of the town had "gone to the principall towne, to speake with their king, and would returne shortly as they told me, and so he did, and brought me a weight and measure, and I sent a man to see that principall towne, and their king" (226).

Despite an abundant mass of gold in these accounts of African trade, there is little corresponding to what Chancellor saw at the Tsar's court. Hakluyt's narrators understood or at least represented African gold as material and commercial, traded as a commodity among others, rather than something bound up with cultural expression and state power. Tangible and weighty, it barely features in the narratives as something seen, worn, or displayed. By contrast, Muscovite gold was represented as visible, social and symbolic. Not only present as an "invaluable huge mass", it was seen and noticed everywhere in its worked, social form; finally, it makes "the eyes of the beholders be dazzled, and their consultations astonished." The language suggests this Russian gold is not just visible but dazzling, perhaps more real as symbol than as commodity, and what it signified was Ivan IV's power. Yet if the English represented Africa as the place of the material, that material was the *sine qua non* of value. Given other European reports, it seems reasonable to wonder whether the narrators may also have underreported seeing gold as a cultural artifact. The difference can be described, but we can't be certain precisely why these African narratives of the 1550's look the way they do.

The other side of the question also remains to be asked: why did the northern trade with Muscovy matter so much, to Hakluyt and others? We can observe that it was the sole tangible result of efforts which had from the 1550's been construed in terms of national prestige, as England's bid to match the discoveries of Portugal and Spain. Within this larger enterprise, the Tsar's glittering court figured the ultimate goal of an Asian empire further to the east. Even in 1600, documents concerning "Cathay and the way thither" took up a significant part of Hakluyt's collection; the longest single items in the first volume are two accounts of fourteenth-century missions to the court of the Khan which, if seemingly outdated, were still being quarried by Hakluyt for information on the human and physical geography of central Asia in the 1590's.[52]

The goal of this hypothetical contact with China was not only or simply commercial profit, but diplomatic, even cultural exchange.[53] The actual account of a further northeast passage search by Arthur Pet and Charles Jackman in 1580 describes an experience both terrifying and monotonous, a long emergency of warping from iceberg to iceberg in freezing fog (*PN* III, 282-303). The instructions for the voyage, however—prepared by Hakluyt's older cousin of the same name—speak eloquently to what its backers hoped to find. Pet and Jackman were instructed to make the kinds of commercial inquiries one might expect: "Take a speciall note of their apparell and furniture, and of the substance that the same is made of, of which a Merchant may make a gesse as well of their commoditie, as also of their wants" (*PN* III, 269). But their instructions presume that the exchange of English and Chinese things will bring not only profit, but delight, to both sides: just as the "seeds of [East Asian] fruits and herbs . . . will delight the fansie of many for the strangenesse," so an English book of plants "may much delight the great Can, and the nobilitie, and also their merchants . . . all things in these parts so much differing from the things of those regions" (*PN* II, 268, 273). Notably, books feature repeatedly both in the instructions given by the elder Hakluyt ("bring thence some old printed booke, to see whether they have had print there before it was devised in Europe") and others by John Dee (*PN* III, 263, 268).

In the instructions for Pet and Jackman, Hakluyt's cousin imagined a culture whose technology, power, indeed civility, might be in advance of Europe. These instructions include, as "Things to be caried with

----

[52] These accounts are by William of Rubruck and John de Plano Carpini (Hakluyt 1903-05, I, 55-79, 229-93). For Hakluyt's use of them, see his letter to Emanuel van Meteren, in Taylor, *Original Writings* II, 418-20.

[53] Hakluyt printed a "Treatise of China" (Macao, 1590), which provided an optimistic account of China's resources in gold: "this region affordeth especially sundry kinds of mettals, of which the chiefe, both in excellencie & in abundance, is gold, whereof so many Pezoes are brought from China to India, into our country of Japon, that I heard say, that in one and the same ship, this present yeere, 2000 such pieces consisting of massie gold . . . were brought unto us for marchandise: and one of these loaves is worth almost 100 duckats. Hence it is that in the kingdom of China so many things are adorned with gold, as for example, beds, tables, pictures, images, litters wherein nice and daintie dames are carried upon their servaunts backs. Neither are these golden loaves only bought by the Portugals, but also great plenty of gold-twine and leaves of gold: for the Chinians can very cunningly beate and extenuate gold into plates and leaves" (VI, 354).

you," not only merchandise and things to delight and entertain the Chinese court, but "Boxes with weights for gold, and of every kind of the coine of gold, good and bad, to shew that the people here use weight and measure, which is a certaine shew of wisedom, and of certaine government settled here" as well as the "coynes of our English monies . . . a thing that shall in silence speake to wise men more then you imagine" (*PN* III, 271). Elsewhere in *Principal Navigations*, lists of weights, measures and money inform the commercial traveller of the standards current in Babylon, Ormuz, or Goa.[54] Something different is envisioned here: reaching past Russia to a court at which the English would demonstrate their *own* apparatus for weighing gold, and its transformation into an authorized medium of exchange bearing the insignia of royal power, a court of "wise men" where their own civility would be triumphantly validated not from below, but from above.

Thomas Hariot and Walter Ralegh both described the New World as populated by peoples prepared to reverence an English book or the portrait of Queen Elizabeth on a coin.[55] China was imagined as not only the other side of the world from the Americas, but also, so to say, the other side of the coin as far as culture. The forms of cultural superiority which English narrators staged at the expense of indigenous Americans, at least on paper, had an evident appeal, and others have been eloquent on this topic.[56] Yet the elder Hakluyt's instructions suggest fleetingly that to have been taken seriously by the Chinese might *also* have been as good as gold to a nation still emerging from a sense of its own backwardness.

We began by considering the travel book as object, and have concluded by considering objects in the narratives which compose the book. Between the bookends of Eden's *Treatyse* (1553) and Hakluyt's *Principal Navigations* (1600), English travel narratives in general became more valuable, in part as a way of asserting national achievement. The two editors' comments and handling of their materials suggest that some appeared more useful to them, for this purpose, than others.

---

[54] John Hasse, who accompanied Chancellor on the voyage of 1553, provided Hakluyt with an account of "The coines, weights and measures used in Russia" (*PN* II, 273). In practice, some of the adjustments necessary must have been not dissimilar to the negotiation of weights and measures between European and African traders.

[55] Thomas Harriot, *A briefe and true report of . . . Virginia* (Frankfurt, 1590), 27; Walter Ralegh, *Discoverie of . . . Guiana* (London, 1596), 81. Both works were reprinted by Hakluyt.

[56] See in particular Jeffrey Knapp, *An Empire Nowhere: England, America, and Literature from* Utopia *to* The Tempest (Berkeley, 1992).

The axis of comparison for editorial treatment and value has been by regions and cultures, rather than whether the voyagers were famous (or not), whether their endeavours were successful (or not), or whether their narratives were well-written (or not). This comparison of African and Russian materials is suggested by the history of trade, but also and especially by the history of the book. I've made two arguments: first, that Russia is privileged by the editors; second, more speculatively, that editors and perhaps also the traveler-narrators understood Muscovy in terms of intangible profit, and Africa in terms of material profit, and preferred the first.[57]

These are arguments about writing, rather than about action; the high-minded disavowals of any greedy desire for tangible profit which pervade travel writing in the period surely don't indicate that anyone was actually turning down the chance to make money, and a general desire for cultural validation was surely not so strong as to override more practical concerns. (After all, the mundane goods Muscovy exported were also very useful). Yet Hakluyt's narratives often tell us far more about failed voyages than about quiet, profitable commercial enterprises abroad. (The Newfoundland fishery would be one example of the latter). Certainly the gold yet to be located in Cathay and the Indies conditions the anthology far more powerfully than the gold English traders purchased with cloth and iron in West Africa. A cautious conclusion to draw from the evidence of Hakluyt's and Eden's collections might be, not that the English in their voyages sought cultural validation more than profit, but that travel *writing* handled the first far more comfortably than the second.

Acknowledgments

This essay draws on research done at the Houghton and John Carter Brown Libraries, the latter supported in part by a grant from the National Endowment for the Humanities; my thanks to NEH, the staff

---

[57] The presence of gold was of course not necessarily an index of actual profit. P.E.H. Hair comments that "up to at least the 1630s trade with Guinea contributed little to the British economy (despite the hopes entertained during the earliest voyages)" ("Attitudes to Africans in English Primary Sources on Guinea up to 1650", *History in Africa* 26 [1999], 47). Conversely, Hakluyt's assertion in the ms. *Discourse of Western Planting* (1584) that the Russia trade had become "beggarly, or dangerous" was according to Willan less a reliable reflection on the trade's success than a piece of propaganda for exploring elsewhere (*Early History of the Russia Company*, 181).

of both libraries, and in particular Richard Ring, reference librarian at the JCB. I'm grateful for opportunities to present earlier versions of this work at Princeton, USC, Trinity College Oxford, and the Musée de l'Homme (Québec). Thanks also to Joyce Millen and Ernest Zitser for their help with unfamiliar sources.

READING TRAVELS IN THE CULTURE OF CURIOSITY: THÉVENOT'S COLLECTION OF VOYAGES

NICHOLAS DEW

McGill University

ABSTRACT

This article explores the circulation and use of travel writings within the seventeenth-century "culture of curiosity", focusing on a figure at the heart of this milieu, Melchisédech Thévenot (? 1622-1692), and his edited *Relations de divers voyages curieux* (1663-1672). The Thévenot case reveals the importance of travel writing for the scholarly community in a period when the modern boundaries between disciplines were not yet formed, and when the nature of geographical knowledge was undergoing radical change. The collection, discussion and publication of the travel collection are shown to be part of the program of Thévenot's experimental "assembly" to investigate the "arts".

John Locke kept abreast of the scholarly news from France through the regular correspondence of Nicolas Toinard, an antiquarian and Biblical scholar from Orléans. In the summer of 1680, a mutual friend added an enquiry of his own. This friend was Melchisédech Thévenot (c. 1622-1692), whom Locke had met during his years in France (1675-79). Thévenot explained that, while reading *Purchas his Pilgrimes*, he had found a reference to some papers of Richard Hakluyt's that had not been printed; Purchas seemed to imply that these texts deserved to be made public, and Thévenot asked Locke to make enquiries as to where these manuscripts might be. Thévenot was already a reasonably well-known collector, who had published a four-volume travel compilation, the *Relations de divers voyages curieux*.[1] He hoped that the missing Hakluyt papers might be found and printed, both for the benefit of the "Public", and as a tribute to Hakluyt, to whom posterity would always be grateful for having brought so many texts to light which would otherwise be lost.[2]

---

[1] Melchisédech Thévenot, ed., *Relations de divers voyages curieux, qui n'ont point esté publiées; ou qui ont esté traduites d'Hacluyt, de Purchas, & d'autres Voyageurs Anglois, Hollandois, Portugais, Allemands, Espagnols; et de quelques Persans, Arabes, et autres Auteurs Orientaux . . .*, 4 vols. large quarto (Paris, 1663-1672); augmented reissue in 2 vols. (Paris, 1696). There was also a shorter octavo volume, supplementing the quarto series: *Recueil de voyages* (Paris, 1681, reissued 1682).

[2] John Locke, *Correspondence*, ed. E. S. de Beer, 8 vols. (Oxford, 1976-89), vol. 2, 229-30 (Toinard to Locke, 14/24 August 1680): Thévenot writes, ". . . Purchas en parle

Thévenot's note to Locke provides an entry point for exploring the circulation of travel writings within the baroque "culture of curiosity".[3] Thévenot, tantalized by a reference to lost Hakluyt papers, hopes to appropriate them within his own series (itself an emulation of Hakluyt); he duly sets about finding them using the method he knows best—by writing to fellow members of the "Republic of Letters". In this note to Locke, most of the key terms and images that we will find recurring as we follow Thévenot's case are present: the encyclopedic compilation, seen as a resource for posterity; the privileging of certain source-texts (usually manuscripts, and often unattainable); and, above all, the desire to bring potentially useful and hitherto hidden knowledge (especially from overseas) into public circulation, via translation and print.

A second example from the Toinard-Locke letters offers a variation on these themes. Toinard and Locke had been discussing Robert Boyle's latest book, in which Boyle described cooking meat and fish in an evacuated air-pump; this prompted Toinard to wonder whether it might be possible to use an air-pump to transform sea water into healthy drinking water. He then relates that Thévenot had once told him that in Holland, some years earlier, a man claimed to have "found this important secret" (i.e. making sea water potable) and had tried to sell his discovery to the Dutch East Indies Company, for the sum of "10,000 écus". The Company refused, and so the secret died with the man. Later, apparently, the Company regretted its decision.[4]

Such stories of ill-fated inventors abound in the correspondence and the periodicals of the time. Thévenot's Dutch anecdote can be connected

---

comme de pieces qui meritent d'estre données au public[.] Il faudroit s'informer en quelles mains peuvent estre tombes ces ecrits, et sauver ces ouvrages en faveur du Public et d'un homme [i.e. Hakluyt] dont on se souviendra tousjours pour l'obligation que nous luy avons de nous avoir sauvé beaucoup de bonnes choses. Il a sauvé des pieces et des ouvrages de quelques uns de nos conquerans François[.] Je vouderois bien estre assez heureux pour luy rendre la pareille et sauver de l'oubly . . . quelques-uns de ses ouvrages." Toinard (or Thoynard, 1628-1706), was an antiquarian and biblical scholar, and one of Locke's most diligent correspondents.

[3] On the "culture of curiosity", see Krzysztof Pomian, *Collectionneurs, amateurs et curieux: Paris, Venise: XVIe-XVIIIe siècle* (Paris, 1987), 61-80; Paula Findlen, *Possessing Nature: museums, collecting and scientific culture in early modern Italy* (Berkeley, 1994); Neil Kenny, *The Uses of Curiosity in early modern France and Germany* (Oxford, 2004).

[4] Toinard to Locke, 24 Sept 1680, in Locke, *Correspondence*, vol. 2, 256: "Mr Tevenot m'a autrefois dit que l'on estoit tres persuadé en Holande qu'un particulier avoit trouvé il y a du tems ce secret important [i.e. of making seawater potable] avec lequel il est mort, parceque la compagnie des Indes Orientales qui s'en est bien repentie, luy avoit refusé dix mille écus qu'il demandoit pour le dire".

with a broader project to "discover" (in the sense of "uncover") hidden knowledge, specifically the "secrets" of the *arts* (artisanal techniques). Discovering the "arts" also meant devising new techniques, new instruments and machines.[5] As we will find, this program for collecting the "arts" is connected with travel and navigation in two senses. First, there is an emphasis on techniques that will be useful for the art of navigation; second, there is the emphasis on using travel itself as a form of *experience* which, if properly accumulated in print, will allow knowledge of nature and of techniques to be discovered and exchanged.

For historians of early modern science, Thévenot figures in the story of the private scientific assemblies that existed just before the establishment of the Académie Royale des Sciences (in 1666).[6] For historians of travel literature, he is known for the *Relations de divers voyages curieux*, the first large-scale French travel collection, frequently cited by early Enlightenment readers. Locke made notes on Thévenot's collection and cites it, along with other travel accounts, in his *Essay on human understanding*.[7] Thévenot's collection also features in the library catalogues of Voltaire, Turgot, d'Holbach, de Brosses, and William Beckford.[8] Usually, these twin aspects of Thévenot's career—his scientific club, and his compilation of travel accounts—are kept apart. If, however, we attempt to read the sources without dividing his interests into present-day categories, a relationship between these activities emerges. As we will see, Thévenot's travel compilation was the product of a particular social network, and of a particular intellectual program.

---

[5] On "secrets" and the "arts" in the scientific culture of the period, see William Eamon, *Science and the Secrets of Nature: books of secrets in medieval and early modern culture* (Princeton, 1994); Pamela O. Long, *Openness, Secrecy, Authorship: technical arts and the culture of knowledge from Antiquity to the Renaissance* (Baltimore, 2001).

[6] Harcourt Brown, *Scientific Organizations in Seventeenth-Century France (1620-1680)* (Baltimore, 1934), 135-60; David J. Sturdy, *Science and Social Status: the members of the Académie des sciences, 1666-1750* (Woodbridge, 1995), 16-21.

[7] John Locke, *An Essay concerning Human Understanding*, ed. Peter H. Nidditch (Oxford, 1975), 71 (I.iii.9), 87 (I.iv.8). On Locke's use of Thévenot, see Gabriel D. Bonno, *Les Relations intellectuelles de Locke avec la France*, University of California Publications in Modern Philology, 38, no. 2 (Berkeley and Los Angeles, 1955), 83-84, 168; John Lough, "Locke's reading during his stay in France (1675-1679)", *The Library*, 5th series, 8 (1953), 229-58, at 239-40. See also Daniel Carey, "Locke, travel literature, and the natural history of Man", *The Seventeenth Century*, 11 (1996), 259-80.

[8] Michèle Duchet, *Anthropologie et histoire au siècle des Lumières* (Paris, 1971), 486; Henri-Jean Martin and Roger Chartier, eds., *Histoire de l'édition française*, 2nd ed. (Paris, 1989-91), vol. 2, 24 (Beckford's copy).

I

Thévenot came from a family of royal office-holders,[9] and it seems that his collecting and scholarly projects were funded largely from private wealth.[10] He is still sometimes confused with his nephew, Jean [de] Thévenot (1633-67), who made two voyages, one to the Levant, one to Persia and India (meeting his death on the way back), and wrote an account of his travels that went through several editions.[11] It needs to be made clear, given the confusion between the two, that Melchisédech never set foot in the Orient himself. However, he did spend some time touring Europe in his youth, possibly in the company of his nephew. Especially important were two diplomatic missions he spent in Italy in the 1640s and 1650s, where he formed friendships with members of the scholarly community, and also developed an interest in Oriental studies, partly through his acquaintance with Abraham Ecchellensis (Ibrahim al-Haqilani), a professor of Arabic at the Maronite College in Rome.[12]

Thévenot was back in Paris by 1655, where he first met Christiaan Huygens.[13] In that period, Thévenot had close links with those Parisian scholars who pursued Skeptical and Epicurean philosophy (the so-called *libertins érudits*), especially the circle around Pierre Gassendi and Henri-Louis Habert de Montmor.[14] Thévenot was frequently described as an

---

[9] On the family, see BN ms fr. 29303, dossier 62724, esp. items 22-31; Thévenot was "Conseiller du Roy en ses Conseils d'Estat"; his grandfather, Melchissédec Garnier (d. 1637), had been "doyen des avocats au Parlement de Paris".

[10] Jean Chapelain, *Lettres*, ed. J. P. Tamizey de Larroque, 2 vols. (Paris, 1880-1883), vol. 2, 616: Chapelain to J. F. Gronovius, 5 Feb. 1669. Chapelain says of Thévenot: "Son application a ceste sorte d'estude est d'autant plus noble qu'elle n'a rien de sordide et qu'au lieu d'y chercher autre interest que celuy de l'avantage du genre humain, il y employe avec son temps la richesse qu'il a héritée de ses pères".

[11] Jean [de] Thévenot, *Relation d'un voyage*, 3 vols. (Paris and Rouen, 1664-1684); "standard" edition, 5 vols. (Paris, 1689), reprinted (Amsterdam, 1727); translations: Dutch (Amsterdam, 1681-8), English (London, 1687), German (Frankfurt, 1693). On Jean de Thévenot, see Lane M. Heller, "Le testament olographe de Jean de Thévenot", *XVIIe siècle*, 167 (1990), 227-234; and the editor's introduction to Jean Thévenot, *Voyage du Levant*, ed. Stéphane Yerasimos (Paris, 1980), 5-27.

[12] On Ecchellensis (1605-1664), see Pieter J. A. N. Rietbergen, "A Maronite mediator between seventeenth-century cultures: Ibrahim al-Haqilani, or Abraham Ecchellense (1606-1664) between Christendom and Islam", *Lias*, 16 (1989), 13-41; and Gérald Duverdier, "Les impressions orientales en Europe et le Liban", in Camille Aboussouan, ed., *Le Livre et le Liban jusqu'à 1900* (Paris, 1982), 157-280.

[13] Jean Mesnard, "Les premières relations parisiennes de Christiaan Huygens", in René Taton, ed., *Huygens et la France* (Paris, 1982), 33-40.

[14] Brown, *Scientific Organizations*; René Pintard, *Le Libertinage érudit dans la première moitié du XVIIe siècle* (Paris, 1943).

honnête homme (indeed "un des meilleurs et des plus honnests hommes de Paris"),[15] and had links with the writers who articulated this particular ethic of sociability. With his private wealth, he was able to create a "cabinet" (a private museum and library, with some scientific instruments) in which he could hold meetings of scholarly friends and play host to foreign scholars when they visited Paris.

In the traditional historiography of French science, Thévenot is known for his role as a member of the Gassendi-Montmor group (the so-called "Montmor Academy"), which Thévenot hosted in the last two years of its existence (1663-1665).[16] Often this group is described a direct ancestor of the Académie Royale des Sciences, although the relationship between the two is more complex.[17] Despite (or perhaps because of) his prominent role as an academy-host, when Colbert founded the Académie Royale des Sciences in 1666, Thévenot was not made a member. For the next eighteen years, he withdrew from Paris intellectual life, pursuing studies at his country house at Issy.[18] The literature's traditional focus on the Académie des Sciences has led historians to "reify" the private academies of the period, to imagine them as "scientific organizations", with a greater degree of programmatic coherence than the sources really support. In many ways, the "assemblies" that met *chez* Montmor and Thévenot were social settings resembling the other clubs and salons of the mid-century, and to some degree sharing participants and projects with them.[19]

---

[15] Huygens to L. Huygens, 7 Dec. 1661, in Christiaan Huygens, *Œuvres complètes*, eds. D. Bierens de Haan and J. Bosscha, 22 vols. (The Hague, 1888-1950), vol. 3, 395.

[16] On the "Montmor academy", see Brown, *Scientific Organizations*, 64-134; Sturdy, *Science and Social Status*, 16-21.

[17] Trevor McClaughlin, "Sur les rapports entre la Compagnie de Thévenot et l'Académie royale des sciences," Revue d'histoire des sciences, 28 (1975), 235-42; idem, "Une lettre de Melchisédech Thévenot," *Revue d'histoire des sciences*, 27 (1974), 123-6; Robert M. McKeon, "Une lettre de M. Thévenot sur les débuts de l'Académie royale des sciences," *Revue d'histoire des sciences*, 18 (1965), 1-6; David S. Lux, *Patronage and Royal Science in Seventeenth-Century France: the Académie de Physique in Caen* (Ithaca, 1989), 29-56.

[18] Erica Harth portrays him as one of Colbert's "mandarins", which is misleading: *Ideology and Culture in Seventeenth-Century France* (Ithaca, 1983), 243-50. It was only at the end of 1684 (after Colbert's death, 1683) that Thévenot received royal patronage, when he was appointed *commis à la garde* of the Bibliothèque du roi, and a member of the Académie des Sciences a month later. He lost the library post in 1691, and died at Issy on 29 October 1692.

[19] Brown, *Scientific Organizations*, tends to over-reify the groups. Contemporary sources make clear the overlapping "membership", e.g. Ole Borch, *Olai Borrichii Itinerarium 1660-1665: the Journal of the Danish polyhistor Ole Borch*, ed. H. D. Schepelern, 4 vols. (Copenhagen and London, 1983), vols. 3 and 4.

Thévenot's group tends to be remembered for the activities of its most celebrated members, Niels Steno, Jan Swammerdam, and Huygens. The Danish naturalist Steno (later known for his work on fossils) first made his name by dissecting a human brain before a large audience at Thévenot's, although he also anatomized insects, along with Jan Swammerdam, the Dutch microscopist, who was lodging with Thévenot at the same time.[20] Huygens was a regular visitor to the Paris group from the mid-1650s, and his letters are a major source for its activities, including the attempts in Paris to replicate experiments with the air-pump.[21] The presence of such relatively canonic figures has meant that Thévenot's group is usually conceived as being primarily, even exclusively, concerned with experimental natural philosophy. However, like most contemporary "scientific" groups, the Thévenot circle set itself a wide remit, which included the improvement of navigation and the use of travellers to collect observations. It seems Huygens conceived of this as akin to Baconian natural history.[22] We find evidence of Thévenot's continued commitment to collecting the arts in the letters he later exchanged with Leibniz, who had made Thévenot's acquaintance in Paris in the 1670s. As well as their diplomatic experiences, the two scholars shared an eclectic, polyhistoric curiosity. Thévenot was among Leibniz's more vociferous supporters in Paris, offering to help bring any of his projects to completion, "sur toute l'Enciclopedie"; Leibniz, for his part, tirelessly commended Thévenot to other correspondents, saying that he was "one of the most universal [men] that I know; nothing escapes his curiosity".[23]

What Leibniz seems to have admired in Thévenot's work was his desire to compile and then preserve in printed form knowledge that

---

[20] J. Schiller and J. Théodoridès, "Sténon et les milieux scientifiques parisiens," in Gustav Scherz, ed., *Steno and brain research in the seventeenth century* (Oxford, 1968), 155-70; Johan Nordström, "Swammerdamiana: excerpts from the Travel Journal of Olaus Borrichius, and two letters from Jan Swammerdam to Thévenot," *Lychnos*, 15 (1954-5), 21-65; G. A. Lindeboom, ed., *The Letters of Jan Swammerdam to Melchisédech Thévenot* (Amsterdam, 1975).

[21] Huygens, *Œuvres complètes*, esp. vols. 3-5; Steven Shapin and Simon Schaffer, *Leviathan and the Air-Pump: Hobbes, Boyle, and the experimental life* (Princeton, 1985), 265-76.

[22] In a note for Colbert attributed to Huygens (c. 1666), Bacon is mentioned as a model for the nascent Académie des Sciences: Huygens, *Œuvres complètes*, vol. 6, 95-6; also in *Lettres, instructions, et mémoires de Colbert*, ed. Pierre Clément (Paris, 1861-1870), vol. 5, 523-4.

[23] Thévenot to Leibniz, undated (autumn 1681), in Leibniz, *Sämtliche Schriften und Briefe* (Darmstadt, 1923-), hereafter cited as *A*, 1 / 3 (series 1, vol. 3), 504; Leibniz to Pellison-Fontanier, 28 March 1692, in Leibniz, *A*, 1 / 7, 293. Thévenot's admiration is often mentioned in letters to Leibniz from other Parisians.

might otherwise be lost. One of the aims of Thévenot's group had been the recovery of forgotten inventions.[24] Leibniz seems to have associated Thévenot with this sort of work, as he explains in a letter of 1678 to Henri Justel, a friend of Thévenot's with similar interests (Justel, too, hosted an "academy", edited a collection of travel accounts, and kept up correspondence with the learned community abroad). For some time, there had been rumours that Justel was working towards a history of inventions.[25] This prompted from Leibniz a long rhapsody on how useful it would be to have a modern version of the elder Pliny's *Historia naturalis*:

> ... for one finds in Pliny an infinity of observations on the origins of the arts...
> There are a great many things which, without Pliny, would be lost. That is why
> I wish that a capable person would leave to posterity a faithful portrait of our
> times, in respect of manners, customs, discoveries, coinage, commerce, arts and
> manufactures; luxury, spending, vices, corruptions, the diseases which reign, and
> their remedies. This person would neglect what one could learn from history, and
> would only attend to that which gets forgotten, and yet deserves not to be—per-
> haps more so than what is normally remarked. But all that requires a person with
> experience, with a vast range of knowledge [consommée en mille belles connois-
> sances]. In a word, more or less the only people I know who are capable of pro-
> viding this are you [i.e. Justel] and Monsieur Thévenot.[26]

He adds that once such a compendious work was complete, posterity would follow their example, and the resulting encyclopedia would constitute "une veritable histoire du Monde". What Leibniz refers to here are the passages in Pliny that give descriptions of the "arts", like the extraction of purple dyes described in book 9, chapter 133, or the accounts of minerals, mining, painting and sculpture that occupy books 33-37. This interest in a "history of trades", or what Bacon called "history mechanical", was a project shared by many in the savant community of the seventeenth and eighteenth centuries, and which forms the background to projects like the Académie des Sciences's *Description des arts et métiers*, the *Encyclopédie* of Diderot and d'Alembert, and eventually the

---

[24] "Project de la Compagnie des Sciences et des Arts" (?1663), in Huygens, *Œuvres complètes*, vol. 4, 325-9, here 328.

[25] Some trace of what Justel's "history of *commodités*" might have looked like can be found in Justel to Locke, 17 Sept. 1679, in Locke, *Correspondence*, vol. 2, 106. Justel edited a *Recueil de divers voyages faits en Afrique et en l'Amerique, qui n'ont point esté encore publiez* (Paris, 1674). On Justel, see Harcourt Brown, "Un cosmopolite du grand siècle: Henri Justel," *Bulletin de la Société de l'Histoire du Protestantisme français*, 82 (1933), 187-201; and Brown, *Scientific Organizations*, 161-84.

[26] Leibniz to Justel, 14 Feb. 1678, in Leibniz, *A*, 1 / 2, 317. Cf. Brown, *Scientific Organizations*, 179.

Conservatoire des Arts et Métiers founded in the Revolutionary period.[27] What is striking is that Leibniz associated this sort of work with Justel and Thévenot.

II

With Leibniz's comments in mind, we can consider the activities of the Thévenot group in its heyday of the early 1660s. One document in particular has been identified as a statement of the Thévenot group's ambitions, an unsigned manuscript entitled "Project de la Compagnie des Sciences et des Arts".[28] This document highlights the importance of travel and geography among the goals of the Thévenot circle. The opening statement is that "the design of the Company is to work towards the perfection of the Sciences and the Arts, and to search comprehensively for everything that could be of some utility or convenience to the human race, and particularly to France". The "Project" then lists various desiderata: experiments will be done, using instruments where possible, to make new discoveries in the heavens and the earth; dissections carried out to improve medicine; new machines will be invented; the secrets of craftsmen and inventors will be made public, proposed inventions will be tested, and "Vulgar Errors" put to the test of experiment. The aim of dispelling popular errors—another familiar theme in the period—is balanced by an emphasis on the mechanical Arts, and the need to acquire and publicize the knowledge of artisans ("les Ouuriers").

A generic feature of such programmatic documents, often written for the benefit of potential patrons, was a rhetoric of utility (for example, in this text, discovering new countries is described as profitable to the state because of the new mines that will be discovered). Even allowing for this, it is worth underlining the prominence given in the "Project" to the facilitation of navigation and the advancement of commerce.

---

[27] For instance, in 1693, Leibniz was excited to hear a rumour that the abbé Bignon was planning to found a royal academy of arts in Paris, which would be a sister to the Académie des sciences. One of the initial projects for this academy was to compile a history of the arts—the first instalment of which was to have been the history of printing. However, the results were so unsatisfactory that the project was shelved. See Leibniz to Bossuet, 29 March 1693 (*A*, 1 / 9, 88); D. Larroque to Leibniz, 14 Nov. 1693 (*A*, 1 / 9, 614). See also Walter E. Houghton, Jr., "The History of Trades: its relation to seventeenth-century thought, as seen in Bacon, Petty, Evelyn, and Boyle", *Journal of the History of Ideas* 2 (1941), 33-60.

[28] "Project de la Compagnie des Sciences et des Arts" (?1663), in Huygens, *Œuvres complètes*, vol. 4, 325-329.

Moreover, the "Project" sets out a scheme to make use of travellers for the collection of information, both natural and technical:

> in all occasions when curious persons travel to, or live in, foreign countries, they shall be given *Memoires* [memoranda/questionnaires], and they will be asked to examine . . . whatever is judged to be remarkable both in Nature and in the Arts.

The Montmor-Thévenot group was able to carry this out, in a fairly limited way, with François Bernier, a student of Gassendi's who had travelled across the Orient and was already living in Mughal India at the time this document was written (and communicating with Paris by letters exchanged with Jean Chapelain).[29] As well as sending specific questions to "curious persons" who happen to be in foreign parts already, the "Project" takes the next step, by suggesting that observers should be sent out with any long-distance voyages:

> and even in long-distance voyages (*les grandes navigations*) we will attempt to send out intelligent persons specifically to remark all that is curious in the New Lands, as much in metals, animals, plants, as in Inventions and Arts.

These expert emissaries should endeavour to exchange technical knowledge with the people they encounter, and in order to improve the terms of artisanal trade, they should take suitable gifts:

> And to that end, when visiting civilized countries (*les pays policés*), travellers will carry models or diagrams of the machines which we use here, so that if the foreigners do not have them, we can teach them how to use some of them, and exchange some of them for those which we do not have, or for the secrets of their arts which we do not know—something which perhaps would be difficult to get by paying money, or by some other means. Also, we will send out [with travellers] all the curiosities of Optics, Dioptrics, etc., of the Magnet, etc., so that the travellers can introduce ourselves by these means, and make themselves esteemed, since we know that it was by such means that entry was gained into some powerful kingdoms.

It seems highly likely that this last suggestion was inspired by the recent experience of the Jesuits in China, who made increasing use of ornate instrument-gifts to improve their position at the imperial court in Beijing.[30] The idea of sending specially-trained scientific observers to distant lands was to be realized by the Académie des sciences, partly at the instigation

---

[29] See Nicholas Dew, *Orientalism in Louis XIV's France* (Oxford, forthcoming), chapter 3.
[30] On the Jesuit astronomers' use of instruments as gifts, see Florence C. Hsia, "French Jesuits and the Mission to China: science, religion, history", University of Chicago Ph.D. diss., 1999.

of Huygens and Adrien Auzout (both members of Thévenot's group who were made members of the Académie).

One reason for accepting that the "Project" is a document from Thévenot's group is that many of the same sentiments are echoed in a "Discours sur l'Art de la Navigation" published by Thévenot as part of the supplementary *Recueil des voyages* of 1681. In this text, one of the few extended published pieces of prose by Thévenot, there is much made of the opposition between artisanal knowledge and the worthless "jeu de l'esprit" of the established sciences. Whereas scholars ("gens de lettres") have filled their libraries with endless commentaries on Aristotle, the art of navigation has advanced by the accumulated experience of pilots on the seas ("ces gens de Mer, ces gens de peu de discours"). The fact that long-distance voyages are now practicable is owed to this accumulation of experiential knowledge:

> We owe this knowledge and these advantages to the useful writings and the exact observations of the navigators of past ages. Geography, and many other Arts, have likewise been improved; and similar progress would have been made in the Sciences, too, if experiments and observations had been employed in the same way.[31]

If seamen had followed the example of the learned, they would never have dared cross the Torrid Zone, America would never have been discovered, and half the world would still be in the "chaos in which the ignorance of past ages had left it". If, conversely, physicians had imitated the navigators in accumulating experience, medicine might have made more progress, and mankind would be enjoying the benefits of a great store of remedies, rather than the ill-founded dogma and false eloquence of the doctors.

It was because of the need for the accumulation of experiential knowledge that Thévenot set himself the task of collecting and translating travel accounts, mainly from English and Dutch long-distance voyages. Because these accounts contained practical navigational matter they could be of use to any future travellers, particularly French merchants. Compiling accounts which were not yet available in French and sometimes not yet even in print into a single collection had the advantage of allowing the seafarer to collate scattered data by leafing through one book. Just like the bubble levels developed in the meetings of Thévenot's group, the collection of travel texts was an instrument designed to be

---

[31] "Discours sur l'Art de la Navigation", in Thévenot, *Recueil de voyages* (1681), sep. pag., 5.

of practical use for navigation.[32] The same concern for publishing technical knowledge that might be useful for seafaring probably lies behind the book on the "art of swimming" that Thévenot later published, and which was read throughout the eighteenth century.[33]

With wonderful optimism, the "Project" proposes that the "compagnie" will enter into communication with "all other Academies", with savants of every country, to share news of books and to exchange local knowledge of both nature and the arts.[34] Correspondence will be needed for the circulation of reports on experiments and observations (including thermometer readings, magnetic variation, tides, eclipses and comets). This will make possible "une histoire de la Nature la plus universelle qui soit possible". This "history of nature" is, clearly, impossible without collective action and transparent communication—even if this ideal might be difficult to realize in practice.[35] Thévenot corresponded with likeminded figures around Europe, especially Huygens (when he was in the United Provinces), Vincenzo Viviani and Lorenzo Magalotti in Florence, and Henry Oldenburg, the intelligencer for the English natural philosophers.[36]

Thévenot's cabinet was not just a meeting place for savants, where experiments were tried, and letters from abroad read out and discussed, but also a private museum, where visitors could examine "curiosities" and rare books. Like most other cabinets, Thévenot's was a site to be

---

[32] Anthony J. Turner, "Melchisédech Thévenot, the bubble level, and the artificial horizon", *Nuncius*, 7 (1992), 131-145.

[33] Melchisédech Thévenot, *L'Art de Nager demontré par figures avec des avis pour se baigner utilement* (Paris, 1696) with reprints 1781 and 1782; English trans: *The Art of Swimming* (London, 1699), reprinted 1764 (twice), 1789, 1838. Thévenot portrays swimming as a "mechanical art" and calls for the establishment of public academies of swimming. It was with Thévenot's manual that Benjamin Franklin taught himself to swim (see *The Autobiography of Benjamin Franklin*, ed. Leonard W. Labaree et al. (New Haven, 1964), 104).

[34] "Project de la Compagnie des Sciences et des Arts", 327 ("s'instruire reciproquement de ce qu'il y a de particulier dans la Nature et dans les arts").

[35] David S. Lux and Harold J. Cook, "Closed circles or open networks? Communicating at a distance during the scientific revolution," *History of Science*, 36 (1998), 179-211; Anne Goldgar, *Impolite Learning: conduct and community in the Republic of Letters, 1680-1750* (New Haven, 1995); Lorraine Daston, "The ideal and the reality of the Republic of Letters in the Enlightenment," *Science in Context*, 4 (1991), 367-86.

[36] Thévenot was writing to Magalotti from 1658 (Brown, *Scientific Organizations*, 135). There are letters from Thévenot to Vincenzo Viviani in the "Galileiana" collection of the Biblioteca nazionale centrale, Florence. The fullest account of Thévenot's links with Florence is W. E. Knowles Middleton, *The Experimenters: a study of the Accademia del Cimento* (Baltimore, 1971), 296-308.

visited by scholars who came through Paris on *voyages littéraires*.[37] His collection included Greek sculpture, and some scientific instruments, but it was best known for its collection of Oriental manuscripts. After his death, the library was put on the market, and a printed catalogue published by Thévenot's friend and sometime assistant, the Arabist, Antoine Galland; after long negotiations, the collection was acquired by the Bibliothèque du roi in 1712. Leibniz, rather late in the day, made an attempt to secure the manuscripts, but in vain.[38]

Rather than separating his collecting activity from his "academy", we should conceive of the "assemblée" as the social use of the cabinet: a collection of *curiosités* and a collective of *curieux*. The savants who met there would discuss the objects, the instruments, the experiments and dissections; and read the correspondence coming in, which often included the travel accounts Thévenot was translating. The cabinets of the *curieux* were the period's sites *par excellence* for contemplating the relationship between nature and art, and for representing materially the Plinian "history" that Leibniz had dreamt of. It is within such as site of knowledge-production that we can locate the production of the *Relations de divers voyages curieux*.[39]

III

In an autobiographical fragment published in the sale-catalogue of his library, Thévenot describes the project to publish a collection of travel texts as a direct offshoot of the work of his "assembly":

---

[37] The Dane, Corfitz Braem, visited Thévenot's cabinet in April 1666 (see Gustav Scherz's introduction to Steno, *Epistolae et epistolae ad eum data* (Freiburg and Copenhagen, 1952), 12). Thévenot's is listed among notable cabinets in Jacob Spon, *Recherche des Antiquités et Curiosités de la Ville de Lyon . . . Avec un Mémoire des Principaux Antiquaires & Curieux de l'Europe* (Lyon, 1675), 217; Charles-César Baudelot de Dairval, *De l'utilité des voyages* (Paris, 1686), vol. 2, 685. Even after his death, Thévenot's collection could be seen *chez* his heir, Girard Garnier (Martin Lister, *Journey to Paris in the year 1698* [London, 1698], 102-4).

[38] Antoine Galland, ed., *Bibliotheca Thevenotiana* (Paris, 1694). See Françoise Bléchet, *Les Ventes publiques de livres en France, 1630-1750* (Oxford, 1991), 67; Margherita Palumbo, *Leibniz e la res bibliothecaria: bibliografie, historiae literariae e cataloghi nella biblioteca privata leibniziana* (Rome, 1993), 153-156; Galland, *Journal parisien (1708-1715)*, ed. Henri A. Omont (Paris, 1919), 129, 131-2.

[39] On Cabinets of Curiosity in general, see Findlen, *Possessing Nature*, and Lorraine Daston and Katharine Park, *Wonders and the order of nature, 1150-1750* (New York, 1998), 255-301.

Each member of the group proposed for himself a task and occupation: mine was to put together and translate into French those things in which other Nations surpass us in the Arts . . . And in order to make Geography more perfect, I put together and gave to the public three [sic] large volumes of a collection of Travels which I had been working on for a long time . . .[40]

Here, as in numerous other sources, the task associated with Thévenot is the "illustration of geography" for the purpose of facilitating commerce. (Navigation was traditionally classified among the arts, rather than the sciences.) Such knowledge is presented as useful, contributing to the well-being of the French people, indeed of the entire human race.[41] The emphasis on utility crops up elsewhere: Thévenot's friend, Jean Chapelain, noted that the goal of Thévenot's collection was to serve as a beacon for French navigators, and to facilitate commerce,[42] but also, as he told a correspondent, to "contribute something to exercise the reasoning of the contemplators of nature".[43] Very similar language is used to describe both the travel-publishing project and the "assembly". Indeed, at one point it is implied that the voyage narratives, along with one of Swammerdam's insect investigations, are being edited *from the records* of the Thévenot group.[44]

The collection of travel accounts was already a genre with a history. Thévenot was following where Ramusio and Hakluyt had led: there had still not been a multi-volume travel collection in French.[45] Thévenot's

---

[40] Thévenot, autobiographical fragment, at head of *Bibliotheca Thevenotiana*, sigs. 2r-3v.

[41] Galland sings the praises of Thévenot's "génie pour tout ce qu'il croïoit pouvoir contribuer au bien & à l'avantage des hommes assemblez pour vivre les uns avec les autres": introductory paragraph to Thévenot's autobiographical fragment, in *Bibliotheca Thevenotiana*, sig. 2r.

[42] Chapelain, "Liste de quelques gens de lettres français vivant en 1662", in *Opuscules critiques de Chapelain*, ed. Alfred C. Hunter (Paris, 1936), 345: "Il a surtout une passion violente pour l'illustration de la géographie, dont il donnera bientôt des preuves au monde par la publication d'un Recueil de voyages anciens et modernes non encore vu des Français, ni quelques-uns même de personne; tous traduits par lui, ou par ceux qu'il a employés pour avancer l'ouvrage, qui a pour but de servir de flambeau à nos navigateurs et la facilité au commerce, ce qu'il accompagne de cartes très sûres qu'il a recouvrées, et qu'il fait graver avec soin à ses dépens, et en l'humeur où il en est on aura de la peine à lui faire avouer ce travail, tant il est désintéressé en cette entreprise . . .".

[43] Chapelain, *Lettres*, vol. 2, 349-50, Chapelain to Carrel de Sainte-Garde, 6 Feb. 1664: ("apporter de quoy s'exercer au raisonnement des contemplateurs de la nature").

[44] The title page of one section of the *Recueil de voyages* reads: "Les Histoires naturelles de l'Ephemere et du Cancellus ou Bernard l'Hermite [. . . par Mr Swammerdam . . .], Tirées *avec les Voyages precedens* du Recueil des Ouvrages de l'Assemblée, qui s'est tenuë chez Mr Thevenot" (my emphasis).

[45] On earlier French travel editors, see Frank Lestringant, *Mapping the Renaissance World: the geographical imagination in the age of discovery* (Cambridge, 1994); Robert O. Lindsay,

Relations were printed in a series of fifty-five fascicles, separately pagi-
nated, bundled into the four parts of the set, each of which had its
own title page and paratext. Although new title pages were printed for
the reissues, it seems that there was really only one impression of each
fascicle.[46]

Thévenot dedicated the collection to Louis XIV.[47] In the dedicatory
epistle we find a series of claims being made: how it is now the turn
of France to establish a trading empire (after the Portuguese and Dutch);
how Louis XIV is the glory of the age, and only France has a large
enough population to colonise effectively; how the extremities of the
world will be drawn out of obscurity by the king; and how it is reserved
to Louis XIV to make "the whole human race . . . richer, more knowledgeable, better informed of all the advantages that men can draw from
the Arts or from Nature". Explorers would bring back "new specific
remedies" unknown to European medicine, and other technical inno-
vations—just as, Thévenot went on, in centuries past, silk, gunpowder
and printing had been transferred from China to Europe. What Thévenot's
rhetoric does is to reemploy the discourse of instauration that we have
seen in the documents surrounding his "academy" within the conventions
for celebrating the *gloire* of the king.

The appearance of Thévenot's collection coincided with a renewed
effort—largely inspired by Colbert—to put French colonial trade on a
better footing. The dedication to the king was added in the same year
that Colbert launched a new Compagnie des Indes orientales (1664), in
deliberate imitation of the Dutch East Indies Company. Likewise, the
contents of Thévenot's series reflect the preoccupation with the need
for France to emulate the Dutch. The title page of the first part makes
plain that some of the texts are translated from Hakluyt and Purchas,
although in the end only seven of the fifty-five texts in the series were
from these English collections; fifteen were from Dutch travel accounts.
Perhaps more importantly, the majority of the texts relate to Asian travels: over forty of the fifty-five items published, compared with only four

---

"Pierre Bergeron: a forgotten editor of French travel literature," *Terrae Incognitae*, 7 (1976),
31-38.

[46] What became the first Part appeared in 1663, the second in 1664, the third in
1666 (together with a reissue of Parts 1 and 2), and the fourth in 1672, again with a
re-issue. Several fascicles were printed subsequently for a projected fifth Part—incomplete at Thévenot's death—and were therefore added to the re-issue of 1696.

[47] Thévenot, *Relations de divers voyages curieux*, part 2 (Paris, 1664), sig. ä, ijʳ-iijʳ, "Au
Roi".

from the Americas (all in the fourth part, 1672). Most of the pieces were extracts rather than complete texts, and most were translations from printed European sources, although there were several texts that were previously unpublished.[48] In addition, the octavo volume of 1681 included other pieces alongside its nine voyage texts, like an account of the *Kunstkammer* of Swammerdam's father, and Thévenot's "Discours on the Art of Navigation".[49] The texts translated included, for example, a "Mémoire sur la Géorgie" by the Italian traveller Pietro della Valle, which had been sent to Urban VIII in 1627; a portion of Thomas Roe's relation of the Mughal empire first published by Purchas; and extracts from John Greaves' *Pyramidographia*, which had first appeared in English in 1646.[50] The collection was not restricted to modern travel narratives, though: the first volume included an extract from the sixth century Byzantine travelogue of Cosmas Indicopleustes (because it included descriptions of animals from the East Indies), and brief extracts from the *Geography* of Abū 'l-Fidā, while the fourth part included the Jesuit Prospero Intorcetta's translation of the Confucian classic, the Doctrine of the Mean, under the title *Sinarum scientia politico-moralis*, along with a life of Confucius. This short text represents the first publication of Confucius in Europe (the Intorcetta text had been printed first at Goa); later, in the 1680s, Thévenot was to be involved in the Jesuits' full-scale publication of Confucian texts, the *Confucius, Sinarum Philosophus* (1687).[51]

Since the workings of the Thévenot group were intimately bound up with the reading and writing of letters to other scholarly circles, it comes as no surprise to find that the collection of travel texts was put together using that correspondence. Chapelain told his contacts abroad to look out for travel accounts suitable for translation.[52] Thévenot made use of his contacts in the United Provinces to get texts relating to the Dutch East Indies trade: it was Huygens, for example, who sent Thévenot

---

[48] For a catalogue of the *Relations*, see Armand-Gaston Camus, *Mémoire sur la Collection des grands et petits voyages [des de Bry] et sur la collection des voyages de Melchisedech Thévenot* (Paris, 1802), 279-341, esp. 286-92. See also "Description of the collection of the voyages of Thévenot," *Contributions to a Catalogue of the Lenox Library*, no. 3 (New York, 1879).

[49] *Recueil de voyages* (Paris, 1681).

[50] On the latter, see Zur Shalev, "Measurer of all things: John Greaves (1602-1652), the Great Pyramid, and early modern metrology," *Journal of the History of Ideas*, 63 (2002), 555-75.

[51] This is discussed in more detail in Dew, *Orientalism in Louis XIV's France*, chapter 5.

[52] Among other examples, see Chapelain, *Lettres*, vol. 2, 349-50 (Chapelain to Carrel de Sainte-Garde, 6 Feb. 1664).

François Caron's description of Japan, which came out in the second part of the collection.[53] Other scholars in Holland were also brought in: Isaac Vossius obtained for Thévenot the text of Cosmas Indicopleustes that appeared in the first part.[54] Meanwhile, Lorenzo Magalotti in Florence sent travel texts and maps to Thévenot, sometimes by the intermediary of travelling scholars, like Lorenzo Panciatichi.[55] The short fragment of Abū 'l-Fidā published in Part 1 was transcribed from a manuscript in the Vatican library by Thévenot's old Maronite friend, Abraham Ecchellensis.[56] This dependence on the correspondence network is occasionally acknowledged in Thévenot's prefatory notes, as a claim for the credibility of the documents he was presenting.[57]

Once the texts had been collected, Thévenot would translate his selections and see them through the press. Like the process of collecting, the business of printing the translations was a function of the social network which Thévenot manipulated: the Royal Censor who signed the *privilège* to publish was his friend Henri Justel (whom we have already met), and the *privilège*'s beneficiary was Thévenot's uncle, Girard Garnier.[58]

---

[53] Huygens, *Œuvres complètes*, vol. 3, 395: Huygens to L. Huygens, 7 Dec. 1661. Huygens was related to Caron by marriage; we might speculate that the Huygens-Thévenot link facilitated Caron's move to Paris in 1665, where he was to play an important role in the history of French trade with India: see Siba Pata Sen, *The French in India: first establishment and struggle* (Calcutta, 1947). Caron's book first appeared as *Beschrijvinghe van het Machtigh Coninckrijcke Japon* (Amsterdam, 1648).

[54] Huygens, *Œuvres complètes*, vol. 3, 347: Thévenot to Huygens, 25 Sept. 1661. However, in his "Avis, Sur le dessein, & sur l'ordre de ce Recueil" (Thévenot, *Relations*, vol. 1 (1663), sig. a ij^r-iv^v, here iij^v) Thévenot states that "Le Fragment Grec du Cosmas vient de Monsieur [Emeric] Bigot, qui l'a copié dans la Bibliotheque de Florence". Presumably both Vossius and Bigot were involved.

[55] Valentin Conrart, *Lettres à Lorenzo Magalotti*, eds. Gabriel Berquet and Jean-Pierre Collinet (Saint-Etienne, 1981), 110 (29 May 1671), 121 (10 Sept. 1671), 132 (22 Jan. 1672).

[56] See the contents page of Part 1, and the short "Avis" to the Abū 'l-Fidā section (vol. 1, sig. i i^v, [sep. pag., 18]), mentioning only "un fameux traducteur . . . Arabe de Nation"; then in the "Avis" to Part 3 (sig. a v^r): ". . . Abulfeda, que le Signor Abraham Echellense avoit commencé à me transcrire d'un Manuscrit du Vatican, & que Messieurs Vossius & Golius m'ont fait copier depuis sur trois Manuscrits Arabes de la Bibliotheque de Leyde".

[57] For example, in the "Avis" to the first part, Thévenot claimed that his collection would be "autant-plus fidele & plus exacte, que ie la feray sur de meilleurs Originaux, & sur la foy de Personnes choisies entre ceux qui les ont courües & obseruées auec plus de soin"; in the "Avis" for the fourth part, he added "j'ay fait chercher dans les plus fameuses Bibliotheques les pieces qui pouvoient l'enrichir, & il y a peu de gens de cette erudition que je n'aye entretenus & consultez sur ce dessein".

[58] Girard Garnier is named as beneficiary in the *privilèges* for all four Parts (misprinted in the first as Garnel). A "Mr Garnier" is identified as Thévenot's uncle in a note attached to a letter from Thévenot to Colbert (BN ms Mélanges de Colbert 152,

This *privilège* was a particularly advantageous one, in that it specified protection for a period of twenty years (rather than the more usual ten), to be counted from the appearance of each volume (rather than the first). This, presumably, was arranged in recognition of the fact that the book would appear in several sections. But because the complete contents of the series could not be specified on the original *privilège*, this meant that the series was effectively open-ended. Such a flexible arrangement was presumably facilitated by Thévenot's friendship with Justel.[59]

Once printed, the instalments of Thévenot's series went out through the circuit of correspondence again. Thévenot would send the fascicles as gifts to those he was in touch with, including Robert Boyle, and the Oxford-based scholars Edward Bernard and Thomas Hyde.[60] They could then circulate them further: Bernard, for instance, sent one copy to Job Ludolf, Frankfurt's celebrated expert on all things Ethiopic.[61] The recipients, if they were in the position to do so, could send copies of their own books in return: Boyle made sure Thévenot got a copy of his *Observations and experiments about the Saltness of the Sea.*[62]

What these examples underline for us is that the *Relations* were produced by collecting texts sent "in" to Thévenot by various correspondents, and then (once translated and printed) circulated back "out" again through the same network. In order to produce the series in Paris,

---

f. 271r), and in Chapelain, *Lettres*, vol. 2, 640. Why Garnier held the *privilège*, and not Thévenot (or a bookseller), is unclear.

[59] On the *privilège* system, see Lucien Febvre and Henri-Jean Martin, *L'Apparition du livre*, 3rd ed. (Paris, 1999), 338-46. This form of "package" *privilège* is described in Elizabeth Armstrong, *Before Copyright: the French book-privilege system, 1498-1526* (Cambridge, 1990), 131-36.

[60] For Boyle, see Henry Oldenburg, *Correspondence*, eds. A. Rupert Hall and Marie Boas Hall, 13 vols. (Madison, 1965-1986), vol. 2, 430 (Oldenburg to Boyle, 4 July 1665): "Monsr Thevenot hath sent you the 2d Tome of his Curious Voyages in folio, fairely bound, wherein are contained, as far as my cursory perusall could informe me, severall things not unpleasing, and instructive both for Navigation, Policy, and Natural Philosophy, though most of it be but Traduction;" and 444 (Boyle's reply): "I have now Receiv'd Monsr Thevenot's Booke of Voyages, where I find some few things Curious enough, & however should find cause to be sensible of the Givers Civilitys". For Bernard and Hyde, see Bodleian ms Smith 8, pp. 3-5 (Thévenot to Bernard, 1673) at p. 4b; Smith 11, p. 15 (Hyde to Thévenot, 24 June 1673).

[61] Bodleian ms Smith 5, p. 151 (Ludolf to Bernard, thanking him for Thévenot's edition of Intorcetta's text, no date); p. 153 (Ludolf to Bernard, 15 Dec. ? 1677, again thanking him: "pro libro La science des Chinois dicto gratias tibi ago . . ."). Ludolf was also in contact with Thévenot (here pp. 155, 157, letters of 20 Mar. 1678 and 31 Dec. 1683).

[62] Oldenburg, vol. 10, 419-24, at 422: Jean-Baptiste Du Hamel to Oldenburg, 6 Jan. 1674.

Thévenot and his associates had to make other people, in remote locations, work for them.[63]

Thévenot's collection of "curious voyages" can be counted as one of his more successful projects. However, as any encounter with the book makes plain, its success in bringing the series of texts together in print was qualified by the practical effects of the publication process. Firstly, the fact that the voyages were printed as independent fascicles meant that the collection as a whole was only a series of discrete fragments. Unlike later travel compendia, the accounts are not organized (either by geography or by date), nor is there an index for retrieving the information. As a result, the volumes are extremely difficult for readers to use. Thévenot *did* publish lists of the contents of the series, but these were probably designed to allow the owner to check that no parts were missing. As we have seen, each fascicle of the series was printed separately, and could be distributed privately. A set of the fragments had to be arranged by the owner before being bound; as a result, the make-up of surviving copies is always slightly different, either because some fragments are missing, or because they are differently ordered.[64]

On occasion, Thévenot alludes to this problem of order within his book. In the list of contents for the first part, he wrote that readers could choose whether to put the extract from Greaves's *Pyramidographia* at the start or at the end of the volume; in his note prefacing the fourth Part, he admitted that he had to abandon his original organizing scheme as he accumulated texts ("il me sera impossible dans la suite de m'ar-rester à l'ordre que je m'estois proposé au commencement"). The problem of order was discussed again in an unsigned "avertissement" prefacing the re-issue of the whole collection that appeared in 1696 (after Thévenot's death). The writer, probably the bookseller Thomas Moëtte, noted that Thévenot was always so busy adding new texts to the series that there was "some confusion in all his works", and that the *Relations* was a collection organized neither by chronology nor by the matters treated (". . . qui n'ont point de suite déterminée par les faits ny par les temps"). The same text makes clear that this textual disorder is partly a function of the book's printing history:

> The large number of different Relations, the interruptions in the sequence of one impression, and [the fact that] several different workers sometimes (for reasons that

---

[63] See Goldgar, *Impolite Learning*; also Lux and Cook, "Closed circles or open networks?".

[64] See Camus, *Mémoire sur la Collection*.

are unclear) worked separately on the same text, produced a kind of disorder, which was very difficult to avoid . . . One should not be surprised, then, if within this Collection one finds false signatures and page numbers which are out of sequence; and one can use the Table to find out whether one has the complete set.[65]

The preface-writer goes on to assert that the disorder within the series is not to be ascribed to any moral failings on Thévenot's part (in particular, the "jealousy" typical of the "curious" ["cette jalousie qui n'est que trop commune entre les Curieux"]). It seems clear that the writer wanted to distance Thévenot from the more negative associations of curiosity. The fact that he was engaged in *commerce littéraire* with so many other respected members of the Republic of Letters is offered as proof of his seriousness. Nonetheless, the problem of order remains, and is explained by referring to Thévenot's constant deferral of bringing the book to a close.

IV

Thévenot's *Relations* is a text which seems constantly to be in danger of collapsing. The difficulties surrounding the ordering of the information presented are inseparable from the book's material composition. Adrian Johns has emphasised the degree to which the familiar bibliographic categories that we take for granted as modern readers (author, text, publisher, and date) become unstable when we consider the world of early modern print. Problems of textual stability were particularly acute, Johns shows, in the case of natural-philosophical publishing.[66] The Thévenot case reminds us that this is especially true of travel-editing enterprises.

The limits to Thévenot's project—the textual disorder that the printed pages reveal—were not unique; such bibliographic problems were shared by other large-scale editorial projects in Paris at that time. Moreover, Thévenot was to experience far greater frustrations with his plan to edit a translation of the *Geography* of Abū 'l-Fidā, which he pursued doggedly from the late 1660s until his death, and which never saw fruition. I have tried to show the importance of travel texts for the "curious" community of the late seventeenth century, and to emphasise that the site of production for Thévenot's travel series was his cabinet—in both the

---

[65] Thévenot, *Relations*, "nouvelle edition" in 2 vols. (Paris, 1696), vol. 1, sig. * i^{r-v}.
[66] Adrian Johns, *The Nature of the Book: print and knowledge in the making* (Chicago, 1998).

spatial-physical sense (a place) and the social sense (as a venue for meetings of scholars). Correspondence and travel between such sites was the most important way in which the Republic of Letters was constituted as an "imagined community"; and by the same token, it was only by harnessing such networks that texts like Thévenot's could be produced at all.

Locke seems not to have replied to Thévenot's enquiry about the missing Hakluyt papers. (Even if he had been able to acquire them for Thévenot, they still may not have seen the light of day.)[67] As we saw, Leibniz was impressed by Thévenot's range of activities, but was also aware of the danger of spreading one's interests too widely and never finishing anything. He jokingly compared Thévenot to Briareus, the hundred-handed monster.[68] Indeed, after Thévenot's death Leibniz regretted how much had been lost with him.[69] This was the one of the dangers of curiosity: too many projects and too little time. There was another danger, though, which seems not to have been articulated, although Thévenot must have been aware of it. This was the fact that the nature of geographical knowledge was changing, partly because of the work of Thévenot's friends at the Académie des Sciences. Huygens and Auzout, for example, were involved in the introduction of new methods of telescopy and timekeeping which would bring unprecedented levels of precision to cartographic and geodesic surveying. In the 1670s and 1680s, the Académie des Sciences established a global cartographic project, sending specially-trained observers with new instrument-driven techniques to destinations around France and the world. In the year Thévenot died (1692), the Académie des Sciences published its "corrected" map of France, showing the difference between the old outline of the country and the new, and the accompanying *cartouche* expressed this difference between old and new as the distinction between a cartography founded on (descriptive) "Relations" and one founded on (quantitative)

---

[67] After all, Jan Swammerdam left his papers to Thévenot, who failed to publish all but a couple of fragments from them before his death. Swammerdam's manuscripts were only saved from oblivion by the diligence of his countryman Boerhaave, who tracked them down in 1727, and published them ten years later as *Biblia Naturæ*.

[68] Leibniz to Thévenot, 23 March 1691, in Leibniz, *A*, 1/6, 410: "vous deuvriés estre *centimanus* comme ce Briarée de la fable. C'est à dire vous deuvriés avoir une centaine de gens propres à executer mille belles veues que vous avés".

[69] Leibniz to Ezechiel Spanheim, 16 April 1696, in Leibniz, *A*, 1/12, 541: "M. Thevenot avoit trop de belles choses à donner, il luy est arrivé ce qui arrive à des femmes qui sont en travail de plus d'un enfant, c'est que souvent l'un empeche l'autre sur tout quand il y a faute d'assistance".

"Observations".[70] It would take many decades before such a change would be completed, and the philological approach to knowledge-making would remain important for geographers; nonetheless, Thévenot's monumental collection was built on foundations which were already, quietly, beginning to shift.

Acknowledgments

My thanks to Peter Burke, Larry Brockliss, Neil Kenny, Simon Schaffer, Karen Henson, and the participants at the USC-Huntington Early Modern Studies Institute Conference "The Early Modern Travel Narrative", for their helpful comments on various versions of this piece.

---

[70] Josef W. Konvitz, *Cartography in France, 1660-1848: science, engineering, and statecraft* (Chicago, 1987); Jordan Kellman, "Discovery and enlightenment at sea: maritime exploration and observation in the eighteenth-century French scientific community", Princeton University Ph.D. dissertation, 1997.

THE CONSTRUCTION OF AN AUTHORITATIVE TEXT: PETER KOLB'S DESCRIPTION OF THE KHOIKHOI AT THE CAPE OF GOOD HOPE IN THE EIGHTEENTH CENTURY

ANNE GOOD

Reinhardt College

ABSTRACT

Peter Kolb (1675-1726), a German astronomer and mathematician, was an unlikely candidate to write the book that became the most well-known source of the Cape of Good Hope and the Khoikhoi in the eighteenth century. This essay uses Kolb's work as a case study for the transformation of one man's personal observations into a variety of works that were quite different from the originals in scope and intention. First, the essay discusses the genesis of Kolb's book, *Caput Bonae Spei Hodiernum*, and focuses on the Khoikhoi. I argue that Kolb's genius lies in emphasizing communalities among Europeans and Khoikhoi, as well as the rationality of Khoikhoi customs. The second part of the essay establishes that Kolb's book did indeed become the most authoritative source of the Cape in the eighteenth century. Over the course of that century, the book was radically modified in translations and abridgements to cover only certain essential topics, and increasingly to emphasize the *otherness* of the Khoikhois.

I. *Introduction: Interpreting Accounts of the Khoikhoi*

In 1746, 27 years after the publication of Peter Kolb's *Caput Bonae Spei Hodiernum*, a dramatically abridged version of it appeared in a popular collection of travel narratives compiled by Thomas Astley in London, titled, *A New General Collection of Voyages and Travels*. In the preface to this work, Astley wrote:

> As touching the Hottentots, of whom so many different and romantic stories have been propagated, we shall be able to fully satisfy the Curiosity of the Public by our Abstract of Kolben's Relation; which is so compleat, that he seems to have left nothing for future Travellers to add. We presume, the Reader will be both surprized and pleased with the agreeable Variety he finds in the Manners and Customs of these People; who the Ignorance or Malice of most former Authors had represented as Creatures but one Degree removed from the Beasts, and with Scarce any Thing human about them except the Shape: Whereas, in Fact, they appear to be some of the most humane and virtuous (abating for a few Prejudices of Education) to be found among all the Race of Mankind.[1]

---

[1] *A New General Collection of Voyages and Travels: Consisting of the most Esteemed Relations,*

These remarks highlight some important perceptions of Kolb's work in the mid-eighteenth century. First, it was generally acknowledged to be the most complete, and therefore authoritative, account of the Cape of Good Hope. Second, this work provided a view of the Hottentots (as the Khoikhoi, the aboriginal inhabitants of the Cape, were called throughout the eighteenth century) that was unlike any that had come before it. But certain corollaries of these two points help to reveal why Kolb's work is so fascinating as a case study for the construction of an authoritative text. Though the original text was "so compleat," indeed, apparently exhaustive in the details it gave of the Cape, in Astley's collection it has been severely cut down to essential details about the Khoikhoi, together with some information about the flora and fauna and the colony in general. Implicitly, therefore, Astley and his collaborators made a distinction between exhaustive details and useful details. Furthermore, though the remarks praise the humanity of the Khoikhoi as represented in Kolb's work, there is a sense that nearly 30 years later, Kolb's positive description was still in competition with negative or bestial descriptions. And, paradoxically, Astley's extremely abridged account tends to emphasize the exotic, outlandish, or even irrational aspects of Khoikhoi social life and customs, which detracts from the assertion that they are "humane and virtuous."

If Peter Kolb's original *Caput Bonae Spei Hodiernum* had not appeared to be exhaustive in its description of the Cape, it is unlikely that the book would have received as much attention as it did. It would not have gained the status of an authoritative text either. This paper is about the "construction of an authoritative text" in at least three ways. First, it looks at the life of this particular traveler to argue that the circumstances of his birth and education made him a careful observer, and one who recognized the worth of discourses on the Khoikhoi in learned circles in Europe. Second, it explores the way that this text, *Caput Bonae Spei Hodiernum*, was compiled, written, and published. Here I examine ways that Kolb creates a sense of authenticity, and then, through his erudite analysis, raises his book above previous accounts of the Cape. Most importantly, however, the paper uses a few examples of Kolb's encounters with the Khoikhoi to delve more deeply into the picture of these people that this book was so instrumental in creating. Kolb drew parallels between European and Khoikhoi society, and allowed his description of the Khoikhoi to criticize European culture. The trope

_____

which have been hitherto published in any Language ..., vol. III, compiled by Thomas Astley (London, 1746), v-vi.

of the critical "Savage" was quite old in European travel narratives, but it was new for the Khoikhoi, and in Kolb's hands seemed more than usually plausible. Third, this paper briefly looks at the afterlife of the text, its translations and its inclusion in many collections of travel descriptions. This afterlife is perhaps the best evidence that *Caput Bonae Spei Hodiernum* became an authority on the Cape, and on the Khoikhoi. And, in examining how the text became authoritative in western Europe, I also attempt to say something about cultural change over the course of the eighteenth century.

Caput Bonae Spei Hodiernum, by Peter Kolb, subtitled "a complete description of the Cape of Good Hope today," was first published in German in Nuremberg in 1719. It became the major source on everything to do with the Cape of Good Hope shortly after its publication, and it maintained that status well into the nineteenth century, even though it received considerable criticism in the later eighteenth century. As with all European accounts of non-European cultures, parts of this book are now quite contested, but it is still considered an important source for studying the Cape in the eighteenth century and the early period of contact between Europeans and the Khoisan peoples. At the time it was published, it was undoubtedly the most exhaustive written account of the Cape available. Its 840+ pages are divided into three sections: the first covers *Physicalia*—i.e. topography, flora, fauna, fish, insects, minerals, etc.; the second is concerned exclusively with the social life and customs of the Khoikhoi; and the third describes the European colony at length and focuses on occurrences during Kolb's own residence at the Cape. These general topics were not randomly chosen. Natural history was an interest avidly pursued by learned men all over Europe in this period, and a close reading of these chapters reveals intellectual and personal connections between Kolb and many "savants" (botanists, zoologists, entomologists—though they cannot be easily separated in this period) who would have been in positions to help and recommend Kolb. Even the section on the colonial intrigues at the Cape had precedents in the European publishing world. Most of the section deals with the rebellion of a group of free burghers against the governor, Willem Adriaan van der Stel, and Ad Biewenga has suggested that for some time in the early eighteenth century there was a vogue in the Dutch Republic for books dealing with this subject.[2] The Khoikhoi, of

---

[2] Ad Biewenga, *De Kaap de Goede Hoop: Een Nederlandse Vestingskolonie, 1680-1730* (Amsterdam, 1999), 34.

course, were particularly current in European learned debates regarding humanity.

Kolb's description of the Khoikhoi was by no means the first. Indeed, there are over 150 European narratives that describe the Cape between 1488, when it was first touched by Bartholomew Diaz, and 1652, when the Dutch set up their refreshment station there. In these narratives, the Hottentots appear as miserable wretches bearing much in common with the animals: they hardly have speech, but instead cluck like turkeys, they smear themselves with rancid fat, wear sheep and cow entrails around their necks, and, worst of all, they have no notion of God or any sort of religion; they are not even idolaters.[3] Between 1652 and 1719, there are well over 100 more narratives, including a handful by men who were residents at the Cape for a number of years.[4] A number of these accounts are more complex and nuanced, reflecting closer familiarity with the area and the people.

At this distance of time and space, it is difficult to know whether we can recover anything of Khoikhoi history and culture in the early period of contact with Europeans. Indeed, many historians and anthropologists repudiate the very idea that European observers of indigenous peoples around the world (from the sixteenth century onwards) could produce anything but hopelessly flawed narratives of what they wanted to see, usually colored by the desire to dominate people they regarded as innately inferior. These criticisms have put much needed checks on the interpretation of travel narratives, and have forced scholars to be more careful in examining both the observers or narrators and the contents of the texts. However, the call to reject travel narratives for anything but the study of European mentalities goes too far. Through careful studies of the people who produced travel descriptions and the contexts in which they were produced, together with sensitivity to the possible counter or parallel narratives produced by indigenous peoples, it is possible to identify descriptions that were of high quality or had greater depth and complexity than others. We may still end up with only shadows and echoes of the lives of indigenous people, but the task of historical practice is to create plausible arguments based on available

---

[3] The best collection of these narratives may be found in Major R. Raven-Hart, *Before Van Riebeeck: Callers at South Africa from 1488 to 1652* (Cape Town, 1967). See also David Chidester, "Bushman Religion: Open, Closed, and New Frontiers," in *Miscast: Negotiating the Presence of Bushmen*, ed. Pippa Skotnes (Cape Town, 1996), 52.

[4] *Cape Good Hope, 1652-1702: The First 50 Years of Dutch Colonisation as Seen by Callers*, Two Volumes, ed. R. Raven Hart (Cape Town, 1971).

sources, and this endeavor is no different. In other words, early modern travelers were not simply creating elaborate fiction out of the impossibility of forming any understanding of non-European peoples and contexts. Joan-Pau Rubiés has argued that the ability of various travelers to learn the "language-games" of non-European cultures meant that it was possible for travelers to become involved at a deeper level, and therefore to interpret what they experienced. Rubiés continues,

> This ability to learn languages, however universal, was of course affected by the travellers' will to understand better, by the empirical means at their disposal and by their diverse critical skills. The existence of different languages is obvious, but insofar as translation seems to have been a possibility, the problem of relativism is only a problem of degree.[5]

In Kolb's case, he must score high marks in terms of the will to understand, and likewise with methodology and critical abilities.

II. *The Education of Peter Kolb*

Let us begin, therefore, with a close look at Peter Kolb's life to explain what sort of a man he was, and, at least in part, the personal agenda he had with regard to describing the Cape of Good Hope. In many ways, Kolb was an unlikely candidate to write the most well-known source on the Khoikhoi in the eighteenth century. He was born in 1675, the son of a blacksmith and toll collector in the small village of Dörflas, outside the walls of the town of Marktredwitz in southern Germany. He describes himself as poor but smart, and with the help of good patrons he was able to rise in the world through education. Indeed, in both the introduction to *Caput Bonae Spei Hodiernum* and in his short autobiography, Kolb's description of his life revolves around two major themes: education (particularly focused on religion and astronomy) and patronage. Kolb's education prepared him to value and connect all kinds of observation and the various branches of knowledge, as was expected of a proper man of letters. He was an ambitious man, and over the course of his life until about age 35, he mainly moved up the ladder of patronage and became better ensconced in the learned world of the Republic of Letters, at least within Germany. However, during the last 15 years of his life, he did not fare as well, and though his book on the Cape became famous, there is simply no evidence that Kolb himself made it big.

---

[5] Joan-Pau Rubiés, *Travel and Ethnology in the Renaissance: South India through European Eyes, 1250-1625* (Cambridge, 2000), xvii.

The first two schools Kolb attended were in the moderately-sized
towns of Marktredwitz and Wunsiedel, within Brandenburg-Prussian
lands. The limited scope of education for children from the lower eche-
lons of society changed over the course of the eighteenth century.[6]
Brandenburg-Prussia was at the forefront of educational reforms, already
getting underway with the Pietist pedagogical reforms in Halle in the
late seventeenth century. As early as 1717 a state law called for com-
pulsory school attendance for children between the ages of six and four-
teen.[7] Kolb participated in this wave of cultural change that encouraged
greater access to education, but it is clear that he was still part of a
much smaller subgroup of men (from all orders of society), and that he
was gifted with the desire and the intellect that allowed him to pursue
a longer course of studies, and consequently improve his position in
society.

With the help of patrons from Marktredwitz and Wunsiedel (particularly after the death of his father in 1691), Kolb was able to success-
fully complete primary and secondary school,[8] and move on to the big
city of Nuremberg. In this period, Nuremberg, an imperial free city,

---

[6] For more on schooling in the late seventeenth century, see R.A. Houston, *Literacy
in Early Modern Europe: Culture and Education, 1500-1800*, 2nd ed. (London, 2002), chapter
two, especially 17 and 56-57; see also, Linda Pollock, "Parent-Child Relations," in *Family
Life in Early Modern Times, 1500-1789*, ed. David Kertzer and Marzio Barbagli (New
Haven and London, 2001), 203-04; and Richard van Dülmen, *Kultur und Alltag in der
Frühen Neuzeit: Dritter Band, Religion, Magie, Aufklärung, 16.-18. Jahrhundert* (Munich, 1994),
171, 174-75, 177.

[7] Houston, *Literacy*, 57. See also, Van Dülmen, *Kultur und Alltag*, bd. 3: 178-79; and
Richard Gawthrop, *Pietism and the Making of Eighteenth-Century Prussia* (Cambridge, 1993).

[8] Neustadt/Aisch, Kirchenbibliothek, MS 129 Autobiography: Kolb writes, "Scholam
Wonsideliensem adivi, ibique Alumnorum Ordini adscriptus eo ipse tempore...." He
was part of a group of scholars called "poor students," or "Pauperes," or "Alumnen"
in Latin. These boys did singing duty in church and in the town, for which they took
in a collection that provided a reasonable stipend for living expenses. Older *alumnen*
might act as tutors to the sons of burgher families with whom they also boarded. It
might seem as though being a "poor student" was an exercise in learning humility and
social distinction from wealthier students, but as Anthony La Vopa points out, both the
practice of tutoring burghers' children and performance in the choir "had the effect of
integrating outsiders into the social fabric and cultural rhythms of local life." Furthermore,
the practice that ambitious pupils got in performing publicly and seeking out patronage
must have been invaluable for young men like Kolb himself, who built the rest of his
career on patronage as well. See August Wolfschmidt, *Magister Peter Kolb: Ein Forscher und
Lehrer aus Franken* (Neustadt an der Aisch, 1978), 6; Hermann Braun, *Der Afrikaforscher
Peter Kolb* (Schriftenreihe der Volkshochschule der Stadt Marktredwitz 21) (Marktredwitz,
1975), vii; Elizabeth Jäger, *Wunsiedel, 1557-1632: Band II/1 einer Geschichte der Stadt Wunsiedel*
(Wunsiedel, 1994), 106-07 and 115-18; Anthony La Vopa, *Grace, Talent and Merit: Poor
Students, Clerical Careers, and Professional Ideology in Eighteenth-Century Germany* (Cambridge,
1988), 22.

was one of the great cities of southern Germany, and well known for publishing and a thriving trade in books.[9] When Kolb left Wunsiedel his intention probably was to study theology and philosophy, and his friends also expected him to do this.[10] However, in 1696, Georg Christoph Eimmart, a prominent Nuremberg artist, mathematician and astronomer selected Kolb to become his *Coobservator* at the state-of-the-art astronomical observatory he had built. Eimmart is relatively unknown outside of Nuremberg now, but in the late seventeenth century he was an important figure in German networks of learned people in general, and for astronomical experiments in particular. The connection with Eimmart brought Kolb into a circle of prestigious savants and artists, who remained important in his life, and were essential in enabling him to take his next academic step of studying at the University of Halle.[11]

Although Kolb spent less than three years in Halle, it was clearly one of the highpoints of his life and crucially influential in the course the rest of his life took. Halle was a new university when Kolb arrived there in 1700. It had been founded in 1691 by Frederick III, the Elector of Brandenburg (who was crowned King in Brandenburg-Prussia in 1701), and was intimately connected with the Pietist movement headed by August Hermann Francke.[12] Most students were enrolled in the

---

[9] Hanns Hofmann, "Endzeit reichstädtischer Selbständigkeit (1650-1806): Kampf um die Selbstbehauptung," and Ingomar Bog, "Endzeit reichstädtischer Selbständigkeit (1650-1806): Wirtschaft und Gesellschaft im Zeitalter des Merkantilismus," in *Nürnberg—Geschichte eine europäischen Stadt*, ed. Gerhard Pfeiffer (Munich, 1971), 308-09 and 317.

[10] Archive of the Friedrich-Alexander Gymnasium (hereafter AFAG) at Neustadt/Aisch 28, Dürr (Kolb's teacher) to Kolb, 16 June 1694, addressed to: "Petro Kolben, der Musen eiferig Er-/ gebenen, Meinem insonders Geliebten/ freund zu beliebiger Entsiegelun/ Bey Hrn. Johan Grafen/ Teutschen Schulmeister/ auf den Laurenzi-Plaz/ zu erfragen. Nürnberg." AFAG 44, Jobsten [or Jobsen] to Kolb, 23 July 1695: "Herrn Hn. Petro Kolben, S.S./ Theol: studioso, Meinen/ Vielgeliebten freundt und Gönner/ werde dieses zu belieblicher ent-/ siegelung [unclear!]/ Zu/ Nürnberg." AFAG 55, Paucker to Kolb, 18 January 1697: "Monsieur/ Monsieur Piere Kolb,/ Estudient en Philosophie/ mon tres cher Amy pour/ le presentement à/ Nürnberg." Jobsten and Paucker were Kolb's friends from the school at Wunsiedel.

[11] On Eimmart's observatory, instruments used there, and important collaborators, see Eric G. Forbes, "Das Eimmartische Observatorium zu Nürnberg (1691-1757)," *Sterne und Weltraum* 9 (1970): 311-313; on the savants and artists in general, see Johann Gabriel Doppelmayr, *Historische Nachricht von den Nürnbergischen Mathematicis und Künstlern* ... (Nürnberg, 1730; reproduction Hildesheim and New York, 1972).

[12] Christopher Clark, "Piety, Politics and Society: Pietism in Eighteenth-Century Prussia," in *The Rise of Prussia, 1700-1830*, ed. Philip Dwyer (Harlow, 2000). In a time when leading German thinkers were coming to regard universities as hopelessly mired in irrelevant tradition, Halle offered an innovative curriculum and academic and religious counseling for its students. Halle also quickly became one of the largest of the

theological faculty, and it is clear that even those who came to study something else did not neglect the opportunity to hear the lectures of Halle's leading theologians.

The most famous of these theologians of the late seventeenth and early eighteenth centuries was August Hermann Francke (1663-1727), then leader of the Pietist movement. Pietists placed emphasis on the devotion of the heart, and developed what Christopher Clark refers to as an "individualized, experience-oriented devotional culture."[13] A corollary of this was an insistence, particularly for theology students at Halle, that each individual should experience a "conversion" where one's personal desires became subordinate to the love of God and the all-encompassing desire to serve Him. Furthermore, the love of God was not something to be guarded in one's heart; rather it was to spur the individual on to an actively good life. But, as Martin Brecht points out, Francke did not see much distinction between lay people and the clergy, or those studying to become clergymen—he urged all people to follow the same pietistic lifestyle.[14] Although some students may have attended the University of Halle simply because of its proximity to their homes, most made a choice to go there and be a part of the Pietist renewal.[15] At the same time, Francke was a serious theologian and a scholar of Oriental languages (the first professorship he held at the University of Halle), and he wanted the university to produce good scholars.[16] Kolb himself was not a theological student at Halle—his "Magister" was conferred by the faculty of philosophy. His dissertation, defended and published hardly a year after his arrival in Halle, in July 1701, was on comets.

German universities with over 500 students already in 1700 (on par with Cologne, Leipzig and Wittenberg), and over 1,500 in the 1710s and 1720s. Charles McClelland, *State, Society, and University in Germany, 1700-1914* (Cambridge, 1980), 28; also Gawthrop, *Pietism and the Making of Eighteenth-Century Prussia*, 173-74. According to McClelland, there were 28 universities in the German states (excluding Austria) in 1700, sharing about 8,000 students among themselves.

[13] Clark, "Piety, Politics, and Society," 72.

[14] Martin Brecht, "August Hermann Francke und der Hallische Pietismus," in *Geschichte der Pietismus, Band I: Der Pietismus vom siebzehnten bis zum frühen achtzehnten Jahrhundert*, ed. M. Brecht, et al. (Göttingen, 1993), 473.

[15] Cf., for example, P. Baumgart, "Leibniz und der Pietismus. Universale Reform-bestrebungen um 1700," *Archiv für Kulturgeschichte* 48 (1966): 364-86.

[16] Brecht, "August Hermann Francke," 471-473; Peschke, "A.H. Franckes Reform des theologischen Studiums," in *August Hermann Francke. Festreden und Kolloquium über den Bildungs- und Erziehungsgedanken bei August Hermann Francke aus Anlaß der 300. Wiederkehr seines Geburtstages 22. März 1963* (Leipzig, 1964), 98.

Having attained this honor, Kolb may have considered taking an academic post, but instead, and again through Eimmart's connections, Kolb was appointed secretary to a noble patron.[17] This man was Baron Bernard Friedrich von Krosick, Privy Councillor to the King of Prussia since 1697, and brother of one of Queen Sophie Charlotte's principal Ladies in Waiting, Christine Antonie von Bülow.[18] Von Krosick, another now little-known figure, was essential in the founding of the Berlin Academy of Sciences. He was the major patron for astronomical projects in Berlin at the beginning of the eighteenth century, and provided crucial resources for the study of astronomy, including a house in Berlin where astronomers were able to live and carry out observations.[19]

III. *Setting Sail for the Cape of Good Hope*

In *Caput Bonae Spei Hodiernum*, Kolb describes Krosick as a great friend to astronomy, and one who was also interested in acquiring fame through the projects he supported.[20] Kolb claims that through their conversations, Krosick came up with the idea of making simultaneous astronomical

---

[17] Johan Wilhelm Wagner, "Brevis Narratio de Ratione ac Methodo Observationum Astronomicarum auspiciis Nobilis Magdeburgensis Dn. Bernhardi Friderici de Krosigk, Berolini & simul in Capite Bonae Spei, per aliquot annos olim institutarum; additis quibusdam hic & illic factis observationibus," *Miscellanea Berolinensia ad incrementum scientiarium* VI (1740): 238.

[18] *Leibniz und seine Akademie. Ausgewählte Quellen zur Geschichte der Berliner Sozietät der Wissenschafte, 1697-1716*, ed. Hans-Stephan Brather (Berlin, 1993), 460. I have not been able to work out whether this connection may have exerted an influence on Krosick, but it is interesting to note that Queen Sophie Charlotte provided a great deal of support for Leibniz's idea of founding the Berlin Academy of Sciences. See, for example, Jürgen Mittelstrass, "Der Philosoph und die Königin—Leibniz und Sophie Charlotte," in *Leibniz in Berlin*, ed. Hans Poser and Albert Heinekamp (Stuttgart, 1990), 9-27, and several other essays with similar themes in the same collection.

[19] *Leibniz und seine Akademie*, ed. Brather, 460. See also J.-H.-S. Formey [?], *Histoire de L'Academie Royale des Sciences et Belles-Lettres, depuis son origine jusqu'à présent (Avec les Pieces Originales)* (Berlin, 1752): "Mais avant que de parler des occupations de la Société, je rappelerai un fait qu'on ne pouroit ensévelir dans l'oubli, sans se rendre coupable d'injustice envers un homme d'une naissance distinguée, qui vers le même tems formoit des entreprises, où l'on dècouvroit autant d'amour pour la vérité, que de gênérosité pour contribuër à ses progrés. Je veux parler de M. Bernard Frideric, Baron de Krosick, sous les auspices duquel se fit un Voyage Astronomique au Cap de Bonne-Espèrance," 54-55.

[20] Kolb writes: "Hierüber [the idea of simultaneous observations] wurde nun von Ihm, als einem klugen, verständigen, weitaussehenden und tiefsinnigen Herrn, sehr lange berathschlaget, welche Kosten dazu erfordert würden: und was vor grossen Ruhm, ein so hoher Liebhaber der Künste und Wissenschafften bey der Welt zugewarten, wenn auch gleich der Endzweck, welcher die Perfection der Astronomie zum Grunde hatte, nicht vollkommen erlangt würde," (*Caput Bonae Spei Hodiernum*, hereafter *CBSH*, 2).

observations in Berlin and at the Cape of Good Hope. The two places were thought to be close to the same meridian of longitude, and the observations were to be made with identical instruments, ideally at the same time of day or night. According to Kolb, Krosick's aim was to help perfect astronomical science as well as to solve the problem of how to calculate longitude accurately at sea (*CBSH*, 2). Kolb does not go into detail about how this was to be accomplished, and indeed, it is not at all clear what he thought his main task was.[21] Once he got to the Cape he may have assessed differently still what he could and could not accomplish.

It was a complex project to get underway, with many practical and logistical necessities and difficulties; it also involved the help of a number of important and learned men in the Dutch Republic. Neither Kolb nor Krosick mention collaborators from either France or England, the more well-known centers for this kind of work; instead, all of their contacts seem to be in northern and central-eastern Europe. In Krosick's letters it becomes clear that he knew many useful men in the Dutch Republic, and he had Kolb meet them for strategic purposes. First among these was Nicolaas Witsen, mayor (*Burgermeister*) of Amsterdam and one of the directors of the Dutch East India Company (VOC), who, later, was also of great importance in connection with the publication of *Caput Bonae Spei Hodiernum*.[22] In addition, Kolb sought out several other learned men who were either involved in the Dutch government, or in the administration of the VOC, as well as Nicolaas Hartsoeker (1656-1725), then living in Düsseldorf, who was known for his work with microscopes and expertise with lenses. Once these preparations were complete, Kolb was given some time to put his own affairs in order before the voyage to South Africa began. He took this opportunity to go to Nuremberg to say good-bye to his mother and to patrons there who continued to support him—but also, as he says, to get advice from the learned mathematicians living there: Eimmart, Wurtzelbau and Doppelmayr (*CBSH*, 3). These meetings suggest the crucial ties that

---

[21] On the complexity of calculating longitude, see the essays collected in *The Quest for Longitude*, ed. William J.H. Andrewes (Cambridge, MA, 1996), and Dava Sobel, *Longitude: The True Story of a Lone Genius Who Solved the Greatest Scientific Problem of His Time* (Harmondsworth, 1995). Interestingly, none of these works mention German contributions to the quest in the late seventeenth or early eighteenth centuries.

[22] Witsen is one of the most interesting polymaths of this period of history. See J.F. Gebhard, Jr., *Het Leven van Mr. Nicolaas Cornelisz. Witsen (1641-1717)* (Utrecht, 1881); and P.J.A.N. Rietbergen, "Witsen's World: Nicolaas Witsen (1641-1717) Between the Dutch East India Company and the Republic of Letters," *Itinerario* 9/2 (1985): 121-34.

existed between Kolb and his first teachers in astronomy, despite the fact that he knew more famous scholars in Berlin and elsewhere by this time.

Kolb left Amsterdam in 1705 as a passenger on a VOC ship bound for the East Indies, with a stop at the Cape of Good Hope. He was now, clearly, well-educated and well-connected (equipped with letters of recommendation), and there was a lot of pressure on him to accomplish great things with his astronomical observations, and to relay these findings to a group of anxious scholars back in Berlin. When he first arrived at the Cape, the governor, Willem Adriaan van der Stel, greeted Kolb cordially and invited him to live in the *Thuyn-huys*[23] in the VOC gardens, at the very heart of the colony. Though Kolb did pursue astronomical observations for at least two years, it appears that he never fulfilled the expectations of his patron. He had difficulty finding an independent place to set up his instruments, then he was hampered by the weather, and finally by the length of time that it took for correspondence to pass between the Cape and Europe. Furthermore, Krosick had trouble relaying funding to Kolb, which strained the relationship. Eventually Krosick stopped providing funds altogether—a decision he apparently did not explain to Kolb. However, it was not unusual for educated men, particularly those who participated in the Republic of Letters, to move from one interest to another, as opportunities appeared. Even before he stopped watching the stars, Kolb started taking notes about all sorts of other things he could observe at the Cape. Indeed, because it was so common for learned men to have a multiplicity of interests, it was rather strange that Krosick discontinued his support. But because of this change in his financial circumstances, Kolb was forced to give up his lodgings and to seek employment. This was probably the low point of his life in terms of patronage, but by late 1710 he had made a small comeback and was working as a secretary to the *Landdrost* (literally, the magistrate, but this person was basically the mayor or leader) of the expansion colonies of Stellenbosch and Drakenstein. However, scarcely two years later, Kolb had another round of bad luck: his eyesight deteriorated so much that he described it as "blindness" in the preface to *Caput Bonae Spei Hodiernum*. He was deemed unable to continue carrying out his secretarial duties, but this decision was at least partly based on the fact that the political faction of which he was a part had

---

[23] Now the official residence of the State President when he is in Cape Town.

fallen out of power again. The combination of circumstances made it easy for the governing council at the Cape to recommend that he should return to Europe, which he did in 1713. Here the quest for patronage began all over again, and the publication of *Caput Bonae Spei Hodiernum* was a vital part of this period of Kolb's life.

During his stay at the Cape, however, Kolb had ample time not just to observe from the outside, but to become a part of the rhythms of life there. In terms of the settler colonies, he was able to experience life at the center and the peripheries. He became involved in the political intrigues within the colony, and had daily contact with the slaves there, as well as individual Khoikhoi and groups of Khoikhoi who lived in and near the areas that the Dutch claimed.[24] Kolb was not an armchair traveler; in fact, he lived at the Cape longer than almost all of the authors who wrote about the Cape in the seventeenth and eighteenth centuries. He knew that the Khoikhoi were part of an on-going European debate about the natural history of man, and therefore had scholarly motivations for deciding to observe them and take notes. However, daily contact meant that he was able to see and hear much more than other travelers, and to develop personal ideas based on relationships of one kind and another, rather than simply on the preconceptions he had brought with him from Europe. This is not to say that Kolb ever fully understood the Khoikhoi or that he was able to present them *as they really were*; however, in the text of *Caput Bonae Spei Hodiernum*, there is constantly at play the aims and motivations of the European man of letters and, equally, a kind of raw data feedback about everything he experienced.

IV. Caput Bonae Spei Hodiernum: *Getting Published*

Kolb's first order of business when he returned to Europe was to seek a cure for his blurred eyesight, and this he found with a well-known doctor in Baden-Baden. It was probably in this period that he first started writing or compiling *Caput Bonae Spei Hodiernum*, and as mentioned before, he must have been partly motivated by the need for steady employment, as well as the desire to vindicate his name among learned men in Germany. There is no evidence that Kolb reconnected with

---

[24] For a detailed consideration of conditions at the Cape of Good Hope in this period and Kolb's part in the complex social order there, please see my dissertation: "Primitive Man and the Enlightened Observer: Peter Kolb among the Khoikhoi," (Ph.D. Thesis, University of Minnesota, 2005).

any of his former patrons. Eimmart had died shortly after Kolb left for the Cape, and Krosick died in 1714. At this point, then, I would like to turn to an examination of the book itself, including issues of patronage and practical questions of how it was actually constructed or put together. From the late seventeenth century onwards, scholars have argued, Germany underwent something of a "reading revolution" (*Leserevolution*) in terms of reading habits, book production, and uses of vernacular languages. Kolb's use of the German language and his method of writing fit into this context.[25]

The first edition of Kolb's work in German was printed in 1719 by Peter Conrad Monath in Nuremberg. This city was the most important center of publishing and communication in southern Germany at this time, with 99 booksellers and publishers active there between 1701 and 1750.[26] The Monath firm published and sold books and art, and seems to have employed engravers.[27] Unfortunately, I have not been able to find detailed information about Monath's business or his relationship with Peter Kolb. Though the firm did not specialize in any particular type of book, we can get a sense of what it published and sold based on the advertisement on the last two pages of *Caput Bonae Spei Hodiernum*. It lists 51 additional titles available from the firm, including works in German, Italian, and Latin. These works are dictionaries, mathematical treatises, a defense of Copernicus, religious treatises, books of sermons and spiritual examples for children, works of natural history (such as ones on insects and flowers), and teach-yourself books on accounting,

---

[25] Book production, or the number of books offered at the yearly book fairs, only reached its pre-Thirty Years' War level around 1768 (of about 1,587 new releases). At the same time, there was a change in the books offered in favor of the use of the German language—by 1692, more German than Latin books appeared at the fairs, and indeed, by 1714 there were twice as many in German as Latin; by 1735 three times more. This change was due in part to the leadership of German intellectuals such as Gottfried Wilhelm Leibniz, Christian Wolff and Christian Thomasius, who consciously strove to elevate German as an academic language, but also to widen the circle of education in Germany over all. See Reinhard Wittmann, *Geschichte des deutschen Buchhandels. Ein Überblick* (Munich, 1991), 76-77 and Schottenloher, *Books and the Western World: A Cultural History*, trans. W. Boyd and I. Wolf (London, 1989), 246.

[26] The city was in third place behind Catholic Augsburg with 150 firms and Leipzig (the main site of the book fairs in this period) with about 145 firms. See Reinhard Wittmann, *Geschichte des deutschen Buchhandels*, 86-87.

[27] David L. Paisey, *Deutsche Buchdrucker, Buchhändler und Verleger, 1701-1750* (Wiesbaden, 1988), 178. Paisey also records that the firm had an office in Vienna, and the title page of their re-translation of Kolb's work in 1745 indicates that they also had outlets in Frankfurt and Leipzig. See pages 329-330 for the full list of publishers active in Nuremberg; pages 302-03 for Augsburg, and 323-25 for those active in Leipzig.

painting miniatures and etching.[28] These titles suggest scholarly con-
sumers but also people of the middle classes, since nobles would have
had tutors available to teach them artistic skills, for example. Two other
books on the list purport to be collections of letters exchanged between
a converted Chinese man living in Europe and his pagan friend living
in Peking. (The letters were translated from Chinese to English and
then to German by Ludwig Ernst von Faramond.) Kolb's book would
have been enjoyed by the same readers who bought both these books
of letters and works on natural history, and certainly Kolb himself was
deeply entrenched in the mentality that produced and pondered such
works.

Caput Bonae Spei Hodiernum is dedicated to Margrave Georg Wilhelm
of Ansbach-Bayreuth, a somewhat less powerful relation of the
Brandenburg family that was building up the kingdom of Prussia in the
same period.[29] It certainly was not unusual for a book, particularly one
that wished to extend knowledge, to be dedicated to a nobleman. Surveys
of English book dedications in the early eighteenth century have shown
that most were addressed to nobles and 14 per cent (of 993) to members
of the royal family itself. Thus there were cultural traditions at work
here too: on the one hand aristocrats still considered book patronage
to be an honorable duty, and on the other hand, the better the patron,
the more prestige that accrued to the book.[30] The association with Georg
Wilhelm may have been another reason that Kolb's work was picked
up in the German regions of the Republic of Letters.

---

[28] The Monath firm seems to have published a lot of work done by Nuremberg sci-
entists: see for examples the entries for Johann Philip von Wurzelbau, Johann Leonhard
Rost, and Johann Gabriel Doppelmayr in Kurt Pilz, *600 Jahre Astronomie in Nürnberg*
(Nuremberg, 1977), 302, 305-07, 316-17, respectively.

[29] Georg Wilhelm was a contemporary of Friedrich III of Brandenburg (1657-1713)
who became King Friedrich I of Prussia (and is responsible for starting to build up
Berlin as a *Residenzstadt*), as well as Friedrich Wilhelm I (1688-1740) who built up the
Prussian army. See *Brandenburgs Kurfürsten. Preussens Könige. Das Taschenlexikon* (Berlin, 1998),
28-31. Kolb first thanks the Margrave for his new job and then turns to his concern
for his book: ". . . auch vor diese geringe Arbeit/ welche ich zeit meines Anwesens in
Euer Hoch-Fürstl. Durchl. Landen/ aus meinen Annotationen zusammen getragen und
verfertiget/ gegen alle Neyder und Feinde/ Deroselben höchsten Schutz und Beystand
implorire" (unnumbered, fifth page).

[30] Richard Yeo, *Encyclopaedic Visions: Scientific Dictionaries and Enlightenment Culture* (Cambridge,
2001), 224. Furthermore, Marion Peters suggests that noblemen, as opposed to mayors
of towns or businessmen, were often in a better position to give real aid (monetary or
in the form of a job) to scholars. See her article, "Nepotisme, Patronage en Boekopdrachten,
bij Nicolaes Witsen (1641-1717), Burgermeester van Amsterdam" *Lias* 25 (1998): 91-92,

V. *Networks of Letter-Writers, Notes and Strategies*

The conceit for each chapter of *Caput Bonae Spei Hodiernum* is that it is a letter to its patron. Other travelers' accounts that Kolb admired used this style, and he said that it also reflected the fact that many of his chapters originated as letters that he had sent to friends back in Europe while he was still living at the Cape. It was one way to couch his narrative in personal terms, helping to establish himself as an eye-witness. At the same time, however, Kolb's general method in most chapters is to first summarize previous accounts that he considered important, then to report his own experiences, and finally to try to draw conclusions. Thus, his method is to offer two kinds of authority: that of personal experience in a first person voice, and the erudition of a researcher, which enabled him to see all sides of a particular issue.

But though these letters were, in a sense, intellectual constructions, since Kolb never wrote to Georg Wilhelm while he was at the Cape, and the chapters were changed and supplemented after the return to Germany, it is certain that Kolb did write letters to many people concerning his experiences. His network of letter-writers reveals something of his position in the Republic of Letters; it also reveals the way that a book on the Cape might gain momentum to reach publication over a number of years. In the preface to *Caput Bonae Spei Hodiernum*, Kolb first challenges his readers to find a more complete travel narrative about the Cape in any language, and then assures them that in his opinion it would be against both honor and reason to entice the money out of their pockets only to serve them "aufgewärmeten Kohls" (warmed up cabbage). He argues that he could prove that this will not be the case with this book, if he could simply show them one of the letters that he sent to "gute Gönner and wehrte Freunde" (good patrons and worthy friends) from the Cape. When he returned from Cape, he found that more had been made of these letters than he could have imagined and he was eagerly pressured to publish his discoveries and share them with the curious world (*CBSH*, unnumbered first page of the Vorrede). A similar reference to letters sent from the Cape occurs in the foreword to the Dutch translation of *Caput Bonae Spei Hodiernum*, with which Kolb was involved just before his death in 1726. Here he states that he wrote many letters to friends in Europe, and that among the learned more

---

where she describes Cornelis de Bruyn's decision to dedicate his book *Reizen over Moskovie* (1711) to Z. von Uffenbach, Duke of Brunswick, rather than Nicolaes Witsen.

was made of these observations than he had expected.[31] He was therefore convinced upon his return home to put all his observations in order
and publish them. Clearly, Kolb wished to view himself as part of an
international class of learned men, and there is a possibility that learned
men wrote directly to him to discuss his work in the early 1720s. But
there is no evidence of this, and during his lifetime, Kolb did not
advance beyond the German and Dutch circles of the Republic of
Letters.

It is unlikely that we will ever know all of Kolb's correspondents, but
we can uncover a fairly large number of them. Kolb mentions in *Caput
Bonae Spei Hodiernum* and in his autobiography that he wrote to Nicolaas
Witsen (mayor of Amsterdam and a Director of the VOC at different
points in his life), mainly about the political troubles during his stay at
the Cape (*CBSH*, 46 and 812).[32] But most of his correspondents seem
to have been German-speakers from the southern regions. Kolb certainly
wrote to Krosick in the early years, but not after 1707. He mentions
writing in Latin to Johannes Gabriel Doppelmayern (or Doppelmayr),
Professor of Mathematics and Natural Philosophy in Nuremberg, about
a strange phase of the moon that he observed during his journey to
the Cape (*CBSH*, 35); he mentions another Latin letter, to Professor
Johan Jacob Scheuchzer of Zurich, about the cloud that covers Table
Mountain, like a cloth, from September to March (*CBSH*, 70 and 73).[33]
There are a few more clues about correspondents in his autobiography,
where he mentions that he wrote to Witsen, Pertsch, Goeckel, Praun,
Leopold and other celebrated men.[34] Pertsch was from a family that
chronicled the history of Wunsiedel; Christian Louis Göckel was the
physician in Baden-Baden to whom Kolb went to have his eyes cured.
The Prauns were a wealthy patrician family in Nuremberg, who had

---

[31] *Naaukeurige en Uitvoerige Beschryving van de Kaap de Goede Hoop* (Amsterdam, 1727),
vol. 1: ". . . van welke brieven veel groter werk onder de Geleerden gemaakt is, als ik
my verbeeld had . . ." (unnumbered ninth page).

[32] He kept up a correspondence with the family of another Amsterdam citizen, Jan
Weysenacker, a merchant and innkeeper—though this was a more personal correspondence. In the AFAG these are letters 22, 32, 34, 38, 75, 76 and 77 by Jan, and 23
and 24 by his daughter, Machtelt (again not chronologically numbered).

[33] However, most of the letters that remain among Kolb's papers in Neustadt an der
Aisch are from friends he knew at school, and they date from before 1700.

[34] Neustadt/Aisch, Kirchenbibliothek, MS 129: "Ab anno itaque [abbreviated in text]
1704 usque [abbreviated in text] ad annum 1714 Germaniam non vidi, sed continuis
peregrinationibus exoticis tempus consumsi, ita tamen, ut etiam cum Viris Celeberrimis
Witzio, Pertschio, Goeckelio, Praunio, Leopold aliisque [abbreviated in text] litteraria
colloquia habuerim" (page 3, verso).

also aided Kolb while he was studying. They engaged in long-distance trade and had links in Bologna and Florence.[35] Kolb mentions a specific letter to Georg Alexander Leopold, pastor of the church in Redwitz (most likely the church Kolb attended before he began his studies in Nuremberg) in the section on Khoikhoi religious practices (*CBSH*, 407). In fact, the letter he mentions is one in which he utterly denied that the Khoikhoi believe in any god—he corrects this position vehemently in the book itself. Except for Witsen, none of these men were known internationally, and probably not even within Germany. Three of them were certainly connections from Kolb's youth. All this suggests that Kolb was not in the first tier, so to speak, of the Republic of Letters, though a few advantageous connections gave him a small foothold.

In addition to Leopold, Kolb mentions several other religious letter-writers in his autobiography—particularly the Pietist missionaries to India, Ziegenbalg and Plütschow; Boeving and Gründler—all of whom mention meetings with Kolb in their letters to August Herman Francke (their director) in Halle.[36] But more remarkable for the question of the construction of *Caput Bonae Spei Hodiernum* is Francke's letter to Kolb in 1709, which contains a request for Kolb to compile observations on the Khoikhoi specifically. The copy of this letter kept by the Franckesche Stiftungen was labeled "Entwurf" (draft) by an archivist, but phrases in the letter suggest that this was not the first exchange between the two men.[37] The press of the orphanage at Halle, under the direction of Francke, published accounts of indigenous peoples and missionary work from all over the world, in the form of newsletters which were bound together later as books. It has been shown that these newsletters were based on actual letters, but they were often edited and rephrased by Francke or his colleagues at the press in Halle. The purpose of such editing was often to heighten the urgency of the call for donations for mission work. As we have seen, Kolb was sympathetic to the Pietist movement and its aims, but oddly, he does not mention Francke or his suggestion for publishing observations on the Cape at any point in *Caput Bonae Spei Hodiernum*.

---

[35] Kolb refers to the family as the "Hoch-Edlen Praunischen Familie" on the first page of the "Dedicatio" of *CBSH*. See also Wolfschmidt, *Magister Peter Kolb*, 9.

[36] See for example, the two letters of Joh. Ernestus Gründler written 1709 (one is a copy of the other, though slightly different) in the Missionsarchiv of the Archive of the Franckesche Stiftungen, Halle, I C II: 8 and I C II: 7.

[37] Francke to Kolbe, "Entwurf," end of 1709, Missionsarchiv of the Archive of the Franckesche Stiftungen, Halle, I C 13a:6.

In his letter, Francke first acknowledges a previous letter from Kolb and thanks him for taking the time to answer so thoroughly the questions put to him by Gründler (which explains the source of the information about the Khoikhoi in Gründler's letters). Furthermore, he expresses his gratefulness for Kolb's willingness to show hospitality to the missionaries traveling to India during their stays at the Cape. It gives Francke joy that one of his former and dear auditors (referring to Kolb's time at the University in Halle) is settled at such a faraway corner of the earth, and he says that Kolb is in his prayers. However, though Francke begins by thanking Kolb for answering Gründler's questions, he wants to know more, and makes a request:

> It would be appropriate for the public if my sir [Kolb] would bring to light a tract about the Hottentots. I think that such a thing would be most pleasant if it came out in the form of letters, and if [it was] (1) first just one letter of 2, 3 or 4 printed pages; if shorter, then it could give the opportunity to formulate questions that would lead to a thorough report, that could be shared in further letters.[38]

None of Kolb's observations were published through the press at the orphanage in Halle, so he probably did not send the requested letters or report. However, it is striking that such a letter should exist, and it opens up further questions about contextualizing Kolb. The letter does indicate that Kolb would have had more than one venue available for publishing his narrative. But he never mentions Francke's part in the matter of collecting his observations for publication, which may suggest that he did not consider this man the primary influence on his subsequent work. Kolb's silence might suggest too a desire to distance himself from the Pietists, and for his book to have a wider European appeal. It starts to become clearer that Kolb's relationship to Pietism was quite complex and not one of simple discipleship.

The only author on South Africa that Kolb mentions as an influence in the preface to *Caput Bonae Spei Hodiernum* is the Pietist missionary Bartholomaeus Ziegenbalg. In many ways, Ziegenbalg's writings provided

---

[38] Francke to Kolbe, "Entwurf," end of 1709, Missionsarchiv of the Archive of the Franckesche Stiftungen, Halle, I C 13a:6, end of 1 (recto) to 2 (or verso): "Dem publico wäre es gar angemesen seyn, wenn mein herr von den Hottentotten einen Tractat ans lichts geben wird. Ich halte davon, daß solcher an angenehmsten seyn werde wenn es in form von briefen her aus käme, und wenn vers [unclear in text] (1) nur ein brief geschrieben würde, [word indeciperable] 2. 3. b[bis?] 4. Gedruckten bogen, wen weniger, so wurde solches gelegenheit geben solche fragen zu formiren deren beantwortung zu einer grundlichen Nachricht dienete, so dann in den folgenden briefen ertheilet werden künte."

negative reasons for Kolb to publish his account. In the preface, Kolb says that he was convinced that he must write about the Khoikhoi at the Cape because of all the mistakes, contradictions and negative assessments he found in other works. He suggests that these mistakes must have been made because the authors had spent too short a time at the Cape or because they were too quick to believe stories told them either by Europeans there or by the Khoikhoi themselves. Kolb mentions Ziegenbalg as one of those who was deceived in this way during his short stay at the Cape. Ziegenbalg was the first of the Pietist missionaries who stopped at the Cape on their way to India, and he met with Kolb in 1706. Most of Ziegenbalg's writings are about his work in India, but he also published some observations on the Cape that appeared in the mission newsletter that was published at the orphanage in Halle: *Kurze Nachricht von seiner Reise aus Ost-Indien nach Europa* (1715-18).[39] Ziegenbalg's main concern was to convert the Khoikhoi, and although Kolb essentially agreed with this aim, most often he uses Ziegenbalg's writings to show how Europeans could be misled when attempting to understand the Khoikhoi—particularly when it came to matters of their belief system.

There is not enough space in this essay to fully explore Kolb's relationships with the Pietist missionaries, and how the writings of each one of them affected the construction of *Caput Bonae Spei Hodiernum*. They were, however, a significant subset of the correspondents who helped to shape his worldview, expectations, and his major work on the Cape. But letters were not the only source Kolb used when he worked on the published version of his description of the Cape. In the dedication to his book, Kolb states that he compiled *Caput Bonae Spei Hodiernum* from his annotations too. When one looks at Kolb's extant notes from the Cape, it is possible to argue that there is a kind of progression in what he decided to do while he was there. From 1705 to 1707 he made rather detailed notes of astronomical observations, and from 1706 to 1707 there are also daily, detailed records of the winds and cloud

---

[39] For more on this newsletter see, Thomas Müller-Bahlke, "Communication at Risk: The Beginning of the Halle Correspondence with the Pennsylvania Lutherans," in *In Search of Peace and Prosperity: New German Settlements in Eighteenth Century Europe and America*, ed. Hartmut Lehmann, H. Wellenreuther and R. Wilson (University Park, PA, 2000), 139-55. On Pietist missionary work generally see, Paul Raabe, H. Liebau and T. Müller, *Pietas Hallensis Universalis. Weltweite Beziehungen der Franckeschen Stiftungen im 18. Jahrhundert* (Halle, 1995). On Ziegenbalg: Brijraj Singh, *The First Protestant Missionary to India: Bartholomaeus Ziegenbalg (1683-1719)* (Oxford, 1999).

coverage. In 1708 Kolb seems to have stopped observing the stars, though he continued to observe the weather. Now, however, the daily entries also record human activities (mostly among the colonists). Unfortunately, even the notes for 1708 are not complete and there are no other leaves for the subsequent years.[40] Later in the book Kolb refers to the loss of many of his papers, but without explaining when or how this happened (*CBSH*, 174 and 190).[41]

In addition to offering clues about the combination of letters and notes he used to reconstruct his experience when he compiled his book back in Germany, Kolb also foregrounds certain strategies he used for finding out information while he was at the Cape that emphasize the reliability of his work. First, the fact that he lived at the Cape for eight years gave him a definite edge over other travelers, but second, he recounts that he tried to record only those things that he had seen himself or had heard from a trustworthy witness. He says that this difficult method cost him "viele tausend Tropffen-Schweisses/ und unbeschreibliche Beschwehrlichkeiten" (many thousand drops of sweat and indescribable difficulties) as well as often putting him in danger from wild animals.[42] Clearly references to hardships and to seeing things with his own eyes

---

[40] These notes may be found in the AFAG. At some point an archivist numbered them in blue pencil, but these numbers are not chronological. These notes are on approximately A4-size paper, often folded together from a larger sheet, and lightly sewn together like a notebook. The astronomical observations are in two copies with slightly different handwritings, most likely both by Kolb, though it is difficult to tell which is the rough and which the neat copy. The archival numbers run from 62 to 70 on the set of notes that is most complete (from late 1705 to 1707); the notes on the wind are numbered 74 (1706) and unnumbered (1707); the notes for 1708 are numbered 61.

[41] In closing the section on birds, Kolb writes: "Und hiemit hat Er auch dasjenige, mein Herr, was ich von der Vögeln observiret, und nach erlittenen Verlust meiner geschriebenen Memoiren noch übrig behalte . . . so ist der Fehler nicht meiner Aufmercksamkeit, sondern der Fatalität zuzuschreiben, die mir noch unterschiedliche andere Papiere entrissen, deren Verlust mich annoch ziemlich kräncket und schmerzet" (*CBSH*, 190).

[42] Though Kolb was not able to learn the language of the Khoikhoi, he does comment that when he felt more comfortable about the language, he began making trips farther away from the Cape and into the countryside around the other European settlements. Kolb says that he sometimes had Khoikhoi traveling with him on these journeys who helped him get around (*CBSH*, 61). On one occasion, when he was traveling to the warm baths in the area called the Land of Waveren, he had three Khoikhoi with him who were acting as his translators. At night, when he was lying in his tent, eleven lions approached them and scared him nearly to death. Luckily, his brave companions chased the lions away by throwing fiery branches at them (*CBSH*, 108-109). It may be that this personal experience of having his life saved by his companions is the main reason that Kolb thought so highly of the Khoikhoi. The fact that he had translators with him may explain why Kolb was able to gather so much information.

are ways that Kolb establishes his own worthiness and authenticity as a writer.[43] In the preface to the Dutch translation of *Caput Bonae Spei Hodiernum* Kolb refers exclusively to his account of the Khoikhoi, with no mention of the other information contained in the book. Here he states even more clearly that he resolved not to set out on paper anything that he did not observe himself or hear from the mouth of a Khoikhoi.[44] Furthermore, Kolb comments on the simplicity of his authorial voice: in the original German text, he remarks that his book does not have the neat turns of phrase that romances have, as this would not have been appropriate to the matter at hand. Indeed, his sentences have a rather Dutch inflection since he spoke Dutch all the time when he lived at the Cape because it was more useful. His language usage certainly allows the reader to hear a particular and personal authorial voice throughout the book—in other words, he seems to emphasize the fact that only he, who had direct personal experience, could have written this book. He goes on to express the hope that his work will be completely clear and that the chapters may be experienced like letters between good friends. This emphasis on simplicity and lack of pretension was not unusual in German travel writing of this period. Stewart, in fact, argues that writers created a self-conscious aesthetic of simplicity.[45]

VI. *The Description of the Khoikhoi*

Caput Bonae Spei Hodiernum was divided into three sections: natural history, social life and customs of the Khoikhoi, and discussion of the settler colony. However, the middle section, on the Khoikhoi, was undoubtedly the part of the book that engaged the most interest. We know this because the learned journals that reviewed the book concentrated most heavily on this part of it; and the translations of the original text most often started with the description of the Khoikhoi, and greatly abridged the rest—especially the section on the settler colony. Kolb, as I have

---

[43] On the importance of authenticity, see William E. Stewart, *Die Reisebeschreibung und ihre Theorie im Deutschland des 18. Jahrhunderts* (Bonn, 1978), 37-39. See also Anthony Pagden, *European Encounters with the New World: From Renaissance to Romanticism* (New Haven and London, 1993), 82-83: he quotes Clifford Geertz, ". . . to be a convincing 'I' witness one must . . . first become a convincing 'I'."

[44] *Naaukeurige en Uitvoerige Beschryving*, vol. 1, ". . . uit den mond en ommegang der Hottentotten zelf, zoude bevinden in der daad alzoo te weezen" (unnumbered tenth page).

[45] Stewart, *Die Reisebeschreibung und ihre Theorie*, 37: ". . . eine selbstbewußte Ästhetik des Schlichten."

mentioned already, wanted to establish his account as attaining a new level of detail and veracity. Thus I want to look at two excerpts connected with the Khoikhoi in part to test how Kolb achieved a sense of being authoritative. In many ways, the original *Caput Bonae Spei Hodiernum* attempted to be an encyclopedic text, but more than this, Kolb wanted to make his account alive so that readers could partake in his reactions. The two texts I have chosen are in some ways arbitrarily picked out, since the section on the Khoikhoi is long and rich in details. The first is a single episode that sheds light on how Kolb communicated with informants. The second is a longer description that allows one to delve into the question of how Europeans reconstructed Khoikhoi belief systems. Both excerpts share important themes: first, the force of personal experience, reinforced by the inclusion of Khoikhoi voices; and second, the competing aims of showing the Khoikhoi to be both like and unlike Europeans. Though these themes involve techniques of textual or literary construction, they also speak to the kind of information gathered in the volume.

Kolb's book offers several fascinating glimpses into the language and people mix at the Cape, including mostly oblique references to how he was able to communicate with the Khoikhoi he met. He was not able to learn the language (though he tried), and so it seems that he usually traveled with at least one translator. He tells one particularly evocative story about interaction with the Khoikhoi later in Part One of *Caput Bonae Spei Hodiernum*, in a section on the waters at the Cape (Letter XVIII). Here he describes the warm baths found in a cave in the Swart Berge (*Schwartzen-Berges*, north and east of Stellenbosch). This incident took place in 1708, at a time when no one knew about the baths and their healing properties—now when you arrive there, says Kolb, you will find at least twenty people in the water.[46] But when he first made the trip, he found that all travelers ended up living like the Khoikhoi (i.e. in moveable structures, hunting game to eat, cooking over fires, etc.)—a remark that could be interpreted as one of the ways Kolb suggests that Europeans are not so different from the Khoikhoi. In addition,

---

[46] Part of the reason for the popularity of the spot by the time Kolb left the Cape, was that his friend Ferdinand Appels was given permission to develop the place a bit and build a house where people could at least use the kitchen. Permission to develop the spot was given by the Council of Policy at the Cape in 1710. See *Suid-Afrikaanse Argiefstukke: Resolusies van die Politieke Raad, Deel IV, 1707-1715*, transcribed and edited by A.J. Böeseken (Cape Town, 1962), 135. On the warm baths generally, see *CBSH*, 379-86.

Kolb discusses several good reasons for carrying wine, brandy and tobacco with one on trips like this: first, these things are good for the stomach (in proper doses), but second, the Khoikhoi one met on such journeys traded sheep or cattle for these products. The Khoikhoi expected to smoke a pipe of tobacco when they met Europeans also as a mark of courtesy. On this particular occasion, Kolb was camping at the warm baths when four Khoikhoi men arrived and approached him to pay their compliments. They also honored him with a rabbit they had killed with their sticks on the way there; in return (as a counter-gift) they asked for brandy and tobacco. Note how Kolb uses the language and usages of polite society here, but does not suggest that there was anything laughable in the situation. The Khoikhoi said that they had been traveling nearly thirty miles in the hopes of finding him and getting some tobacco, since they had neither seen nor tasted it for a very long time. Kolb was happy to oblige them, and after they had smoked a while, the Khoikhoi gathered some wood, made a fire and stayed with him that night. They told him stories, first about a Portuguese ship that had been wrecked on the coast by De la Goa Bay some years earlier, and which Kolb had heard about. He seems to take this verifiable element as a reassurance that he could believe the other things they told him. The Khoikhoi said that the ship could still be seen, but was now so full of sand that it was no longer possible to get goods out of it. In addition, they described their land to him, and, he says, many other remarkable things about their way of life, which would be described elsewhere in his book. He enjoyed their company and their stories so much, that he gave them all another piece of tobacco when they set off on their way again.[47] If Kolb had several Khoikhoi translators with him, it is even more likely that he would have learned a lot from an encounter like this. His ease in this situation also seems rather remarkable, and if one can speak of his general attitude toward the Khoikhoi,

---

[47] Kolb writes, "Einsmals kamen ihrer 4. zu mir, welche erfahren hatten, daß mich bey dem warmen Bad aufhielte, und machten ihr compliment; verehreten mir auch einen Hasen, den sie unter Wegs mit ihren Küris oder Stöcken todt geschlagen hatten. Diese verlangten nichts anders zur GegenGifft, als nur Brandwein und Toback; sagten auch, daß sie sonderlich darum einen so weiten Weg von ungefähr 30. Meilen, nach mir zugekommen wären: und bathen, ich möchte doch ihren Tobacks-Hunger sättigen, da sie schon eine geraume Zeit herwärts keinen gesehen, geschweige denn gehabt hätten. Da ich nun ihre Bitte erfüllet und ihnen Toback gegeben hatte, brachten sie Holz herbey und blieben selbige Nacht bey mir; machten auch nachgehends in der Nacht eine Erzehlung von dem Portugiesischen Schiff, welches vor einigen Jahren bey der Bay de la Goa gestrandet: und sagten daß man noch etwas davon sehen könte, aber wegen des

this friendly exchange of stories and personal products is it.[48] But he also records passages that are remarkable for their insensitivity, and even in this pleasant encounter by the warm baths, one wonders how aware Kolb was that the exchange taking place had been translated at least twice—once from one Khoikhoi man to another (most likely from a different tribe), and then into German or Dutch that Kolb could understand. At other points in the book he suggests that Khoikhoi occasionally deliberately misled Europeans who were questioning them about culture (Ziegenbalg, for example)—but this in itself indicates that Kolb did not think that he had been fooled.[49] It was certainly enough, however, for most of Kolb's eighteenth-century audience to hear this story and grasp that Kolb had had real conversations, with real Khoikhoi, outside of the major European settlement, and yet in terms that were not so foreign after all to exchanges in sitting rooms across Germany. But today we would like to know: where did these four Khoikhoi come from and to which tribes did they belong? Were they really seeking Kolb, and if so, why? If we read these Khoikhoi men as cultural brokers with personal reasons for accompanying this European man on his journeys, could we suppose that Kolb had become known as the man who was recording everything there was to know about the world at the Cape? Might there have been prestige or fun involved in seeking out this man and telling him stories? These questions cannot be answered fully, but it is clear that these cultural brokers enabled Kolb to write a deeper and more complex account of the Khoikhoi than any that had gone before him, and helped make this book authoritative.

At the beginning of the section devoted to the social life and customs of the Khoikhoi, Kolb first lays to rest two persistent myths about them:

---

hinein geworffenen vielen Sandes, könte man nun nichts mehr heraus bekommen. Weil mir nun von demselbigen Schiff bewust war, daß es viele Kostbarkeiten geführet hatte, war mir ihre Erzehlung, wie auch ihres Landes Beschreibung, samt andern vielen merckwürdigen und zu seiner Zeit vorkommende Sachen, ihre Lebens-Art belangende, desto angenehmer: und gab ihnen noch ein Stück Toback mit auf den Weg" (*CBSH*, 285).

[48] An interesting parallel might be drawn to G.A. Robinson, Protector of the Aborigines (in Australia) in the 1840s: see Inga Clendinnen, "Reading Mr. Robinson," *Australian Book Review* 170 (1995): 34-42. I thank Rhys Isaac of Latrobe University for bringing this fascinating article to my attention.

[49] During the first thirty years of the colony, official translators for the VOC administration—especially Eva, Harry and Doman—held considerable status. Greater familiarity among Khoikhoi and Europeans meant that less dependence had to be placed on the very few individuals who were at first able to achieve bilinguality. Things had changed by the eighteenth century. Kolb, for example, seems to have traveled with three or four translators. On the early translators, see Elphick, *Khoikhoi and the Founding of White South Africa* (Johannesburg, 1985), esp. 103-110.

that they eat raw intestines and that they wear entrails around their necks. He says that he has never seen any of them wearing entrails. However, they do rub themselves with sheep's fat or butter to protect their skin and as a sign of wealth. Also, the women wear many leather anklets (*CBSH*, 482-83) and the men sometimes wear the bladders of wild animals (inflated) in their hair to show their prowess as hunters (*CBSH*, 485)—but never stinking entrails just for the fun of it. Furthermore, they do eat intestines, but only after cleaning them thoroughly and cooking them. Kolb even says that he tried the dish and it was good (*CBSH*, 367). Though the issues of wearing entrails and eating intestines may seem like rather silly details to address, these were two of the things that eighteenth-century Europeans were most likely to have heard about Khoikhoi.[50] Kolb's rejection of these accepted beliefs, based on his personal experience, was one way that he established his work as being at a new level of veracity in observation, but more importantly he also completely overturned the commonly held assumption that the Khoikhoi believed in no god or gods at all.

But it is not just veracity that he was aiming for; Kolb also crafted his description of the Khoikhoi to talk back to European culture. In other words, his narrative was part of the emerging trope of the Noble Savage, influenced directly by Baron de Lahontan's narrative of travels in Canada (which Kolb mentions in the preface to his book).[51] It is doubtful whether Kolb fully agreed with the kind of skepticism expressed by writers such as Lahontan, but he was certainly struck by the idea that a "savage" could answer questions about the customs of his own people and that his answers could call western civilization into question. Kolb recounts several stories in which Khoikhoi raised in European households finally reject European clothing, dwellings, and religious beliefs and return to their ancestral kraals. In the text, Kolb expresses an inability to understand why the Khoikhoi would choose to reject the civilization that had been bestowed on them, and with it the Christian

---

[50] See the excellent article by M. Van Wyk Smith, "'The Most Wretched of the Human Race': The Iconography of the Khoikhoin (Hottentots) 1500-1800," *History and Anthropology* 5/3-4 (1992).

[51] Lahontan, *Nouveaux voyages de M le Baron de Lahontan dans l'Amérique septentrionale*, 2 vols. (The Hague, 1703). See also Felipe Fernández-Armesto, *Civilizations: Culture, Ambition, and the Transformation of Nature* (New York, 2001), 135, where he adeptly summarizes Lahontan's work: "The mouthpiece for his [Lahontan's] freethinking anti-clericalism was an invented Huron interlocutor—a sort of sober Pookie called Adario, with whom he walked in the woods, discussing the imperfections of Biblical translations, the virtues of republicanism, and the merits of free love."

revelation that had been granted them. In particular, he was surprised that they laughed at people who tried to talk to them about God, and he was similarly puzzled by their unwillingness to talk about their own beliefs.[52] He often states that the Khoikhoi were not stupid people, and yet he was equally certain that Christianity was not foolishness and that the Khoikhoi should accept its truth. Many unexplained and unresolved pieces of dialogue and interaction serve to oddly subvert the author's controlling assumptions, which would seem to be that Europeans possess a higher degree of civilization and their religion is the only true one. It could be argued that one of the reasons Kolb set out to try to understand the Khoikhoi point of view was because he was unable to make them accept his. But like most people, Kolb had to use what he knew to explain what he did not understand, and this give-and-take can be seen in his reconstruction of Khoikhoi religious beliefs.

First, it should be noted that in contrast to the paragraph, or at most a page, that previous authors spent on explaining Khoikhoi religion, Kolb devotes a whole chapter (thirteen large pages) to his explanation. In this chapter he deals only with their concepts of God and various worship practices, but in the rest of the section on the Khoikhoi he makes it clear that he understands various rites of passage and other practices to be connected with religious observation as well. In Kolb's explanation, the one God of the Khoikhoi is called the Great Captain, that is Gounia, or sometimes Ticquoa Gounia, God of all Gods. They also call the moon Gounia, and they honor the moon as the visible manifestation of the invisible God (*CBSH*, 408). Kolb gives an animated description of the Khoikhoi dancing before the new and full moon, which he sees as their worship service:

> It is especially rare and unusual to see what strange grimaces these people make at the same time. At times they lay themselves on the ground with their bare bodies, as they are accustomed to always being, and they yell and sing with full voice a number of unintelligible words. At times they stand up again and look to the

---

[52] He quotes an informant when he is trying to understand the Khoikhoi practice of honoring certain places. Kolb says that he asked a Khoikhoi man called Kamma (whom he persuaded to talk by offering him a pipe of tobacco) to tell him why he had been dancing in apparent joy on the top of a certain hill. Kamma replied that he had been sleeping there the night before when a lion had passed by and had not smelled him and attacked him. He was therefore dancing to thank whoever had saved him. Kolb then tried to persuade Kamma that it was in fact God's holy angel who had protected him, but all Kamma would say is, "Kamme niet verstaan" or "Kamma doesn't understand" (*CBSH*, 419), and as soon as he finished the pipe he jumped up and walked away. So much for being drawn into a long conversation.

moon with hefty cries, and sing out these words: Mutschi Atzé, that is: Be greeted
or welcome/Senihar eatzé, that is: Make it so that we may get much honey;
Choraqua-kahá chori Ounqua, that is: Make it so that our cattle may find much
to eat and give much milk . . .

When they are tired of yelling and dancing, they stand up straight, look at the
moon and murmur a few unintelligible words somewhat softly; but still clapping
their hands, and stamping their feet for joy, so that it shakes; turning and moving their bodies at the same time, now to this, now to that side, now forward,
now backward, indeed so that one cannot understand what they actually want to
indicate with that: next they begin to sing their Mutschi Atzé again, and once
more yell so strongly, that one must hold the ears closed if one is near to them.[53]

Notice that Kolb's understanding of this event is predicated on what
he knows: Europeans have worship services and pray to God, and Kolb
sees an analogous event in this singing and dancing.[54] Furthermore,
when he speaks about the moon as the visible manifestation of God,
under which the Khoikhoi recognize the invisible God, one can hear
faint echoes of the Christian, and for Kolb Lutheran, ritual of holy
communion, where the bread and the wine blessed by the minister are
seen as physical attributes under which the body and blood of Christ
should be understood. Also, unlike previous authors, Kolb does not simply call this event "raving." And though he does not understand all that
is said or done, he has either listened or made inquiries to find out
what sorts of things the Khoikhoi sing out before the moon. Finally, it
should be mentioned that Kolb connects this singing and dancing before
the moon to ancient Jewish practices of praising God (part of the on-
going argument about what happened to the lost tribes of Israel).

Kolb's explication of Khoikhoi religion does not end with his account
of the position of the moon in their beliefs. He also touches on three
other significant points: the existence of an apparently lesser God or
Captain, whom the Khoikhoi believed to cause harm, their veneration
of the praying mantis, and the practice of considering certain hills or
groves of trees as special, if not precisely hallowed. Kolb found out
about the lesser Captain by asking Khoikhoi whether they had cause

---

[53] My translation from Kolb, *CBSH*, 411.

[54] In the 1920s and 1930s, the ethnographer/anthropologist Dorothea Bleek also
believed such singing and shouts to be prayers, mainly for food. She translated one of
these in this way: "Ho, Moon lying there,/ Let me kill a springbok/ To-morrow,/ Let
me eat a springbok;/ With this arrow/ Let me shoot a springbok/ With this arrow;/
Let me eat a springbok,/ Let me eat filling my body/ In the night which is here,/ Let
me fill my body." Partially quoted from I. Schapera, *The Khoisan Peoples of South Africa:
Bushmen and Hottentots* (London, 1930), 172. See also Elizabeth Elbourne, "Early Khoisan
Uses of Mission Christianity," in *Missions and Christianity in South African History*, ed. Henry
Bredekamp and Robert Ross (Johannesburg, 1995), 76.

to fear Gounia, the Great Captain. The Khoikhoi answered that they had no cause to fear the Great Captain, who always did good things, but there was a lesser Captain, called Touquoa, who caused them harm, and who they therefore feared and served (*CBSH*, 414). Kolb says that he follows Böving in (predictably) assigning this figure the position of the devil in Khoikhoi religion.

On the other hand, the Khoikhoi practice of honoring the praying mantis as an omen of favor and good fortune is completely foreign, bizarre, and foolish to Kolb.[55] After describing how the Khoikhoi dance, sing, feast, and sprinkle an herb called *buchu* on their heads when one of these insects enters their kraal or huts, he then describes a confrontation between a German settler's son and the Khoikhoi who lived nearby and worked on the farm. The son caught a praying mantis and threatened the Khoikhoi that he would kill it. According to Kolb, they answered the boy (in pidgin Dutch): "You have caught this little creature, and now you want to just kill it, is that right? Just wait, if you do that, we are all going to walk."[56] Though Kolb may not be quoting directly, I want to highlight this inclusion of the voices of the Khoikhoi in his account. It is a brilliant strategy for giving his work the feel of immediacy; it is also a technique used more in Kolb's work than in any others. This suggests his superior desire to learn by listening, even in a situation that he considered strange. Furthermore, his mention of buchu in this situation reminds one of his description of this herb in the section on plants. Kolb was not a trained botanist, and learned most of what he knew while he was at the Cape. The first aim of his descriptions was clearly to give an idea of what the living plant was like, and to describe various uses of it, including simple decoration. He begins with the Latin phrase name, "Spiraea Africana odorata, foliis pilosis" and translates this into German as, odiferous African *Spiraea*, with hairy leaves—called buchu by the Khoikhoi.[57] He then connects the plant to

---

[55] See Schapera, *The Khoisan Peoples*, 177-78; also the very interesting article by Sigrid Schmidt, "Die Mantis religiosa in den Glaubenvorstellungen der Khoesan-Völker," *Zeitschrift für Ethnologie* 98 (1973), 102-27. Schmidt looks at both the historical and the modern position of the mantis in Khoisan beliefs. She suggests that though the mantis often was given the name of the High God in Khoisan folk beliefs, this did not mean that it was identical with God, but instead acted as an oracle—that is, the mantis brought omens and could also carry certain prayers to God.

[56] "Gy dit Beest fangum zoo, en nu dood makum zoo, is dat braa? Wagtum, ons altemaal daarvan loopum zoo" (*CBSH*, 417-18).

[57] Kolb writes, "Diese Gattung der Spireae, wird von den Hottentotten Buchu genennet; welche sie im Sommer, wenn die Kräuter dürr zu werden anfangen, und vollkommen verblühet haben, häuffig sammlen und gantz dürre werden lassen, daß sie selbige zur

certain social practices of the Khoikhoi: in the summer, when the herb has finished blooming and begins to dry out, the Khoikhoi collect the plants, dry them completely and then grind the plants down to a fine powder. The Khoikhoi sprinkle their heads with this powder both for cosmetic purposes and when they have headaches. Kolb then adds two further points: first that buchu powder has a function similar to hair powder in Europe, and secondly that it smells good. This description also shows that Kolb was not interested in enforcing points of difference between Europeans and the Khoikhoi; rather he draws upon what he saw as a common practice: the cosmetic use of a perfumed powder. This is a major theme of Kolb's book as a whole, and perhaps one of the reasons that it had such a strong resonance all across Europe in the eighteenth century.

And finally, Kolb's description of Khoikhoi religion also turns back on the European audience and criticizes their lukewarm-ness and lack of faith. Indeed, one of the main themes in his description of the social life and customs of the Khoikhoi is that they shame Europeans in many ways—including the way that they serve God. Here we seem to see again the glimmerings of Kolb's Pietist background which emphasized so strongly the need for personal conversion to the will of God. Kolb writes:

> Who then would now be able to deny that this dancing, singing and shouting at the time of the new and full moon is not a worship service? I for my side am completely sure of it, and I know as an infallible truth, that in the manifestation of their zeal, which they show at that time, they shame millions of Christians... [who] are so lukewarm, cold, lethargic and listless when they complete the same [worship of God], that it is not only a scandal before God, but also before such blind heathens... (*CBSH*, 412).

Kolb believed that the greatest barrier to bringing Khoikhoi to the Christian faith was not the lack of missionaries or the language barrier, but instead the horrible example that the Christians set for these people.

VII. *Textual Afterlife*

At this point I want to turn away from content and finally focus on what might best be called issues of distribution surrounding the book—

Pulver zerklopffen können: mit welchem sie so wohl zur solchen Zeit, wenn sie Koppf-Schmertzen, als auch sonsten zur Zierde, eben gleich wie wir etwa die Haar-Pulver gebrauchen, den Kopff bestreuen, und sich schön machen. Es siehet dieses Pulver Gold-gelb aus, und riechet sehr wohl" (*CBSH*, 254).

or the clearest indications we have that it did indeed become the authoritative book about the Cape. I have already mentioned that *Caput Bonae
Spei Hodiernum* was translated into Dutch, and published shortly after
Kolb's death in 1726 and 1727. This version was a nearly exact translation, with a new foreword by the author, in two deluxe volumes with
more maps and illustrations than the original, executed in ways that
were more technically sophisticated than the original. After the Dutch
version, however, all subsequent translations were also abridgements.

In 1731, the first English translation, done by Guido Medley, appeared
in London, published by the print shop of William and John Innys.
This shop was quite closely connected to the Royal Society and specialized in books on science and medicine as well as natural and experimental philosophy. Hans Sloane, President of the Royal Society at the
time, was a patron of the book, but it seems that Medley was never
himself accepted as a fellow of the Society. The book was subsequently
reprinted in 1738 by the same firm. The English translation was published in two small volumes: the first deals briefly with the topography
of the Cape, and then concentrates on the section on the Khoikhoi;
the second is concerned with the flora and fauna of the Cape. Though
Medley praises Kolb for the exactness of his account, he is probably
the first author to also criticize Kolb for the great length of his work.
Medley writes, "He [Kolb] is very tedious in some Relations, and here
and there runs out in Reflections that are neither very entertaining, nor
very much to the Purpose."[58]

In 1741, the first French translation appeared, done by Jean Bertrand,
published by the Amsterdam firm of Jean Catuffe. The French translation is divided into three beautiful little volumes: the first deals with
the description of the Khoikhoi; the second deals with various aspects
of geography, such as topography, geology, winds and water, as well as
the layout of the European colonies and their habits of government
there; the third describes the natural history of the Cape region. This
translation was reprinted twice in 1742 and 1743. Bertrand too acknowledges that he cut those of Kolb's stories that seemed too long or dull,
but he does not call Kolb's intellect into question, as Medley did. Instead,
he goes to some trouble to emphasize that Kolb was an educated man

---

[58] *The Present State of the Cape of Good Hope*, vol. I (London, 1731), xvii. On the English
translation, see Linda Merians, *Envisioning the Worst. Representations of "Hottentots" in Early
Modern England* (Newark, DE, 2001).

of good taste, who was supported by an aristocratic patron, and therefore not just an adventurer out to make a quick buck.[59]

In 1745, the Monath firm decided to retranslate the French version into German, indicating that the original, though very popular, was just too long-winded for many readers. In Monath's preface to the new edition, he states that after the popularity achieved by the French translation, he thought it wrong that non-Germans should be benefiting so much from Kolb's work while nothing similar existed for the pleasure of his compatriots. It is significant that Monath emphasizes Kolb's nationality, since this is probably the only time that happened.

After Monath's translation, a new vogue started among those publishing travelers' accounts: multi-volume collections of all the "best" narratives, in abridged forms so that readers would not have to spend a great deal of time to gather information about places and people. One of the first of these was published in London by Astley and Green: *A New General Collection of Voyages and Travels* (1745), quoted at the beginning of this essay. The purpose of the collection was not to unearth new material, but rather to compile what the editors considered to be the best accounts of the various regions of the world. This series was translated very quickly into French and German, with a lot of intrigue and back-biting going on among the publishers. The French version, under the direction of the famous Abbé A.F. Prévost, was called *Histoire generale des Voyages, ou Nouvelle Collection de Toutes les Relations de Voyage Par Mer et Par Terre . . .*, beginning publication in 1746; the German version was called *Allgemeine Historie der Reisen zu Wasser und Lande: oder Sammlung aller Reisebeschreibungen . . .*, beginning publication in 1747. Kolb's work appeared in all of these, drastically reduced. The effect of this, on the one hand, was to distill the information in his narrative into a chunk that was easily readable and could be quickly absorbed, catering to the new, enlarged and perhaps less educated reading public. But on the other hand, the nuances of Kolb's work, the doubts expressed, and the reluctance to pass judgments and tie up all loose ends, are all lost; the resulting narrative seems brash, and, with regard to the Khoikhoi in particular, less balanced and respectful.

The primary audience for Peter Kolb's work probably was learned men and the readers of the literary journals—who were not necessarily

---

[59] On the French translation, see François Fauvelle-Aymar, *L'Invention du Hottentot: Histoire de regard occidental sur les Khoisan (XVe-XIXe siècle)* (Paris, 2002), 239.

identical.[60] As mentioned earlier, Kolb himself speaks of the fact that a great deal of fuss was made among learned men over the letters that he sent back from the Cape. Another way that the Republic of Letters communicated was through the learned or literary journals that started being published in the late seventeenth century and became a mainstay of the Republic of Letters in the eighteenth century. The main purpose of the journals was to share reviews of books (usually called *extraits*), though some journals included articles on questions (theological, philosophical) as well as sharing discoveries (scientific, archaeological or geographical). The journals allowed scholars to gather information about what was going on in the Republic of Letters more rapidly than simply through their own correspondents. Furthermore, as the production of books increased during the century, it allowed learned men (the main audience) to gather knowledge quickly about books they either could not afford to buy or would not have time to read.[61] The great majority of the journals were in the French language and many were printed in the Dutch Republic (either in The Hague or in Amsterdam) where there was a large population of immigrant Huguenots and greater freedom of the press. There were also important journals in Latin, as well as some in German, Dutch and English. However, the French journals certainly helped boost the position of French as the international language of Enlightenment, beginning at an early stage in the eighteenth century.[62]

Reviews of Peter Kolb's works appeared in the learned journals of this period. These essays were not critiques, however, but usually summaries of the book. It is possible to get some sense of what the authors found most interesting in Kolb's writings by noting what they chose to mention and what they chose to skim over or leave out completely.

---

[60] Around 1700, there were about 100,000 people in Germany who had completed a higher education and therefore certainly formed the reading public. Contemporaries, however, complained that the book market was aimed almost entirely at learned people. See Wittmann, *Geschichte des deutschen Buchhandels*, 105 and 104. In 1690 Adrian Beyer, a legal scholar who was concerned with reforming the book trade, claimed about the book market: "Seine Wahren sind von = und vor niemand als Gelehrten/ kaufft iemand von and'n Professionen zu Zeiten ein Teutsch= oder bey anderen Nationen in seiner Mutter = Sprach gesteletes Büchlein/ so geschiehets zufälliger Weise und selten/daß daruf keine Rechnung oder Staat zu machen."

[61] Anne Goldgar, *Impolite Learning. Conduct and Community in the Republic of Letters, 1680-1750* (New Haven and London, 1995), 55-56.

[62] Godlgar, *Impolite Learning*, 55, 58, 60. See also, Hoftijzer and Lankhorst, *Drukkers, boekverkopers en lezers tijdens de Republiek. Een historiografische en bibliografische handleiding*, 2nd ed. (The Hague, 2000) 140-43.

Using the Rare Books collection of the University of Minnesota, I have only been able to look through ten journals with complete or nearly complete runs for the period from 1719-1746, and therefore my conclusions are necessarily incomplete. Reviews of Kolb's work may be found in two major German journals: *Acta Eruditorum* (1720) (published in Latin) and the *Deutsche Acta Eruditorum* (1720) (published in German); however, these journals do not review any of the later translations. Unfortunately, I have not been able to consult any Dutch-language journals or French ones focused on Dutch subjects, and I have not found any reviews of the Dutch translation in the other journals I have perused. For the English translation, I have not found reviews of the work as such, but authors in the *Grub Street Journal* (18 February and 4 March 1731) picked up on some of Kolb's stories about the Khoikhoi; the *Gentleman's Magazine* mentions the stories in the *Grub Street Journal* and the *Weekly Register*. These English journals were not pitched solely at a learned audience, and therefore probably reached more people—especially since they were all weeklies. The French translation, which one might have expected to resonate more loudly in the learned journals, was only reviewed in one French journal, the *Journal des Sçavans* (1741). Nevertheless, this was the oldest literary journal and therefore the best established and most prestigious. Notices for the publication of the French translation also occurred in volumes 25 and 26 of the *Bibliotheque Raisonné*, but it was not reviewed.[63] All of these journals may have been read widely across national borders in the Republic of Letters, but it seems clear that journals based in particular countries did not review books published in other countries.

As noted earlier, one thing these journal reviews seem to have in common is a primary fascination with the Khoikhoi, followed by an interest in the plants and animals of the Cape. In general, the *Acta Eruditorum* and the *Journal des Sçavans* seem to highlight more traditionally scholarly material, and do not delve much into speculations about Biblical connections or ways that Khoikhoi customs might be compared to those of Europeans. It could be argued, therefore, that these two journals were aimed particularly at traditionally scholarly groups. On the other hand, the *Deutsche Acta Eruditorum*, the *Grub-Street Journal* and the *Weekly Register* focus on exactly this sort of religious and social material. German readers appear to have enjoyed Kolb's observations about

---

[63] I have also been able to look through the *Bibliothèque Ancienne et Moderne*, *Bibliothèque Française* and *Mercure Historique et Politique*.

physical things and the ways he tried to connect them to stories from the Bible.[64] English readers in the 1730s enjoyed the portrayal of the social lives and customs of the Khoikhoi and the ways that the words could be used for laughter-inducing comparisons with English society.[65] The material highlighted in these journals may indicate that the editors were trying to reach a larger pool of less highly educated readers, or less serious scholars. Thus it seems appropriate, first, to note that based on the evidence from the journals too, Kolb's work had quite a large appeal; and second, that this evidence also makes one question the parameters of the Republic of Letters.

In conclusion, then, Kolb's book provides an excellent case study for the construction of a text that became authoritative over the course of the eighteenth century. Kolb himself was well-educated, and yet of a low enough social class that he had to be ambitious to gain patronage and to achieve any sort of recognition. His book on the Cape reflects his own polymathic interests, as well as coverage of those topics that he would have known to be important to his European audience. His education allowed him to employ rhetorical devices that imbued his account with a particular sense of veracity. Indeed, the naïve and yet authoritative voice of this eye-witness still retains much persuasive power. In personal terms, it is difficult to know whether Kolb achieved the recognition he sought in the Republic of Letters, even after the publication of *Caput Bonae Spei Hodiernum*. At the end of his life he held a secure position as the rector of the Latin School in Neustadt an der Aisch, but he was not well-off, and there is also no evidence that he was the center of a correspondence network. Nevertheless, after his death, the fame of his book spread as it was translated and abridged. It was successful because it tapped into currents in European thought about travel and foreign peoples—currents that reveled in the exotic and yet desired to see commonalities. Kolb's exhaustive construction of the social life and customs of the Khoikhoi, who, in his hands, were at once primitive and perspicacious, was irresistible.

---

[64] For the later eighteenth century, Stewart notes that contemporaries emphasized that the genre of travel narratives was free from class- or profession-specific ties: *Die Reisebeschreibung und ihre Theorie*, 191.

[65] "Strange! The different nations entertain of the same thing! the force, the witch-craft of custom! To be piss'd upon in Europe is a token of the highest Contempt; To be piss'd on in the Hottentot Ceremonies is a token of the highest honour. Pissing is the glory of all the Hottentot Ceremonies," *Grub-Street Journal* 59 (18 February 1731).

AFRICANS IN THE QUAKER IMAGE: ANTHONY BENEZET, AFRICAN TRAVEL NARRATIVES, AND REVOLUTIONARY-ERA ANTISLAVERY

JONATHAN D. SASSI

Associate Professor, Department of History
College of Staten Island and the Graduate Center, City University of New York

ABSTRACT

This article compares Anthony Benezet's influential 1771 antislavery tract, *Some Historical Account of Guinea*, with the sources from which he gleaned his information about Africa and the slave trade, the narratives published by European travelers to West Africa. Benezet, a Philadelphia Quaker and humanitarian reformer, cited the travel literature in order to portray Africa as an abundant land of decent people. He thereby refuted the apology that cast the slave trade as a beneficial transfer of people from a land of barbarism and death to regions of civilization and Christianity. However, Benezet employed the travel narratives selectively, suppressing contradictory evidence as well as controversial material that could have been used to construct an alternative depiction of African humanity. Nonetheless, Benezet's research shaped the subsequent debate over the slave trade and slavery, as antislavery writers incorporated his depiction into their rhetorical arsenal and proslavery defenders searched for a rebuttal.

How could an eighteenth-century Quaker abolitionist appeal to the authority of an English slave trader? Captain William Snelgrave's *A New Account of Some Parts of Guinea and the Slave-Trade*, published in 1734, would seem to offer a most unlikely place to look for material to use against the Atlantic slave trade. It provided, in the assessment of a modern scholar, "a justification of the slave trade which became standard" for its time.[1] Nevertheless, Philadelphian Anthony Benezet found in Snelgrave's book a short excerpt that he could use in his influential antislavery tract, *Some Historical Account of Guinea*, which was first published in 1771. The following essay analyzes exactly why and how Benezet deployed evidence from the accounts of European travelers to West Africa— most of whom, like Snelgrave, were directly involved in the slave trade— and with what consequences both for his own work and the broader,

---

[1] P. J. Marshall and Glyndwr Williams, *The Great Map of Mankind: Perceptions of New Worlds in the Age of Enlightenment* (Cambridge, Mass., 1982), 233. The preface notes that Williams authored the chapter from which this comment is taken.

© Koninklijke Brill NV, Leiden, 2006
Also available online – www.brill.nl

JEMH 10,1-2

eighteenth- and early nineteenth-century campaign against slavery. Some historians have noted Benezet's references to the travel literature in his publications.[2] However, no one has undertaken a thorough analysis of the subject, without which we miss an important dimension of the Revolutionary-era debate over slavery.

Snelgrave's book contained a concise defense of the slave trade. It was largely based on his experiences during two voyages to the Slave Coast of West Africa in 1727 and 1730. Snelgrave plied the triangular route for the purpose of exchanging English manufactured goods with African merchants for ivory, gold, and, above all, slaves, the last of which he could vend in the West Indies. He offered a number of reasons that not only legitimated the slave trade but also demonstrated its mutual benefits to Africans and Englishmen. First and foremost, he claimed, "It is evident, that abundance of Captives, taken in War, would be inhumanly destroyed, was there not an Opportunity of disposing of them to the *Europeans*. So that at least many Lives are saved, and great Numbers of useful Persons kept in being." The Africans thereby spared would, in his estimation, enjoy a better life in the West Indian sugar islands than they would have had they remained in their homeland. African societies gained further from the transaction by being able to sell off the undesirables who were unable to pay either their debts or criminal fines. For its part, England benefited from having its overseas

---

[2] David Brion Davis, *The Problem of Slavery in Western Culture* (Ithaca, N.Y., 1966), 464-72, contains a perceptive section on the multivalent images of African peoples and cultures contained in the travel narratives, which ranged from frank admirations to the crudest racial stereotypes, but he mentions Benezet's use of them only in passing on 467. Similarly, Anthony J. Barker, *The African Link: British Attitudes to the Negro in the Era of the Atlantic Slave Trade, 1550-1807* (London, 1978), 100-54, provides an overview of the images of Africa that the travel narratives conveyed to their readers, although he too only notes Benezet's appropriations very briefly; see in particular the references on pages 109 and 112. Roger A. Bruns, "Anthony Benezet's Assertion of Negro Equality," *Journal of Negro History* 56 (1971): 230-38, did discuss Benezet's use of the travel narratives, particularly on 233-35, but without a thoroughgoing analysis of just what he did and did not take from those tomes. The same can be said of Maurice Jackson, "The Social and Intellectual Origins of Anthony Benezet's Antislavery Radicalism," *Pennsylvania History* 66 (1999): 86-112, which mentions Benezet's reference to the travel literature on 96-98. For another brief reference, see also Winthrop D. Jordan, *White over Black: American Attitudes toward the Negro, 1550-1812* (Chapel Hill, 1968), 286. David L. Crosby contends that "Benezet shifted the reformist argument from generalizations to particulars, from matters of principle to matters of fact" ("Anthony Benezet's Transformation of Anti-Slavery Rhetoric," *Slavery and Abolition* 23 [2002]: 39-58, quote on 49). Since his focus is on Benezet's innovative "rhetorical style" (p. 42), Crosby does not examine specifically how Benezet mined the travel narratives.

possessions developed by laborers well suited to a tropical climate. "In a word," Snelgrave concluded, "from this Trade proceed Benefits, far outweighing all, either real or pretended Mischiefs and Inconveniencies."[3]

When Snelgrave described West African society, he did so in shocking and disgusting terms. His arrival on the Slave Coast in 1727 came shortly after the fall of Whydah to the forces of Dahomey. His visit to the king of Dahomey's camp provided the *raison d'être* for his book, since few Europeans had traveled so far inland from the coast. There Snelgrave claimed to have seen a pile of four thousand human heads, the result of the slaughter of prisoners from Whydah. He recounted witnessing ritual human sacrifices, and inferred the practice of cannibalism from the absence of corpses the following day. In addition, according to Snelgrave, "it is common for some inland People, to sell their Children for Slaves, tho' they are under no Necessity for so doing." Such a seemingly incredible assertion, one evidencing a total lack of the normal bonds of affection between parents and children, Snelgrave pronounced himself "inclined to believe." He also depicted pre-conquest Whydah as a pagan civilization where snakes were revered as sacred beings.[4]

Anthony Benezet took aim at all these defenses of the slave trade and negative depictions of Africa in *Some Historical Account of Guinea* by constructing a series of countervailing images. He described Africa as a land well-suited for human habitation and its people as well behaved and sociable, cast the slave trade as a rapacious and corrupting practice, and exposed the brutality of West Indian slavery. From Snelgrave's *A New Account of Some Parts of Guinea and the Slave-Trade*, he salvaged one quote that he could use to portray Africa in a positive light. Benezet repeated Snelgrave's observation that "The country [in the vicinity of Whydah] appears full of towns and villages; and being a rich soil, and well cultivated, looks like an entire garden."[5] Whatever social disorder

---

[3] William Snelgrave, *A New Account of Some Parts of Guinea and the Slave-Trade*, Cass Library of African Studies, Slavery Series, no. 11 (London, 1734; reprint, London, 1971), 158-61, quotes on 160-61.

[4] Ibid., 11-12, 26-52, 159, quote on 159.

[5] Anthony Benezet, *Some Historical Account of Guinea, Its Situation, Produce, and the General Disposition of Its Inhabitants. With an Inquiry into the Rise and Progress of the Slave Trade, Its Nature, and Lamentable Effects*, 2d ed., Cass Library of African Studies, Slavery Series, no. 2 (London, 1788; reprint, London, 1968), 24. The first edition was published at Philadelphia in 1771. In the dozen years prior, Benezet had published at least three other works that all dealt with Africa and made similar use of the travel literature. I focus in this essay on *Some Historical Account of Guinea*, because it culminated the preceding works and represented the fullest expression of this strand of Benezet's thought.

existed in West Africa by the eighteenth century Benezet laid at the feet of avaricious European slave traders who had corrupted the inhabitants' original innocence. He found no evidence to support the claim that war captives would be slaughtered were they not sold into slavery. In short, he reversed the conventional formulation by depicting the corrupting influence of European barbarism on African civilization.

A comparison of Benezet's quote with Snelgrave's original text reveals, however, that "Benezet was, in fact, highly selective" in what he took from his sources.[6] The larger passage from which Benezet took his quotation reads as follows:

> The Custom of the Country allows Polygamy to an excessive degree; it being usual for a great Man to have some hundreds of Wives and Concubines, and meaner Men in proportion; whereby the Land was become so stock'd with People, that the whole Country appeared full of Towns and Villages: And being a very rich Soil, and well cultivated by the Inhabitants, it looked like an intire Garden. Trade having likewise flourished for a long time, had greatly enriched the People; which, with the Fertility of their Country, had unhappily made them so proud, effeminate, and luxurious, that tho' they could have brought at least one hundred thousand Men into the Field, yet so great were their Fears, that they were driven out of their principal City, by two hundred of their Enemies; and at last lost their whole Country, to a Nation they formerly had contemned.[7]

Evidently Benezet plucked his positive depiction of Whydah from a surrounding context that had actually been designed to illustrate the moral degradation of the area's inhabitants.

Not only did Benezet selectively excerpt or silently pass over evidence in the travel narratives that contradicted his arguments for the Africans' innocence and civilization, but he also refused to follow other paths within the literature that would have brought him to his desired destination of having people see Africans as fully and equally human. For instance, Benezet downplayed the power and autonomy of African rulers and traders for fear of acknowledging their complicity in the slave trade. He neglected to point out the Africans' cultural richness or even the frailties they had in common with the rest of mankind. He also declined to attack assertions of African barbarism from the vantage of cultural relativism, despite the fact that the travel narratives sometimes explicitly offered this option. Benezet's Quaker beliefs and abolitionist values pre-

---

[6] David Brion Davis came to this conclusion with regard to Benezet's quotations from the Scottish jurist George Wallace's *A System of the Principles of the Law of Scotland* (Edinburgh, 1760) and the anonymous pamphlet, *Two Dialogues on the Man-Trade* (London, 1760). See Davis, "New Sidelights on Early Antislavery Radicalism," *William and Mary Quarterly*, 3d ser., 28 (1971): 592.

[7] Snelgrave, *New Account of Some Parts of Guinea and the Slave-Trade*, 3-4.

cluded him from developing any of these more audacious suggestions on behalf of the full human equality of Africans. Thus, Benezet channeled his antislavery arguments from the travel literature along a narrow course and declined to launch his attack along the broader front available to him. Still, the path that he blazed was soon followed by a host of other antislavery figures, which, in turn, called forth the renewed efforts of proslavery writers. By appealing to the authority of the African travel narratives, Anthony Benezet cast a paradigm that would influence writers on slavery, for and against, white as well as black, well into the nineteenth century.

Benezet turned to the African travel literature in order to counter the argument, epitomized by William Snelgrave, that since Africa was a place of such utter barbarism, endemic warfare, and pagan darkness, its people were actually better off coming to American regions of civilization and Christianity, notwithstanding their enslaving chains. He realized that in order to combat this prevailing view, he would have to fight fire with fire: he would have to research the travel narratives himself in order to show that Africa was a place of natural richness and decent, orderly people. Indeed in Benezet's rendering, Africans were made to exemplify a whole range of Quaker virtues. Benezet also drew upon natural rights theory and warned of divine wrath in a multifaceted critique of slavery in *Some Historical Account of Guinea*, but the book's overriding concern was to revise his readers' understanding of the contemporary state of Africa. In fashioning a new, complimentary picture of Africa, Benezet had to turn a blind eye to many statements to the contrary that were to be found in the travel literature. As a result, he left the door open to other writers who had their own, very different reasons for casting Africa in a less flattering light.

For information about West Africa and the slave trade, Benezet consulted a select group of books published in London during the first half of the eighteenth century. His Philadelphia location would also have afforded him the opportunity to speak in person with native Africans, travelers, and especially seamen with knowledge of the Guinea coast. Benezet's close links with the city's black community would certainly have brought such individuals to his attention, so it is not clear why Benezet did not avail himself of such oral testimony.[8] Most likely Benezet

---

[8] "Ten percent of the slaveowners in Philadelphia in 1767 were mariners, men who frequently owned a slave before they owned a home" (W. Jeffrey Bolster, *Black Jacks:*

stuck to the printed page so that his evidence could be independently
verified by anyone who wanted to follow his footnotes. The five works
that he referenced repeatedly in *Some Historical Account of Guinea* were
the second volume of John Green's four-volume compilation, *A New
General Collection of Voyages and Travels* (London, 1745-1747), known by
its publisher's last name as the Astley collection, Jean Barbot's *A Description
of the Coasts of North and South-Guinea*, which took up most of volume five
in Awnsham and John Churchill's six-volume compilation, *A Collection
of Voyages and Travels* (London, 1732), William Bosman's *A New and Accurate
Description of the Coast of Guinea* (London, 1705), Francis Moore's *Travels
into the Inland Parts of Africa* (London, 1738), and William Smith's *A New
Voyage to Guinea* (London, 1744). Three other travel narratives that Benezet
cited were Michel Adanson's *A Voyage to Senegal, the Isle of Goree, and the
River Gambia* (London, 1759), Peter Kolb's *The Present State of the Cape of
Good-Hope*, 2 vols. (London, 1731), and William Snelgrave's aforemen-
tioned *A New Account of Some Parts of Guinea and the Slave-Trade* (London,
1734). These books were all well known and constituted what Philip
D. Curtin has termed "a canon of West African knowledge."[9]

Most of their authors were a hardbitten lot of traders and administrators
employed by one of the European firms engaged in the slave trade and
other varieties of commerce on the African coast. Even the two writers
who traveled primarily for scientific discovery, Adanson and Kolb,
depended on the trading companies for patronage, transportation, and
logistical support. The authors of these eight works came from a variety
of nationalities, Dutch, French, and German, as well as English, although
demand was such that non-English books were soon reprinted in translation. These travelers wrote for a few different, but interrelated goals
that included facilitating subsequent traders, correcting the errors of previous writers, and, in general, adding to the stock of knowledge in this
age of the Enlightenment. William Smith best summarized their common objective of writing to satisfy "the present Curiosity of the Publick

---

African American Seamen in the Age of Sail [Cambridge, Mass., 1997], 26). For Benezet and
Philadelphia's black community, see Julie Winch, *A Gentleman of Color: The Life of James
Forten* (New York, 2002), 15, 24-25. I thank Alison Games in particular for raising the
question of why Benezet relied on printed sources to the exclusion of oral ones.

[9] Philip D. Curtin, *The Image of Africa: British Ideas and Action, 1780-1850* (Madison,
1964), 11. G. R. Crone and R. A. Skelton concluded that "the circumstantial evidence
that John Green, the cartographer, was the editor of Astley's collection appears to be
strong" ("English Collections of Voyages and Travels, 1625-1846," in *Richard Hakluyt and
His Successors: A Volume Issued to Commemorate the Centenary of the Hakluyt Society*, ed. Edward
Lynam [London, 1946], 100).

for whatever may contribute to the rend[e]ring the Produce of distant Countries and the Manners of Foreign Nations, fully and certainly known." None of these writers simply recounted the details of his journey; they also included a smorgasbord of other information about the people and places they visited. Benezet especially focused on the details of the slave trade and the wealth of ethnographic observation they reported. P. E. H. Hair's evaluation of Jean Barbot's travel narrative pertains equally to most of the other books as well. While Barbot included a slew of "culturally and morally biased comments," it was also true that "partly because he wrote at enormous length, there was no consistency in his judgements, and Africans were at times credited with intelligence and virtue." Benezet was able to exploit his sources' inconsistency as he fashioned his particular, antislavery portrayal of Africa.[10]

Benezet realized that relying on the reports of these men carried some inherent risks. For one thing, he cautioned, "how unsafe it is to form a judgment of distant people from the accounts given of them by travellers, who have taken but a transient view of things." Indeed, while some accounts, such as Bosman's, represented the fruits of several years' residence in West Africa, others, such as Barbot's, were based on only a couple of voyages. More critical, these writers were hardly disinterested observers, but men deeply implicated in the slave trade. As Benezet pointed out, "the accounts we have of the inhabitants of Guinea, are chiefly given by persons engaged in the trade, who, from self-interested views, have described them in such colours as were least likely to excite compassion and respect, and endeavoured to reconcile so manifest a violation of the rights of mankind to the minds of the purchasers." Nevertheless, the same authors, almost in spite of themselves, "cannot but allow the Negroes to be possessed of some good qualities, though

---

[10] William Smith, *A New Voyage to Guinea: Describing the Customs, Manners, Soil, Climate, Habits, Buildings, Education, Manual Arts, Agriculture, Trade, Employments, Languages, Ranks of Distinction, Habitations, Diversions, Marriages, and Whatever Else Is Memorable among the Inhabitants. Likewise, an Account of Their Animals, Minerals, &c. With Great Variety of Entertaining Incidents, Worthy of Observation, That Happen'd During the Author's Travels in That Large Country. Illustrated with Cutts, Engrav'd from Drawings Taken from the Life. With an Alphabetical Index*, Cass Library of African Studies, Travels and Narratives, no. 22 (London, 1744; reprint, London, 1967), iii; P. E. H. Hair, "Introduction," in *Barbot on Guinea: The Writings of Jean Barbot on West Africa, 1678-1712*, ed. Hair, Adam Jones, and Robin Law, Works Issued by the Hakluyt Society, 2d ser., vols. 175-176 (London, 1992), 175:liv. For more on the genre of African travel narratives published in Britain during the first part of the eighteenth century, see Marshall and Williams, *Great Map of Mankind*, 229-239; Barker, *African Link*, 16-22.

they contrive as much as possible to cast a shade over them."[11] In other words, the travel narratives that Benezet had to work with were certainly not antislavery texts in and of themselves. Yet this very fact gave their observations an added credibility as coming from men with no part in the abolitionist project.

Benezet would have had access to the books that he cited in *Some Historical Account of Guinea* either from his personal collection or through one of Philadelphia's libraries. The 1770 catalog of the Library Company of Philadelphia listed all of the travel narratives cited above and all but eight of the other, lesser works referenced. His younger brother, the merchant Daniel Benezet, was listed there among the members of the Library Company, so Anthony could have used that connection for borrowing from its holdings.[12] Anthony Benezet could have consulted other books on account of his part-time work as a librarian. He was "the first Librarian of the Friends Library in Philadelphia," and he also served as an assistant librarian for four years at the Loganian Library. At the latter institution, for example, he would have been able to read the lovely and expensive two-volume set of Sir Hans Sloane's *A Voyage To the Islands Madera, Barbados, Nieves, S. Christophers and Jamaica, with the Natural History of . . . the last of those Islands* (London, 1707, 1725). In sum, Philadelphia was a city enmeshed in the transatlantic world of books, which gave Anthony Benezet ready access to the requisite source materials for his research about Africa.[13]

Benezet's first order of business was to rehabilitate Africa and its people from the accumulated stereotypes that had clustered around them like barnacles. He began with someone like William Snelgrave in mind by acknowledging that "too easy credit is given to the accounts we frequently hear or read of their barbarous and savage way of living in their own country." Because Europeans and Americans alike believed these tales of savagery, they were "naturally induced to look upon [the

---

[11] Benezet, *Some Historical Account of Guinea*, 85, 83.

[12] *The Charter, Laws, and Catalogue of Books, of the Library Company of Philadelphia. With a Short Account of the Library Prefixed* (Philadelphia, 1770). George S. Brookes, *Friend Anthony Benezet* (Philadelphia, 1937), 19, identifies Daniel Benezet as Anthony's younger brother. According to the Library Company of Philadelphia's present librarian, "any member of a shareholder's family or household could borrow in his name with a note in his hand" during the eighteenth century (James N. Green, e-mail to the author, March 16, 2005).

[13] Henry J. Cadbury, "Anthony Benezet's Library," *Bulletin of the Friends Historical Association* 23 (1934): 63-75, quote on 64; Edwin Wolf II, *The Library of James Logan of Philadelphia, 1674-1751* (Philadelphia, 1974), xlix, 455; idem, *The Book Culture of a Colonial American City: Philadelphia Books, Bookmen, and Booksellers*, Lyell Lectures in Bibliography, 1985-6 (Oxford, 1988).

Africans] as incapable of improvement, destitute, miserable, and insensible of the benefits of life; and that our permitting them to live amongst us, even on the most oppressive terms, is to them a favour." In order to counter these erroneous and prejudicial views, Benezet too appealed to "authors of credit," the writers of the travel narratives, who "have been principal officers in the English, French, and Dutch factories, and who resided many years in those countries."[14] What followed was virtually a point-by-point refutation of each aspect in the stereotyped image of African barbarism.

Benezet first attacked the notion that the West African coast was a malignant torrid zone, virtually unfit for human habitation. While he admitted that Europeans did indeed suffer high mortality there, Africans nevertheless found it a healthful and agriculturally fruitful place. He piled up eyewitness descriptions that testified to the agricultural productivity of West Africa from Senegambia to the Slave Coast, the former of which, for instance, "abounds with grain and fruits, cattle, poultry, &c." Thanks to the care and industry of the local inhabitants, this fertile coastline yielded its crops in abundance. Sounding like a modern-day booster from the chamber of commerce, Benezet also extolled the economic vitality of non-agricultural sectors such as metalworking, textiles, the fishery, and overland trade.[15]

In addition to their industriousness, Benezet presented evidence that complimented West Africans for other virtues as well. He quoted Francis Moore, who had written that "they [the Fulis of the Gambia River region] were rarely angry, and that he never heard them abuse one another." Likewise, at Whydah, William Smith reported that "the natives here seem to be the most gentleman-like Negroes in Guinea, abounding with good manners and ceremony to each other." Similar reports came from Benin, where the citizens were said to be scrupulously honest, and other points along the coast. Most important, Benezet cited several authors who all concurred that the Africans loved their children as normal people everywhere did and would not offer them for sale as slaves.[16] All of these comments obviously contrasted with descriptions of lying, bloodthirsty savages.

Governing a populace of such integrity and decency proved not much of a challenge. Benezet reprinted a description of circuit-riding judges

---

[14] Benezet, *Some Historical Account of Guinea*, 1-3.
[15] Ibid., 3-7, 11-12, 15, 19-25, quote on 5.
[16] Ibid., 9, 25, 30-33, 83-84, quotes on 9 and 25.

dispensing justice along the Gambia, which would have seemed familiar to his readers in both Britain and America. Such violations of the law as did occur were "severely punished."[17] Moreover, Benezet frankly admired the social safety net that he learned was in place in these societies. Local rulers made sure that "the old, the blind, and lame, amongst themselves" were provided for. This he contrasted with Europe, where beggars were a common sight. Finally, these West African states were generally peaceable, despite assertions to the contrary of "some modern authors," at least prior to the arrival of European powers on the coast.[18]

Even in the area of religion, which one might expect a pietistic Quaker to have found especially problematic, Benezet identified a number of positive attributes to contrast with the stereotype of snake-worshiping idolaters. The Islamic faith of the peoples of Senegambia he credited with fostering literacy and abstention from alcohol.[19] Farther to the south and east, along the Gold and Slave Coasts, Benezet quoted Bosman's testimony that "the Whidah Negroes have a faint idea of a true God" but also the false doctrine that God had delegated the governance of this world to a range of lesser deities. Throughout those two coasts, Benezet added hopefully, "some authors say, the wisest of these Negroes are sensible of their mistake in this opinion, but dare not forsake their own religion, for fear of the populace rising and killing them."[20] Finally, he also noted that there were many Christians among the residents of the kingdoms of Kongo and Angola on account of prior Portuguese missionary endeavors.[21]

In short, Benezet presented West African peoples as proto-Quakers in their virtues of industry, honesty, and integrity, their social ethic and peacefulness, and their promising, if still incomplete, religious beliefs. Africa became in this portrayal an almost Edenic land. Benezet quoted the French naturalist, Michel Adanson, who had written, "Which way soever I turned my eyes on this pleasant spot, I beheld a perfect image of pure nature. . . . the whole [landscape] revived in my mind the idea of our first parents, and I seemed to contemplate the world in its primitive state. . . . I was not a little pleased with this my first reception; it convinced me that there ought to be a considerable abatement made in the accounts I had read and heard every where of the savage character

---

[17] Ibid., 7-8, 31, quote on 31.
[18] Ibid., 9, 28-29, 51, quotes on 9 and 51.
[19] Ibid., 9-11.
[20] Ibid., 27-28.
[21] Ibid., 33.

of the Africans."[22] Adanson's quote summarizes Benezet's argument regarding the natural abundance and decency of Africa and Africans.

Of course, it would have been impossible for Benezet to try to deny completely that West Africa in his day suffered terribly from warfare and petty tyrants. Instead, he placed the blame for these and other social ills squarely on European intruders. The Africans, he concluded, "might have lived happy, if not disturbed by the Europeans; more especially, if these last had used such endeavours as their christian profession requires, to communicate to the ignorant Africans that superior knowledge which providence had favoured them with."[23] However, European traders did anything but spread the light of the gospel among the "ignorant Africans," but rather seemed to specialize in manipulating them. European merchants plied the Africans with liquor, fanned sparks of enmity into all-out war, and corrupted native leaders, all toward the goal of increasing the number of people available for sale into slavery. As Benezet concluded, quoting William Smith, "the discerning natives account it their greatest unhappiness, that they were ever visited by the Europeans."[24] If Africans shared any blame for this sorry state of affairs, it was because some local rulers had "invaded the liberties of their unhappy subjects, and become their oppressors." But even these petty tyrants Benezet exculpated, since he contended that they had fallen prey to "the excessive love of spirituous liquors, and the tempting baits laid before them by the factors."[25] Europeans, in short, had debauched an innocent land and victimized its populace. In addition, there was no reason to credit the slave traders' assertion that they were rescuing war captives from mass slaughter. Far from relocating enslaved people from savagery to civilization, European slave traders had despoiled what had been a more-than-tolerable place to live prior to their arrival. It was they who were the savages.[26]

Taken together, the travel narratives resembled an abundant garden, from which Benezet could pick the passages that best suited his purposes. This garden, however, also sprouted numerous weeds. In other words, there was a great deal of material contained in the travel accounts that flatly contradicted Benezet's portrayal. William Bosman's *A New and*

---

[22] M. Adanson, *A Voyage to Senegal, the Isle of Goree, and the River Gambia* (London, 1759), quoted in Benezet, *Some Historical Account of Guinea*, 13-14.

[23] Benezet, *Some Historical Account of Guinea*, 2.

[24] Ibid., 50-55, quote on 52.

[25] Ibid., 82.

[26] Ibid., 51, 55.

Accurate Description of the Coast of Guinea, for example, could just as easily
have been used to refute all of Benezet's aforementioned points about
the Africans' virtues, good government, or religion. Regarding the people
of the Gold Coast, Bosman reported,

> The *Negroes* are all without exception, Crafty, Villanous [*sic*] and Fraudulent, and
> very seldom to be trusted; being sure to slip no opportunity of cheating an *European*,
> nor indeed one another. A Man of Integrity is as rare among them as a white
> Falcon, and their Fidelity seldom extends farther than to their Masters.... The
> degenerate Vices are accompanied with their Sisters, Sloth and Idleness; to which
> they are so prone that nothing but the utmost Necessity can force them to Labour:
> They are besides so incredibly careless and stupid, and are so little concerned at
> their Misfortunes, that 'tis hardly to be observed by any change in them whether
> they have met with any good or ill Success.[27]

Regarding the indigenous religion of the same region, Bosman sneered,
"the Priests, who are generally sly and crafty, encouraged by the stupid
Credulity of the People, have all the opportunity in the World to Impose
the grossest absurdities and fleece their Purses; as they indeed do
effectually." Their government he dismissed as "licentious and irregular . . . and frequent Wars are occasioned by their remiss Government
and absurd Customs."[28] Bosman also included a hideous description of
a general from "Adom" by the name of "Anqua," who drank the blood
of vanquished foes.[29] These comments were a far cry from Benezet's
depictions of peaceful, well-ordered inhabitants and institutions.

Jean Barbot's well-known travel account provided an even clearer
example of a source cited by Benezet that could also have been used
to contradict every one of the points he made. Similar to Bosman's
description of the Gold Coast, Barbot assailed the governments of
Senegambia as despotic. Regarding the area's religion, he dismissively
characterized the people as "gross superstitious pagans, living after the
wildest manner." In striking contrast to Benezet's depiction, Barbot
heaped scorn on the Senegambians' character. In a remarkable assem-
blage of adjectives, he wrote, "They are generally extremely sensual,
knavish, revengeful, impudent, lyars, impertinent, gluttonous, extrava-
gant in their expressions, and giving ill language; luxurious beyond
expression, and so intemperate, that they drink brandy as if it were

---

[27] William Bosman, *A New and Accurate Description of the Coast of Guinea, Divided into the
Gold, the Slave, and the Ivory Coasts* (London, 1705; reprint, New York, 1967), 117.
[28] Ibid., 152, 164.
[29] Ibid., 22-24. Bosman described the state of Adom, p. 22, as "This Republick, or
Common-wealth, or rather Common Plague to Man-kind, (as being an Assembly of
Thieves and Villains)."

water; deceitful in their dealings with the *Europeans*, and no less with their own neighbours, even to selling of one another for slaves, if they have an opportunity." He gave basically the same derogatory sketch of the inhabitants of the Gold Coast. In short, European slave traders were doing people a favor by transporting them from Africa, "for aboard ships all possible care is taken to preserve and subsist them for the interest of the owners, and when sold in *America*, the same motive ought to prevail with their master to use them well, that they may live the longer, and do them more service. Not to mention the inestimable advantage they may reap, of becoming christians, and saving their souls."[30] Despite Benezet's numerous citations to Barbot's *Description*, the book as a whole is closer to William Snelgrave's point of view with regard to the legitimacy of the slave trade and its assessment of African people.

Accordingly therefore, Barbot's *Description* had been the principal informant for Arthur Lee, whose 1764 *Essay in Vindication of the Continental Colonies of America* excoriated Africans as utter savages.[31] Lee, a member of one of Virginia's first families, had taken umbrage at a remark in Adam Smith's *Theory of Moral Sentiments* that contrasted the enslaved "heroes" of Africa with their American masters, whom Smith labeled "the refuse of the jails of Europe." Lee actually argued that Americans should divest themselves from slavery, since it could never be morally justified, discouraged manufacturing, and meant living with the constant

---

[30] John Barbot, *A Description of the Coasts of North and South-Guinea; and of Ethiopia Inferior, vulgarly Angola: Being A New and Accurate Account of the Western Maritime Countries of Africa. In Six Books. Containing A Geographical, Political, and Natural History of the Kingdoms, Provinces, Common-Wealths, Territories, and Islands belonging to it. Their Product, Inhabitants, Manners, Languages, Trade, Wars, Policy and Religion. With a full Account of all the European Settlements; their Rise, Progress, and Present Condition; their Commerce, and Measures for improving the several Branches of the Guinea and Angola Trade. Also of Trade-Winds, Breezes, Tornadoes, Harmatans, Tides and Currents, &c. And a New Relation of the Province of Guiana, and of the great Rivers of Amazons and Oronoque in South-America. With an Appendix; being a General Account of the First Discoveries of America, in the fourteenth Century, and some Observations thereon. And a Geographical, Political, and Natural History of the Antilles-Islands, in the North-Sea of America. Illustrated with a great Number of useful Maps and Cuts, engraven on Copper; very exactly drawn upon the Place* (London, 1732), 56-58, 34, 235-236, 270, quotes on 58, 34, and 270. Barbot's *Description* was vol. 5 in Awnsham and John Churchill, comps., *A Collection of Voyages and Travels, Some Now first Printed from Original Manuscripts, Others Now first Published in English. In Six Volumes. With a General Preface, giving an Account of the Progress of Navigation, from its first Beginning. Illustrated with a great Number of useful Maps and Cuts, Curiously Engraven* (London, 1732).

[31] An American [Arthur Lee], *An Essay in Vindication of the Continental Colonies of America, from a Censure of Mr. Adam Smith, in His Theory of Moral Sentiments. With Some Reflections on Slavery in General* (London, 1764). For further background information on this text, see Davis, *Problem of Slavery in Western Culture*, 440-441, and Jordan, *White over Black*, 309-10.

fear of uprisings and amidst the slaves' corrupting influence. Nonetheless, he was just as sure that "the barbarous Africans" were no "nations of heroes." Citing Barbot, he portrayed them as hopelessly depraved, untrustworthy, sadistically cruel and bloodthirsty, and "stupid," snake-worshiping pagans. As if all that were not bad enough, Lee also noted that the Africans were the most uncouth diners, who would eat anything "in the most voracious and filthy manner."[32] Arthur Lee's *Essay* demonstrates that the travel narratives, so full of inconsistent evidence, could support divergent opinions regarding Africa and the slave trade.

In *Some Historical Account of Guinea*, Anthony Benezet made unprecedented use of the limited number of books that Americans had at their disposal for learning about Africa. He exposed the defamations of African society that propped up the slave trade and instead portrayed African people as much like his Philadelphia neighbors in their virtues. It was the savage, European slave traders who were responsible for degrading African civilization. Yet Benezet sampled from the travel literature only selectively. Unfavorable elements he left behind, where other writers could pick them up. Of course, Benezet was under no obligation to provide ammunition to the other side in the debate over slavery by disclosing everything in the travel literature, but he did not build the strongest case available to him for the full human equality of African people. Instead he confined himself to depicting the Africans' "innocent simplicity."[33] Therefore, *Some Historical Account of Guinea* turns out to be as much a story of what Benezet left out of the book as what he chose to include.

Anthony Benezet's abolitionist priorities and Quaker values both influenced how he chose to portray African people in *Some Historical Account of Guinea*. They also kept him from developing other arguments for African equality that were latent in the travel literature. Four such alternatives stand out. In the first place, the African rulers and traders

---

[32] [Lee], *Essay in Vindication*, 11-13.
[33] Benezet, *Some Historical Account of Guinea*, 2. Benezet had also carefully chosen his extracts when he had portions of Arthur Lee's 1767 antislavery newspaper essay republished. He omitted Lee's discussion of the threat of a slave rebellion, and thereby in the assessment of one historian, "the Quaker abolitionist emasculated the slave when he excised the scenes of violence and bloodshed from the picture of slavery sketched by Arthur Lee" (Richard K. MacMaster, "Arthur Lee's 'Address on Slavery': An Aspect of Virginia's Struggle to End the Slave Trade, 1765-1774," *The Virginia Magazine of History and Biography* 80 [1972]: 147-148, quote on 148).

described in the travel narratives were no innocent victims or ignorant dupes, but smart and aggressive business partners. Some writers also emphasized the Africans' common humanity by noting their common human failings. Third, the travel accounts provided many examples of the richness of African cultural expression in such areas as music or dance. Finally, travel writers sometimes openly confessed their prejudices and concluded that judgments of cultural superiority or inferiority were all relative to the observer's values.

The accounts of every European trader who traveled to Africa testified to the Europeans' lack of power relative to local African governing authorities and traders. Merely for the privilege of coming ashore to re-provision with wood and water, a European ship captain would have to pay a fee. The compensation for the requisite native boatmen, sawyers, and porters would also have to be negotiated. In addition, before any bargaining for commodities could begin, customs duties and "presents" had to be handed over to the proper authorities. As the Astley collection reported regarding some potentates along the Senegal River, "If they can get nothing by way of Gift, they will borrow; and in case of Refusal, forbid Trade, or load it with Exactions. The Neighbourhood of these Kings is therefore very troublesome, as they constantly expect new Presents; to which if you once accustom them, they take Care to keep-up their Demands." Likewise, Jean Barbot described a portion of the eastern Gold Coast where Dutch, English, and Portuguese forts stood close together. Regardless of their imposing edifices, "The three *European* forts have but little authority over the *Blacks*, and serve only to secure the trade, the *Blacks* here being of a temper not to suffer any thing to be imposed on them by *Europeans*; which, if they should but attempt, it would certainly prove their own ruin." In short, African rulers were no pushovers, but were in a position to set the terms of interaction with European visitors. Of course, to acknowledge the Africans' autonomy and power also would have been for Benezet to abandon his contention that they were merely the innocent victims of European greed.[34]

Both Europeans and Africans carried out their negotiations with a mixture of hospitality and threats. Violence hung in the background as

---

[34] [John Green, ed.], *A New General Collection of Voyages and Travels, Consisting of the Most Esteemed Relations Which Have Been Hitherto Published in Any Language, Comprehending Everything Remarkable in Its Kind, in Europe, Asia, Africa, and America*, Cass Library of African Studies, Travels and Narratives, no. 47, 4 vols. (London, 1745-1747; reprint, London: Cass, 1968), 2:56 (all subsequent citation are from vol. 2); Barbot, *Description of the Coasts of North and South-Guinea*, 181; John Thornton, *Africa and Africans in the Making of the Atlantic*

a very real possibility should the two sides fail to come to terms. Andre Brüe, a French trader traveling up the Senegal in 1698, encountered a situation where two rival claimants to local rule each expected tribute. When Brüe paid the one he surmised was more powerful, the disappointed one sent his son to Brüe and told him "to pay the Customs, otherwise his Father would stop his Trade, and prevent his returning down the River." In reply, Brüe stated that "he would pay no Customs; that he would trade as he pleased, and if the King offered him the least Insult, he would burn his Town, and send him a Slave to *America*." His threat succeeded in making this deposed African king back down, and Brüe resumed his business. At other times, of course, Africans came out on top in such standoffs. Once in the vicinity of Cape Three Points, the Dutch attempted to take over an abandoned Danish outpost and refused to pay rent to the local "caboceer," an African known as John Conny. When the Dutch landed a detachment of forty troops, Conny counterattacked "with greater Force, [and] cut them in Pieces, paving the Entrance of his Palace, soon after, with their Skulls."[35] Apparently, Anthony Benezet as a Quaker pacifist did not want to make the argument that Africans were as skilled as Europeans in the rough-and-tumble realities of power politics.

African merchants also earned the grudging respect of their European counterparts. Jean Barbot—not one, as we have seen, given to favorable comments about Africans—admitted that African merchants "examine every thing with as much prudence and ability as any *European* trader can do." Often these Africans astutely played one trading partner against another to obtain better prices or more desirable goods. For instance, Andre Brüe realized that the long-distance traders he encountered along the Senegal River could also take their wares to the Dutch at Arguin, the English along the Gambia, or the Arabs who came down to Timbuktu, instead of dealing with his French company.[36] A female trader whom Brüe met along the Gambia embodied this multinational trading regime and the important place of "Atlantic creoles" along the coast. "Signora

---

World, 1400-1800, 2d ed. (New York: Cambridge University Press, 1998). As David Brion Davis adds, "the power and disciplined organization which evidenced a high level of cultural development also proved that Negroes played a larger part in the slave trade than abolitionists wished to believe" (*Problem of Slavery in Western Culture*, 467). See also Bruns, "Anthony Benezet's Assertion of Negro Equality," 235.

[35] [Green], *New General Collection of Voyages and Travels*, 70, 449-450.

[36] Barbot, *Description of the Coasts of North and South-Guinea*, 274; [Green], *New General Collection of Voyages and Travels*, 61, 70.

Belinguera" was an African woman who had been married to a Portuguese man, and she both spoke and wrote fluently in English, French, and Portuguese. "No Woman knew better the Art of making herself agreeable, or of ruining those who had to deal with her," Brüe had learned. "Some of the *Europeans* had found this to their Cost: However, it was always the Interest of the Company's Factors to keep well with her by frequent Presents."[37] In other words, any trader on the Guinea coast could have testified that his African counterparts had to be treated with respect and bargained with as equals, or he ran the risk of the failure of his venture. For Benezet to discuss the power and shrewdness of such African traders as Signora Belinguera certainly would have put the lie to casual assertions of their savagery or ignorance. However, at the same time it would have raised the issue of their complicity in the slave trade. Perhaps also Benezet, as the only one of four brothers who had not pursued a mercantile career, felt awkward with building a case for Africans' equality on the basis of their sharp trading practices.[38]

Francis Moore provided another, exquisite tale that further demonstrated the relative weakness of Europeans in relation to Africans once the parties were ashore. He described his dealings with the King of Barsally, who apparently relished flaunting his power over Moore and his fellows from the Royal African Company. One day the king showed up at the English factory with a hundred of his men, and he proceeded to take "Possession of [Moore's colleague] Mr. *Roberts*'s own Bed, and then having drank Brandy till he was drunk, at the Persuasion of some of his People, order'd Mr. *Roberts* to be held, whilst himself took out of his Pocket the Key of his Storehouse, into which he and several of his People went, and took what they pleased." Moore and the other, vastly outnumbered Englishmen had no choice but to let the king and his henchmen do as they pleased. The king's arrogance only increased, until one day he spat a mouthful of water in Moore's face. At this point Moore concluded that he had to take a stand, because "if I suffer'd such Insolence from Black Men, it would make them the more bold and insulting, and that it was better to venture dying once, then to be continually abused, and the Occasion of other *Englishmen* being contemn'd, so I took the Remainder of the Water, and threw it into his

---

[37] [Green], *New General Collection of Voyages and Travels*, 83; Ira Berlin, "From Creole to African: Atlantic Creoles and the Origins of African-American Society in Mainland North America," *William and Mary Quarterly*, 3d ser., 53 (1996): 254-263.
[38] Brookes, *Friend Anthony Benezet*, 19-28.

Breeches." The king grabbed for a knife with which to kill Moore, but fortunately for Moore, one of the king's aides intervened and rebuked him for his outrageous behavior in getting drunk and spitting in Moore's face. "Upon which," Moore concluded this account, "he was so much ashamed, that he came and lay down upon the Floor, with his Garment off, and took my Foot and placed it upon his Neck, and there lay till I desired him to rise: After which, no Man was a greater Friend to me, nor more willing to oblige me in any respect than he was."[39] Moore's account abundantly manifests the Englishman's lack of strength on the ground in West Africa.

It is also a fully human story involving haughtiness, anger, shame, and reconciliation, and as such it suggests that Benezet could have pursued a second line of argument that Africans were just like Europeans in all their human foibles and emotions. Jean Barbot on several occasions qualified his derogatory comments toward Africans with the admission that Europeans were guilty of the same things. For example, he noted that justice in Senegambia was sometimes corrupted, so that "rich and powerful criminals" went unpunished. However, he admitted that such injustice was part of "the corruption of human nature every where. Many instances of corruption among these people might be brought, but that I think it superfluous, that crime being too notoriously practised among christians; and therefore none will question its prevailing among unpolished infidels, who have less ties to secure them against interest and human respects." On the Gold Coast, he remarked, wealth had fueled the merchants' vanity "as is too common to the generality of mankind." And while European traders there liked to complain that Africans cheated them, in fact Barbot pointed out that Europeans swindled Africans too with rigged scales. He lamented that "self-interest and covetousness, which is called the root of all evil, are vices too common to all the corrupt race of mankind, either christians or pagans." Indeed, Barbot again portrayed the Europeans as more blameworthy than Africans

---

[39] Francis Moore, *Travels into the Inland Parts of Africa: Containing a Description of the Several Nations for the Space of Six Hundred Miles up the River Gambia; Their Trade, Habits, Customs, Language, Manners, Religion and Government; the Power, Disposition and Characters of Some Negro Princes; with a Particular Account of Job Ben Solomon, a Pholey, Who Was in England in the Year 1733, and Known by the Name of the African. To Which Is Added, Capt. Stibbs's Voyage up the Gambia in the Year 1723, to Make Discoveries; with an Accurate Map of That River Taken on the Spot: And Many Other Copper Plates. Also Extracts from the Nubian's Geography, Leo the African, and Other Authors Ancient and Modern, Concerning the Niger, Nile, or Gambia, and Observations Thereon* (London, 1738), 83-85.

in this instance, since "christians ought to remember the words of St.
Paul, to the *Roman* christians in his days, on the like occasion: chap. ii.
v. 24. *That for their evil practices the name of God is blasphemed among the
Gentiles.* And that *double weights and double measures are an abomination to
God.* Levit. xix. 36. and Prov. xi. 1."[40] Other examples could illustrate
further Barbot's observation that Africans' faults were merely an aspect
of their fallen humanity. Corruption, pride, covetousness, and other
impurities were sins that befell men and women universally, without
regard to race or creed. As a French Huguenot refugee, Barbot apparently retained a robust sense of the general depravity of mankind from
his Reformed background.[41] Benezet, as a Quaker, was either not attuned
to such arguments or rejected them on theological grounds, for he did
not build a case for the Africans' common humanity from their common
depravity.

Benezet missed a third opportunity to refute stereotypes of the Africans'
savagery when he neglected to recognize examples of their cultural richness that were to be found in the travel narratives. Barbot, to use
another example from him, opined that the drums and other percussion
instruments at Benin "together afford a disagreeable and jarring sound."
However, he also commented that there was "another instrument, . . .
a sort of harp; being strung with six or seven extended reeds, on which
they play very artfully, sing finely, and dance so justly to the tune, that
it is agreeably diverting to see it; and really the *Benin Blacks* are the
best dancers of all the *Guineans.*" Brüe and other travelers to Senegambia
usually noted the griots who entertained honored guests with their pan-
egyrics. Thousands of miles to the south at the Cape of Good Hope,
Peter Kolb stated "as my Opinion, that the *Gom Gom,* as insignificant
a Piece of Work as it is, was it to be studied by a judicious *European*
Musician, would be found to have as fine Musick in it as any Instrument
we have, and be as much admir'd." In addition, the excerpt in the
Astley collection from Richard Jobson's *The Golden Trade,* which was
based on his 1620-1621 voyage to the Gambia, contained a wonderful
vignette of his visit to a festival that reminded him of "a Country Fair
in *England*" where people ate, drank, and made merry. In order to rec-
iprocate the hospitality he had received from the local ruler, Jobson
dropped in on his house that evening, and found a group of people
dancing to the music of the balafon, another instrument that European

---

[40] Barbot, *Description of the Coasts of North and South-Guinea,* 58, 234-235.
[41] P. E. H. Hair notes Barbot's Huguenot background in *Barbot on Guinea,* 175:ix-x.

travelers were apt to comment upon favorably. Jobson seized the moment "and to let them see the *English* used such Diversion, he took-out one of the young *Blackmoor* Girls, and danced with her, which pleased them all exceedingly." Such passages might have suggested to Benezet a comment about musical proficiency or accomplishments in dance, but he did not attempt to make an argument for the Africans' artistic achievements or cultural beauty. Perhaps he assumed that contrary stereotypes of wild music and indecent dances were already too deeply ingrained.[42]

From an appreciation of aspects of African culture it would have been a short step to cultural relativism, which offered a fourth possibility for establishing the equal humanity of Africans. Two trends combined to sow doubts about the usually presumed superiority of European civilization. The encounter of European men with African people— especially African women, as in the case of Jobson and his "*Blackmoor* Girl"—led some travelers to question their reflexive assumptions about African inferiority. In addition, the Enlightenment's assaults on tradition and prejudice reinforced skepticism about conventional opinions and mores. The travel literature here and there contained bold declarations of the relativity of cultural standards, which led directly to the corollary that African peoples and cultures stood on a level equal with European. Anthony Benezet read these passages, but apparently decided that their affirmations and implications were just too radical for him to embrace.

Prolonged contact with Africans on their native soil suggested to some observers that their condescending judgments were merely rooted in narrow prior experience. The French naturalist, Michel Adanson, discovered that his physical appearance struck Africans as just as odd as theirs did Europeans. At one Senegal River village in 1749, he encountered children who had never seen a white man before and marveled at his complexion, the texture and style of his hair, and his clothing. "It came into my head," Adanson wrote, "that my colour, so opposite to the blackness of the Africans, was the first thing that struck the children: those poor little creatures were then in the same class as our infants, the first time they see a Negroe." Traveling among "the Hottentots" of the Cape of Good Hope—a group whose name was a byword for

---

[42] Barbot, *Description of the Coasts of North and South-Guinea*, 372; [Green], *New General Collection of Voyages and Travels*, 48 (griots) and 187 (Jobson); Peter Kolb, *The Present State of the Cape of Good-Hope*, trans. Guido Medley, Landmarks in Anthropology, 2 vols. (London, 1731; reprint, New York: Johnson Reprint Corporation, 1968), 1:273.

African savagery—led Peter Kolb to see "that the *Hottentots* have a great many idle ridiculous Customs." "But," he continued, "where is the Nation that has not, in one Corner or other of it, Customs, in many Particulars, as idle? And where is the Wise Man, who has not a ridiculous Side? Give the *Hottentot* Sense but fair Play, and 'twill appear like other People's."[43] In these instances, in other words, familiarity bred not contempt, but appreciation for African people and their cultures. Astute observers realized that many casual judgments of African barbarism were solely based on prejudice.[44]

Nothing worked like sexual attraction to break down the barriers between people. Adanson had remarked of the women of Senegal that "some of them [are] perfect beauties." A footnote added, "The vast numbers of children, and children's children, the French begat by them, and left there, prove our author is not singular in his opinion." Jean Barbot, ever the Calvinist, had noted disapprovingly that there were "many leud *Europeans*; who not regarding complexions, say, *all cats are grey in the dark*." While such European-African sexual liaisons could be exploitative or merely for temporary convenience, there were also men who found African women genuinely alluring. The resulting mixed-race offspring often played key roles as commercial and cultural intermediaries along the coast.[45] Moreover, some European men preferred the sexual conventions in African culture to their own. While traveling from the Gambia River overland to the Portuguese settlement at Cacheu in 1700, Andre Brüe met a Spanish native of Cuba named Juan Maldonado. "Don *Juan* was not married, yet made himself easy, as the Custom of the Country allowed him as many Wives as he thought fit to take." For Maldonado to reject Christian Europe's prohibitions against multiple wives in favor of African marriage conventions at least implied the

---

[43] Adanson, *Voyage to Senegal*, 74; Kolb, *Present State of the Cape of Good-Hope*, 1:249.

[44] On the eighteenth-century "discovery of prejudice," see Jordan, *White over Black*, 276-280.

[45] Adanson, *Voyage to Senegal*, 39; Barbot, *Description of the Coasts of North and South-Guinea*, 238; Robin Law and Kristin Mann, "West Africa in the Atlantic Community: The Case of the Slave Coast," *William and Mary Quarterly*, 3d ser., 56 (1999): 307-34. This sexual encounter between Europeans and Africans was quite similar to that between Europeans and Indians as described in travel accounts of the North American backcountry, where "explorers and early colonists had often commented on native beauty and provided those who followed with a tantalizing portrait of Indian sexual culture as uninhibited and permissive" (Richard Godbeer, "Eroticizing the Middle Ground: Anglo-Indian Sexual Relations along the Eighteenth-Century Frontier," in *Sex, Love, Race: Crossing Boundaries in North American History*, ed. Martha Hodes [New York, 1999], 91-111, quote on 95).

alternative possibility of those norms. For their part, Africans were report-
edly just as shocked and puzzled over the European ideal of monogamy
as European observers typically were over African polygamy. During
one of Brüe's voyages up the Senegal, a local king offered to him one
of the princesses in marriage. When Brüe declined, saying that he already
had a wife back home in France, "This occasioned much Discourse
among the King's Wives, on the Happiness of the *European* Women.
One Thing puzzled them, how the Sieur *Brüe* could live so long without his Wife; and what he thought of her Fidelity in his Absence."[46]
The idea and the reality of sex across the cultural divide and of alternative forms of marriage rendered assertions of European superiority
less confident and could have been used to advocate equal African
humanity.

A long passage in William Smith's *A New Voyage to Guinea* united stories of sexual encounter with a broader critique of European civilization from an Enlightenment perspective. During his return voyage back
home to England, Smith had the "Satisfaction" of "the Company of
Mr. *Charles Wheeler*, who had been a Factor to the Royal *African* Company
for Ten Years in *Guinea*, and was now returning Home in our Ship."
Over two dozen pages Smith recorded at length some of Wheeler's
remarks. Smith's travel companion expressed admiration for the Africans'
multiple wives and other aspects of their sexual culture and also praised
African burial practices as superior to European. Most remarkably,
Wheeler stated plainly that Europeans' judgments against these African
customs as uncivilized merely reflected back on the Europeans' "Prejudice
of a different Education."[47] In both his "irreligion and sexual rampancy,"
Wheeler typified the eighteenth-century libertine.[48] Whether or not his
discourse is based in reality remains open to question. The editor of
the Astley collection, John Green, did not include it in the large selection
from Smith's travel narrative that he reprinted, judging—on what grounds
we do not know—the "Dialogue between that Gentleman [Wheeler]
and his Negro Mistress . . . to have been composed at Fancy, than to
have any real Foundation in Nature." Modern scholars likewise pronounce
at least some of it "improbable."[49] The important points, however, are

---

[46] [Green], *New General Collection of Voyages and Travels*, 87, 59.

[47] Smith, *New Voyage to Guinea*, 242-244.

[48] James G. Turner, "The Properties of Libertinism," in *'Tis Nature's Fault: Unauthorized
Sexuality During the Enlightenment*, ed. Robert Purks Maccubbin (New York, 1987), 75.

[49] [Green], *New General Collection of Voyages and Travels*, 464; Marshall and Williams,
Great Map of Mankind, 235.

that the passage is there in Smith's original volume, which Anthony
Benezet read and quoted often, but that he chose to ignore it. His silence
on Wheeler's commentary is deafening.

Wheeler's first startling remarks concerned the topic of polygyny,
which Europeans routinely invoked as the epitome of African savagery.
He discussed a variety of reasons that favored the practice (at least from
a man's point of view), such as the example of the biblical patriarchs,
longstanding African tradition, the idea that it gave a man an alternative
when his wife was indisposed on account of either pregnancy or men-
struation, and "as a Man may have Variety at Home, he is not so
prone to seek it Abroad." Regarding the last point, he added that he
"often thought that the Practice of too many *Europeans* was more liable
to Censure, who besides a Wife keep two or three Harlots." Here
Wheeler explicitly voiced an opinion in favor of the Africans for he
continued, "Nay, the *European* is really in a very dangerous Fault, for
he is taught, that such an Action is contrary to the Religion he pro-
fesses, and for which he is liable to Damnation; nothing of which the
Negroe believes, or is taught to believe; so far from which, that he herein
follows the Example of his Ancestors, and treads in the Path of *Abraham*
the Patriarch, which undoubtedly was right."[50]

Moving on to another aspect of Africans' sexual culture, Wheeler discussed in a positive light the practice of providing high-status male
houseguests with a concubine, so that the man would not be tempted
to have illicit relations with any of the wives of the house. This was a
privilege that Wheeler himself had often enjoyed as a European at a
royal African court. During his first encounter, Wheeler was paired
"with a young Lady in her Prime, her Stature was tall, and she was
well proportion'd, and I must acknowledge, that the Sight of her, pro-
duc'd some Emotions in me in her Favour." To make a long (and fairly
graphic) story short, Wheeler slept with his companion that night, "and
in that Situation I soon forgot the Complexion of my Bedfellow, and
obey'd the Dictates of all-powerful Nature. Greater Pleasure I never
found, and during my Stay, if Paradise is to be found in the Enjoyment
of a Woman, I was then in the Possession of it."[51] Of course, during
slavery powerful white men often availed themselves sexually of black
women.[52] But here was a rare find, inasmuch as Wheeler frankly praised

---

[50] Smith, *New Voyage to Guinea*, 244-245.
[51] Ibid., 250-254, quotes on 251, 254.
[52] Philip D. Morgan, "Interracial Sex in the Chesapeake and the British Atlantic

both the beauty of his African partner and the sexual conventions that put them together.

The language attributed to Wheeler in this discourse employs some key Enlightenment concepts. As historians have uncovered, the Enlightenment entailed a questioning of traditional sexuality, in the same way that it questioned, for example, religious orthodoxies or arbitrary government.[53] Most obviously, Wheeler's inclination to follow "the Dictates of all-powerful Nature" showed the same exaltation of "Nature" as found in other categories of Enlightenment thought. The goal of "Pleasure" also served as the guiding principle for Enlightenment ethics. "The pursuit of pleasure, leading to happiness," writes Roy Porter, "became seen in Enlightenment writers, from Locke and Addison to Chesterfield and Bentham, as the behaviour dictated by Nature to man."[54]

Wheeler furthermore spoke positively about African courtship, marriage, and child-rearing customs, and ended with a comparison of funerary practices. Both European and African societies had "ridiculous" mourning rituals, but the Africans had the advantage in Wheeler's estimation of at least burying their dead a few miles out of town along a riverbank, unlike the European practice of using the churchyard. "I am of Opinion," he concluded, "that we should bury our Dead in the same Manner, if it were not for the following Reasons: The Gain of the Parish Priest, and the absurd and ridiculous Notions of the Efficacy of Christian Burial, and the Resurrection of the same Body at a Day of Judgment." Obviously, Wheeler's anticlericalism was also standard for Enlightenment radicals. Benezet passed silently over this and Wheeler's other heretical statements, of course, but he then quoted the immediately following remark about how "The discerning Natives account it their greatest Unhappiness, that they were ever visited by the *Europeans*," so he could not have failed to have read Wheeler's radical opinions.[55]

The Wheeler discourse ended with this stunning paragraph: "Upon the Whole, Whether the Manner of Action in this Country is so good

---

World, c. 1700-1820," in *Sally Hemings & Thomas Jefferson: History, Memory, and Civic Culture*, ed. Jan Ellen Lewis and Peter S. Onuf (Charlottesville, 1999), 52-84.

[53] I have learned a great deal about the Enlightenment's sexual implications in a superb essay by Roy Porter, "Mixed feelings: the Enlightenment and sexuality in eighteenth-century Britain," in *Sexuality in eighteenth-century Britain*, ed. Paul-Gabriel Boucé (Manchester, Eng.: Manchester University Press, and Totowa, N. J.: Barnes & Noble Books, 1982), 1-27. See also G. S. Rousseau and Roy Porter, eds., *Sexual Underworlds of the Enlightenment* (Chapel Hill, 1988).

[54] Porter, "Mixed feelings," 4.

[55] Smith, *New Voyage to Guinea*, 259-66, quotes on 265-66.

as that of *Europe*, ought to be judg'd by its Consequents. And I doubt not but upon an impartial Examination of the Premises, it would be found, that we Christians have as many idle ridiculous Notions and Customs as the Natives of *Guinea* have, if not more."[56] Wheeler had explicitly made an argument for the equality and humanity of the Africans based on cultural relativism, but the pious Benezet was unwilling to advocate Wheeler's sexual and religious heterodoxy. The entire section nevertheless remains striking, and serves as a reminder that such a radical argument was possible as early as the mid-eighteenth century.

The travel literature offered at least four potential claims to Africans' equality with Europeans that Anthony Benezet declined to exploit. As a committed Quaker, he was not open to either the Calvinist tenet of total depravity or the radical Enlightenment notion of the relativity of cultural norms. As an abolitionist, he also wanted to shield Africans from any involvement in the slave trade, even if that meant denying their skills and power in military or economic affairs. Suggestions of African talents in music and dance he did not develop either. Benezet must have calculated that his straightforward picture of African civilization and innocence would find a more sympathetic audience than anything more radical, and it did exert a strong influence on both sides of the Atlantic. But his partial method of excerpting from the travel narratives also left him open to criticism from those who did not share his abolitionist aims.

In a May 1774 letter to one of the premier English abolitionists, attorney Granville Sharp, the Philadelphia doctor Benjamin Rush exulted that "the cause of African freedom in America continues to gain ground." In large measure Rush attributed this progress to the "indefatigable" labors of "our worthy friend Mr. Benezet." He lauded their mutual friend as a man who "appears in every thing to be free from prejudices of all kinds, and talks and acts as if he believed all mankind however diversified by color—nation—or religion to be members of one grand family. His benevolence and liberality are unbounded."[57] Rush certainly knew his man, inasmuch as Benezet was remarkably free from his society's racial prejudices and no one could gainsay Benezet's "benevolence." As this essay has demonstrated, Benezet also pressed the idea of "one

---

[56] Ibid., 266-267.
[57] Rush to Sharp, May 13, 1774, in John A. Woods, ed., "The Correspondence of Benjamin Rush and Granville Sharp, 1773-1809," *Journal of American Studies* 1 (1967): 5.

grand family" of humanity to an extreme when he depicted West Africans
as much like Pennsylvania Quakers, flattening cultural differences in the
process. Rush's letter itself illustrates the transatlantic nature of eighteenth-century antislavery, as correspondence and publications went back
and forth between Philadelphia, London, and numerous other points
along the North Atlantic littoral. As a result of his "indefatigable" efforts,
Benezet gained a hearing from influential people, and a place for his
travel-literature themes in the abolitionists' rhetorical arsenal. He also
earned both a rebuttal from proslavery apologists and the enduring
memory of the new nation's free black community.

Some Historical Account of Guinea made a splash that rippled throughout the North Atlantic world after its publication in 1771. Benezet had
compiled it, since his previous publications were running out of stock
and he wanted to influence further "the rising generation." He had also
learned more about slavery and the slave trade, so there was additional
material to include.[58] Most important, he aimed "to set this weighty
matter in a true point of view."[59] Benezet had a Quaker faith in the
power of the light of truth to prevail over ignorance and iniquity. As
he remarked in a letter to Irish Quaker Richard Shackleton,

> How an evil of so deep a dye has so long passed uncensured, and has even received
> the countenance of a Christian government and been supported by law, is sur-
> prising; and I apprehend must, in a great measure, have arisen from a false rep-
> resentation being made of the case to those in whose power it would have been
> to put a stop to the trade, who have been unacquainted with the corrupt motives
> which give life to it, and the groans, the dying groans which daily ascend to God,
> the common Father of mankind, from the broken hearts of these our distressed
> fellow-men; or, I think, we could not have so long continued in a practice so incon-
> sistent with British ideas of liberty.[60]

In short, Benezet believed that if he could acquaint people in power
with the true turpitude of slavery, there was hope for change. In the
judgment of Thomas Clarkson, he largely succeeded. Writing in 1808
in his retrospective history of the British movement to abolish the slave
trade, Clarkson deemed Benezet's Some Historical Account of Guinea "instrumental, beyond any other book ever before published, in disseminating
a proper knowledge and detestation of this trade."[61]

---

[58] Benezet to Samuel Fothergill, Oct. 24, 1771, in Brookes, *Friend Anthony Benezet*, 280-81.
[59] Benezet to John and Henry Gurney, Jan. 10, 1772, in ibid., 284.
[60] Benezet to Shackleton, June 6, 1772, in ibid., 294.
[61] Thomas Clarkson, *The History of the Rise, Progress, and Accomplishment of the Abolition of*

In no small part the impact of *Some Historical Account of Guinea* was due to its author's energetic promotional efforts. Benezet did not count on the chance circulation of his book, but rather he commenced a far-reaching correspondence that sought to place copies into the hands of influential people. He drew first upon his Quaker contacts for introductions to prominent Friends overseas.[62] He also asked Quakers to extend his reach by contacting someone else on his behalf. The letter to Shackleton, for example, had the further aim of reaching Edmund Burke, an associate of Shackleton's.[63] By no means, however, did Benezet limit his collaboration to fellow Quakers. He counted the Presbyterian Benjamin Rush as a valuable yokefellow, and he initiated communications with the Anglican Granville Sharp in a letter of May 14, 1772, that had copies of *Some Historical Account of Guinea* enclosed. Benezet's relationship with Sharp had a multiplier effect, as Sharp distributed copies of the London reprint of *Some Historical Account of Guinea* to "all the Judges, to several of the Nobility, & many others."[64] Benezet also suggested to some of his correspondents that they excerpt his work for publication in their newspapers.[65] He used whatever methods seemed to offer an opportunity for spreading his message. No doubt he would have been gratified to learn that the student taking the antislavery side in a 1773 Harvard commencement debate on the legality of slavery had excerpted portions of his book. Likewise, Benezet derived "much satisfaction" in seeing a substantial chunk of *Some Historical Account of Guinea*, even without attribution, in John Wesley's *Thoughts upon Slavery*, which he then arranged to have reprinted in Philadelphia. Had he lived long enough, he would have been proud too to see his book footnoted

---

the *African Slave-Trade by the British Parliament*, Cass Library of African Studies, Slavery Series, no. 8, 2 vols. (London, 1808; reprint, London, 1968), 1:169.

[62] For example, Benezet used his acquaintance with Joseph Oxley as an opening to write to John and Henry Gurney (Benezet to John and Henry Gurney, Jan. 10, 1772, in Brookes, *Friend Anthony Benezet*, 283-84). Likewise, his letter to Richard Shackleton began by mentioning their mutual friend, Samuel Neale (Benezet to Shackleton, June 6, 1772, in ibid., 293-96).

[63] Benezet to Shackleton, June 6, 1772, in ibid., 296. In the same way, Benezet had Virginia Quaker Robert Pleasants deliver a copy of *Some Historical Account of Guinea* to Patrick Henry (Henry to Pleasants, Jan. 18, 1773, in ibid., 443-444; Benezet to Pleasants, April 8, 1773, in ibid., 298-99).

[64] Benezet to Sharp, May 14, 1772, in ibid., 290-93; Sharp to Rush, Feb. 21, 1774, in ibid., 447.

[65] Benezet to John and Henry Gurney, Jan. 10, 1772, in ibid., 286; Benezet to Sharp, May 14, 1772, in ibid., 291.

as a reliable authority on West Africa and the slave trade in Olaudah Equiano's *Interesting Narrative.*[66]

Benjamin Rush's *An Address to the Inhabitants of the British Settlements, on the Slavery of the Negroes in America* clearly shows how Benezet's arguments from the African travel literature quickly entered the repertoire of anti-slavery rhetoric. This is not to say that the travelers' accounts moved into the front rank, but they took their place alongside other arguments grounded in the Bible, natural rights, or reports of the cruel conditions on West Indian plantations. For starters, Rush noted that slavery was sometimes justified by assertions of Africans' moral and intellectual inferiority. However, he replied with obvious recourse to *Some Historical Account of Guinea,* "The accounts which travellers give us of their ingenuity, humanity, and strong attachment to their parents, relations, friends and country, show us that they are equal to the Europeans, when we allow for the diversity of temper and genius which is occasioned by climate. We have many well-attested anecdotes of as sublime and disinterested virtue among them as ever adorned a Roman or a Christian character." He also drew upon Benezet's excerpts about West Africa's agricultural richness in addressing the frequent claim that only Africans were naturally suited to work in the climate of the West Indian sugar islands. Actually, Rush countered, Africans were less suitable laborers than Europeans, since "such is the natural fertility of soil, and so numerous the spontaneous fruits of the earth in the interior parts of Africa," that Africans were habituated to "live in plenty at the expence of little or no labor." Rush made a third appeal to "the testimony of historians and travellers" in order to rebut the claim that the slave trade saved African captives from being slaughtered. Instead, echoing Benezet, he wrote "that wars were uncommon among them, until the christians who began the slave trade, stirred up the different nations to fight against each other."[67] In sum, Benezet's publication provided a few more arrows for abolitionists' rhetorical quiver.

[66] [Theodore Parsons and Eliphalet Pearson], *A Forensic Dispute on the Legality of Enslaving the Africans, Held at the Public Commencement in Cambridge, New-England, July 21st, 1773. By Two Candidates for the Bachelor's Degree* (Boston, 1773), 36-39, 42-43; Benezet to Wesley, May 23, 1774, in Brookes, *Friend Anthony Benezet,* 318; John Wesley, *Thoughts upon Slavery* (London, 1774; reprint, Philadelphia, 1774), 6-33; *The Interesting Narrative of the Life of Olaudah Equiano, Written by Himself,* ed. Robert J. Allison, Bedford Series in History and Culture (Boston, 1995), 35, 40, 95. Equiano's *Interesting Narrative* was first published in London, 1783; the Bedford edition is from the first American edition, New York, 1791.
[67] A Pennsylvanian [Benjamin Rush], *An Address to the Inhabitants of the British Settlements,*

"A West-Indian" then residing in Philadelphia, Richard Nisbet, replied forthwith to Rush's *Address* with a range of arguments that included a biblical case for slavery's legitimacy, a reassertion of Africans' superiority for labor under the tropical sun, and a defense of West Indians planters in general from abolitionists' demonization. It is of particular note that Nisbet attacked Rush, and by extension Benezet, for how they employed the travel narratives. In the first place, Nisbet questioned the reliability of the travel literature, warning that "one ought to be cautious in trusting to the relations of voyagers into distant countries. There are very few authentick histories of the west coast of Africa; and the inland parts, I believe, have hardly ever been visited by an European." Moreover, in a clear swipe at the integrity of Benezet's compilation, Nisbet wrote, "*Some people*, with a view to palliate the beastly customs and gross stupidity of the natives, give us an account of the nations contiguous to the Moors, and a few on the Gold coast, who may be somewhat more civilized than the rest. They must be pretty much at a loss, when they have recourse to the Hottentots, to prove the civilization of the Africans." In other words, Nisbet charged Benezet with sifting the travel accounts for a few choice examples and burying other evidence that did not conform to his thesis. Regardless of his just having warned of the unreliability of the travel literature, Nisbet added that "Other writers represent the Africans in different, and probably their real colours." Bringing the depictions of Jean Barbot or William Snelgrave to mind, although without specifically naming either one, Nisbet wrote that "Africa, except the small part of it inhabited by those of our own colour, is totally overrun with barbarism."[68] The arguments that Rush had derived from *Some Historical Account of Guinea* had obviously achieved some salience if Nisbet felt compelled to offer such a refutation.

Before the year was out, Benjamin Rush answered Nisbet in a follow-up pamphlet. After further examining biblical precedents and elaborating stories of West Indian cruelty, Rush addressed Nisbet's claims about African barbarism. He granted that "Few Travellers possess Abilities, Introductions, or Languages, proper to acquire a complete knowledge of National Characters." He also conceded that many Africans "are

---

on the *Slavery of the Negroes in America*, 2d ed. (Philadelphia, 1773; reprint, New York, 1969), 1-2, 8, 17-18.

[68] A West-Indian [Richard Nisbet], *Slavery Not Forbidden by Scripture. Or a Defence of the West-India Planters, From the Aspersions Thrown out against Them, by the Author of a Pamphlet, Entitled, "An Address to the Inhabitants of the British Settlements in America, Upon Slave-Keeping"* (Philadelphia, 1773), 20-22.

inferior in Virtue, Knowledge, and the love of Liberty to the Inhabitants of other parts of the World," but he accounted for this with reference to the hot climate and geographic isolation of Africa. As for African idolatry, Rush pointed out that false religious notions were to be found everywhere around the globe and throughout history, so this was no proof of inherent African inferiority. Instead of simply reasserting a picture of Africa's innocence, Rush turned to the argument from cultural relativism that Benezet had declined to exploit. "Where is the difference," Rush asked rhetorically, "between an African Prince, with his face daubed with Grease, and his Head adorned with a Feather; and a modern Macaroni with his artificial Club of Hair daubed with Powder and Pomatum? . . . Where is the difference between the Mahometan Negro who maintains three or four Wives agreeable to the Religion of his Country; and the European Christian who keeps three or four Mistresses contrary to the Religion of his Country?" Finally, Rush asked, did alleged barbarism justify enslavement anyway?[69] Nisbet's critique, therefore, elicited a stronger, more nuanced statement from Rush than Benezet had originally advanced.

Another critique of *Some Historical Account of Guinea* appeared in *A Treatise upon the Trade from Great-Britain to Africa; Humbly recommended to the Attention of Government*, which was published in London in 1772. The work was primarily a polemic directed against the African Committee that administered the British forts on the Gold Coast, alleging mismanagement and advocating reforms. In discussing the trade with Africa, however, the anonymous author felt it necessary to preface his remarks with a justification. His central contention took the form of a syllogism: Britain's power and prosperity depended on commerce; the African trade was a key part of British commerce; therefore, Britain's power and prosperity depended on the African trade. In trying to legitimate the African trade, the author had to brush aside abolitionists' objections. "What vain pretence of liberty can infatuate people to run into so much licentiousness," he scoffed, "as to assert a trade is unlawful, which custom immemorial, and various acts of parliament have ratified and given a sanction to?"[70] Writing one year after the publication of

---

[69] A Pennsylvanian [Benjamin Rush], *A Vindication of the Address, To the Inhabitants of the British Settlements, on the Slavery of the Negroes in America, in Answer to a Pamphlet entitled, "Slavery not Forbidden by Scripture; or a Defence of the West-India Planters from the Aspersions thrown out against them by the Author of the Address"* (Philadelphia, 1773; reprint, New York: Arno Press and the New York Times, 1969), 24-33, quotes on 24-25, 30-31.

[70] An African Merchant [John Peter Demarin?], *A Treatise upon the Trade from Great-*

Some Historical Account of Guinea, he trained his fire on Anthony Benezet in particular. The author criticized Benezet's selective excerpts from the travel literature, saying "he gives partial extracts from the history of Africa, and omits whatever makes against him." As shown above, *Some Historical Account of Guinea* was vulnerable to this criticism, and the anonymous merchant made the most of it. He mockingly noted, for instance, that "Benezet represents the Africans as people endowed with great talents and virtue.... He mentions that the Fuli, a nation on the Gambia, sell no slaves. What an exact character of the British nation would an author give, who should assert, that we would not fight, because one sect among us refused to bear arms!" In addition, the author resorted to British jingoism, in order to tar Benezet and other American abolitionists as Revolutionary zealots. Their "unnecessary and impracticable scheme of universal freedom," he charged, was merely "the device of the Puritans of North America, who now cry out for *perfect* liberty, as they once did for *perfect* purity, till they destroyed all real religion, and ruined both church and state; and who began these their last outcries, as appears by the dates of their works, only on our asserting our jurisdiction over them."[71] Whatever the strengths or weaknesses of these arguments, the fact that this author deemed it necessary to attempt a refutation further testifies to the powerful and immediate impact that *Some Historical Account of Guinea* made on both sides of the Atlantic. The book also made the reliability of evidence from the travel narratives a prominent point of contention.

In the next decade, Thomas Jefferson joined these defenders of slavery in casting doubt on the African travel literature. It seems likely that Jefferson too had read Benezet or come in contact with his arguments as he wrote *Notes on the State of Virginia*. In Query XIV on "Laws," Jefferson infamously asserted the inferiority of blacks for a variety of reasons. In one well-known sentence he wrote, "Comparing them by their faculties of memory, reason, and imagination, it appears to me, that in memory they are equal to the whites; in reason much inferior, as I think one could scarcely be found capable of tracing and comprehending the investigations of Euclid; and that in imagination they

---

Britain to Africa; Humbly recommended to the Attention of Government (London, 1772), 7. The attribution of this work's possible authorship comes from J. D. Fage, *A Guide to Original Sources for Precolonial Western Africa Published in European Languages, for the Most Part in Book Form*, rev. ed. (Madison, 1994), 84.

[71] [Demarin?], *Treatise upon the Trade*, Appendix D, quotes on 31 and 33.

are dull, tasteless, and anomalous." In his very next two sentences, Jefferson may have been anticipating Benezet's critique when he added, "It would be unfair to follow them to Africa for this investigation. We will consider them here, on the same stage with the whites, and where the facts are not apocryphal on which a judgment is to be formed." Apparently Jefferson was trying to head off abolitionists in the mode of Benezet by dismissing all evidence from Africa as "apocryphal" and thereby unreliable. Nevertheless, while Jefferson tried to deny African material from the defenders of African Americans, he himself tossed in a remark sometimes found in the travel literature that blacks preferred whites sexually "as uniformly as is the preference of the Oran-ootan for the black woman over those of his own species." It would appear that Jefferson recognized the power of Benezet's researches into the African travel narratives and tried to deny them to his opponents.[72] But they would not be denied.

Anthony Benezet's use of the African travel literature in his publications thus changed the trajectory of the Revolutionary-era debate between pro- and antislavery writers. His work could not be ignored, especially given his efforts to distribute copies to influential readers. Abolitionists added his findings to their catalog of denunciations, while defenders of slavery scrutinized Benezet's work for flaws that might negate his impact.

Benezet's publications, preeminently *Some Historical Account of Guinea*, also appear to have informed the new nation's free black intellectuals as they launched "what was arguably the first African American-initiated literary genre in the early republic, the short-lived but significant series of addresses beginning in January 1808 commemorating the abolition of the slave trade by the United States and Britain."[73] These orators shared a number of Benezet's depictions of Africa, including his vision of the continent's abundance, its people's "simplicity, innocence, and contentment," and the slave trade's depredations.[74] In addition, Benezet's contributions to the African American community continued to garner memorials of praise long after his death.

---

[72] Thomas Jefferson, *Notes on the State of Virginia*, ed. William Peden (1787; Chapel Hill: University of North Carolina Press, 1955), 138-139. Smith, *A New Voyage to Guinea*, 51-52, for example, contained the following remark: "I shall next describe a strange Sort of Animal, call'd by the White Men in this Country [Sierra Leone], a Mandrill . . . It is said, that the Males often attack and use Violence to the Black Women whenever they meet them alone in the Woods."

[73] Dickson D. Bruce, Jr., *The Origins of African American Literature, 1680-1865* (Charlottesville, 2001), 106.

[74] Peter Williams, Jr., "An Oration on the Abolition of the Slave Trade; Delivered

In language reminiscent of Benezet's, the January 1st speakers, typically up-and-coming leaders in urban, Northeastern free black communities, described how perfidious European slave traders had used a variety of underhanded techniques to despoil an African paradise. They portrayed their ancestral land in glowing terms. "Africa in its primitive state," according to New York's Henry Sipkins, "exhibits the most blissful regions, productive of all the necessaries and even luxuries of life, almost independent of the arm of husbandry. Its innocent inhabitants regardless of, or unacquainted with the concerns of busy life, enjoyed with uninterrupted pleasure the state in which, by the beneficent hand of nature, they were placed." Because of these "habits of ease which they derived from the natural fertility of their own country," the drudgery of plantation life was all the more unbearable for those later enslaved, or so claimed the Philadelphia clergyman, Absalom Jones.[75] With what were then already a series of stock images, every speaker painted a dramatic verbal picture of how wily slave traders used either naked force or duplicity to obtain their human cargoes. In the words of New Yorker William Hamilton, for example, "They set to work that low, sly, wicked, cunning, peculiar to the Europeans, to the creating of jealousies and animosity, one horde or nation with another. To those princes who were proof against their vile craftiness they administered draughts of their intoxicating spirituous liquor and then distilled in them their base purposes." As a result, they converted Africa into "one continued scene of suspicion, mad jealousy, confusion, war, rapine, blood and murder."[76] Given the obvious similarities between these statements and the portrayals in *Some Historical Account of Guinea*, one wonders whether these orators were drawing directly on Benezet's book. Probably they were

---

in The African Church, in The City of New York, January 1, 1808," in Dorothy Porter, ed., *Early Negro Writing, 1760-1837* (Boston:, 1971), 346.

[75] Henry Sipkins, "An Oration on the Abolition of the Slave Trade; Delivered in The African Church, in The City of New York, January 2, 1809," in ibid., 367; Absalom Jones, *A Thanksgiving Sermon, Preached January 1, 1808, in St. Thomas's, or the African Episcopal, Church, Philadelphia: on Account of the Abolition of the African Slave Trade, on that Day, by the Congress of the United States* (Philadelphia, 1808), 12. See also Russell Parrott, *An Oration on the Abolition of the Slave Trade, Delivered on the First of January, 1812, at the African Church of St. Thomas*, Rhistoric Publications, no. 229 (Philadelphia, 1812; reprint, Philadelphia, 1969), 6.

[76] William Hamilton, "An Oration, on the Abolition of the Slave Trade, Delivered in The Episcopal Asbury African Church, in Elizabeth-St. New York, January 2, 1815," in Porter, ed., *Early Negro Writing*, 395. For similar depictions, see also Jones, *Thanksgiving Sermon*, 11; Parrott, *Oration*, 4-5; Sipkins, "Oration," 368; Williams, "Oration," 347-348.

combining information from Benezet with that from other literary sources as well as the African American oral tradition.[77]

What is certain is that these orators paid homage to Benezet as one of the leading figures in the abolitionist struggle and as the great proponent on behalf of education in their community. "Had not a Benezet, a Sharp, a Wo[o]lman, a Delwin, a Clarkson, a Rush, a Wilberforce, and many other worthies, been zealous in vindicating the rights of the injured Africans," commented Philadelphia printer Russell Parrott, "we still should have to lament the existence of a trade, the bare mention of which, fills the soul with horror."[78] New York's Peter Williams, Jr. lauded "the useful exertions of Anthony Benezet," who "sensible of the equality of mankind, rose superior to the illiberal opinions of the age; and, disallowing an inferiority in the African genius, established the first school to cultivate our understandings, and to better our condition." Williams reminded his listeners that "a due sense of his meritorious actions [should] ever create in us a deep reverence of his beloved name."[79]

Anthony Benezet's publications established a paradigm for numerous nineteenth-century authors in their use of evidence from African travel narratives. In a story that is beyond the scope of this article, both pro- and antislavery writers continued to cite travelers' accounts in order to substantiate their conflicting claims. Perhaps more than any other group, proponents of African colonization appealed to the travel literature.[80] They had to walk a fine line in both extolling Africa's potential for settlement and decrying its ongoing paganism and lawlessness, which, of course, justified colonization. Following the 1799 publication of Mungo Park's celebrated *Travels in the Interior Districts of Africa*, a steady stream

---

[77] Bruce, *Origins of African American Literature*, 58-59, 106-109.

[78] Parrott, *Oration*, 8. See also Sipkins, "Oration," 370; Hamilton, "Oration," 398. The identification of Parrott as a printer comes from Julie Winch, *Philadelphia's Black Elite: Activism, Accommodation, and the Struggle for Autonomy, 1787-1848* (Philadelphia, 1988), 189, n. 21.

[79] Williams, "Oration," 350-351.

[80] Two pro-colonization works that made extensive use of the African travel literature, for example, were Frederick Freeman, *A Plea for Africa, Being Familiar Conversations on the Subject of Slavery and Colonization, [Originally Published under the Title "Yaradee."]*, 3d ed., rev. and enl. (Philadelphia, 1838), and Joseph Tracy, *Colonization and Missions. A Historical Examination of the State of Society in Western Africa, as Formed by Paganism and Muhammedanism, Slavery, the Slave Trade and Piracy, and of the Remedial Influence of Colonization and Missions* (Boston, 1844). William Lloyd Garrison sought to rebut colonizationists' claims with his own references to African travel narratives in *Thoughts on African Colonization* (Boston, 1832; reprint, New York, 1968), 35-36.

of travelers' and missionaries' accounts of Africa rolled off British and American presses. They provided plenty of fresh grist for the debates over slavery and colonization, even as such old standards as Barbot, Bosman, and Snelgrave continued to be cited as authorities.[81]

In *Some Historical Account of Guinea*, Anthony Benezet depicted West Africans in a Quaker image, in order to counter the self-serving justifications of slave traders that they were rescuing Africans from a miserable existence of bloodshed and barbarism. By contrast, in Benezet's rendering, Africans enjoyed their continent's abundance in peace and simplicity, and they exhibited numerous other Quaker virtues such as reverence, charity, and industry. Only European slave traders had spoiled this picture of innocence. Thus, Benezet reversed the stereotypical polarity between civilization and savagery. The African travel narratives upon which Benezet rested his claims, however, contained all sorts of comments about the land and its people, complimentary and derogatory alike. Benezet's Quaker values and abolitionist aims both screened out negative comments and inhibited him from pursuing some of the bolder arguments for African equality that were present in the travel literature. Nevertheless, *Some Historical Account of Guinea* influenced a number of other antislavery leaders and blazed a rhetorical path that they soon followed. Proslavery critics tried to cast doubt on Benezet's use of the travel literature, while African American orators incorporated his depictions of Africa and the slave trade into their emerging identity. No doubt the former's criticism he would have brushed off; the latter's praise he would have humbly relished.

Acknowledgments

Jonathan D. Sassi is associate professor of history at the College of Staten Island and the Graduate Center of the City University of New York. Earlier versions of this essay were presented at the USC-Huntington Library Early Modern Studies Institute's conference on "The Early Modern Travel Narrative: Production and Consumption," Los Angeles, May 1, 2004, and the Omohundro Institute of Early American and History and Culture's tenth annual conference, Northampton, Massachusetts, June 12, 2004. The author is grateful for the feedback received there. He also wishes to thank Ruth H. Bloch, David L. Crosby,

---

[81] One proslavery work that referenced all three publications was David James McCord, *Africans at Home* (offprint of an essay from the *Southern Quarterly Review* of July 1854).

James N. Green, Phillip Lapsansky, Peter Mancall, Joseph C. Miller, David Waldstreicher, and the anonymous readers of the JEMH for their comments and suggestions. The research for this article was supported (in part) during 2003-04 by a grant from the City University of New York PSC-CUNY Research Award Program and by a one-month Andrew W. Mellon Foundation Fellowship at the Library Company of Philadelphia and the Historical Society of Pennsylvania during July 2004.

TRAVEL WRITING AND HUMANISTIC CULTURE: A BLUNTED IMPACT?

JOAN-PAU RUBIÉS

London School of Economics and Political Science

ABSTRACT

An influential historiographical tradition has opposed the accounts of extra-European worlds produced by sixteenth-century travel writers to the concerns of humanists and other European men of learning, even detecting a 'blunted impact' up until the eighteenth century, when the figure of the philosophical traveller was proclaimed by Rousseau and others. It is my argument that this approach is misleading and that we need to take account of the full influence of travel writing upon humanistic culture in order to understand how the Renaissance eventually led to the Enlightenment. A first step consists in analysing the collective impact of accounts of America, Africa and Asia, rather than opposing the 'New World' to other areas. Moreover, whilst quantitative estimates offer a route for the assessment of 'impact', it is the qualitative aspect which is most clearly central to the cultural history of the period. Even 'popular' observers were often subtly influenced by concepts and strategies formulated by the intellectual elites. Under close scrutiny, it appears that humanists—and here I adopt a broad definition—had a crucial role in the production and consumption of travel accounts, as editors and travel collectors, as historians and cosmographers, and eventually—from the turn of the seventeenth century—as 'philosophical travellers'. The article seeks to illustrate these roles with reference to some examples from the first phase of the encounter. In particular, the early accounts of the Columbian expeditions by Nicolaus Scyllacus and Peter Martyr of Anghiera can be shown to have elaborated Columbian material more faithfully than is usually understood to be the case. Similarly, the historiography of conquest published after the middle of the sixteenth century reveals the widespread application of humanist standards to the literature of encounter produced in the previous sixty years.

> In the two or three centuries since the inhabitants of Europe have been flooding into other parts of the world, endlessly publishing new collections of voyages and travel, I am persuaded that we have come to know no other men except Europeans.
>
> Rousseau, *Discourse on the origins and foundations of inequality among men* (1754).

Rousseau's claim that European travellers, mostly sailors, merchants, soldiers and missionaries, that is, men of limited education or (in the latter category) imbued with a profound bias, had failed to be philosophical enough to appreciate what the real differences between men were, expressed an aspiration to a new universal and scientific anthropology which had deeper roots than he would have granted. Already in 1604, in a letter to Scaliger, the humanist historian La Popelinière (1541-1608) declared his intention to become a traveller—a philosophical traveller like Marco Polo or Vespucci had *not* been—in order to bring perfection to universal history. His aim, imbued by a cosmopolitan ideal, was the full knowledge of men, whether civilized or savage (however improper, La Popelinière added, the latter term possibly is).[1] Although La Popelinière did not manage to get very far, if we consider the accounts of travellers like Ogier de Busbecq, Jean de Léry, George Sandys, Pietro della Valle, François Bernier, Jean Chardin, Paul Rycaut, Gemelli Careri, Jean-Baptiste du Tertre or the baron of Lahontan, it appears that Rousseau's statement was rather unfair, revealing the casualness of his own engagement with this kind of literature: the philosophical traveller that he asked for had already been born in the previous two centuries. What is less clear is whether a humanistic, antiquarian and philosophical education was the requisite for a better understanding of cultural difference, or rather, as Montaigne had suggested in his essay *Des cannibales*, an obstacle to empirical ethnography.[2]

Whilst the transformation of European culture after the Renaissance is often seen in relation to the 're-discovery' of the pagan civilization of classical antiquity, set of course in the complex political and social contexts of the period, in the long term the impact of accounts of 'new worlds' exerted an equally crucial influence. The new awareness of geographical diversity often acted in combination with the deep antiquarian perspective derived from a fresh assessment of the culture and learning of the ancient world, to create the grounds for a new theory of civilization. It will be my argument that we need to take full account of the influence of travel writing upon humanistic culture in order to understand how the Renaissance eventually led to the Enlightenment. Here I am not interested in interpreting the production of the travel accounts

---

[1] As quoted in George Huppert, *The Idea of Perfect History: Historical Erudition and Historical Philosophy in Renaissance France*, (Urbana, Ill. 1970), pp. 195-96. La Popelinière's intellectual project, explicitly 'modern', was to write a general history which was also cultural, that is, with an ethnographic and antiquarian component. It had been developed in his remarkable *Idée de l'histoire accomplie* (1599).

[2] 'For clever people [*les fines gens*] observe more things and more curiously, but they interpret them; and to lend weight and conviction to their interpretation, they can not help altering history a little. They never show you things as they are, but bend and disguise them according to the way they have seen them; and to give credence to their judgment and attract you to it, they are prone to add something to their matter, to stretch it out and amplify it. We need a man either very honest, or so simple that he has not the stuff to build up false inventions and give them plausibility; a man wedded to no theory'. Montaigne, *The Complete Works*, translated by Donald Frame, with an introduction by Stuart Hampshire (London, 2003), p. 184.

per se (as I did in a previous study), but rather their influence upon European intellectual culture, through a number of specific images, practices and debates. However, it is also part of my argument that the relationship between primary narratives and their contexts of production can help illuminate the wider issue of the role of this literature in the transformation of European culture.

A tradition of historiography concerning the discovery of the New World has focused on the issue of 'impact', and in particular has developed the theme of a 'blunted impact'. In the words of John Elliott, whose highly inspiring *The Old World and the New* (1970) can be considered as the classic statement of this tradition, if we consider the principle that 'the absence of influence is often as revealing as its presence', the picture which emerges is one of a widespread reluctance to 'accept the New World into consciousness', as veneration for antiquity, combined with a sense of superiority, created obstacles to a rapid response and full appreciation of the magnitude of the discovery. In this account the humanists, led by Peter Martyr of Anghiera with his famous identification of the condition of Caribbean peoples encountered by Columbus with the classical 'golden age' of innocent simplicity, were singled out for 'projecting onto America their disappointed dreams', with the consequence that they closed the door to 'understanding an alien civilization'. At a deeper level the problem also affected issues of perception: Elliott argued that sixteenth-century Europeans 'all too often saw what they expected to see', or, as David B. Quinn put it a few years later, 'men saw in the new the old, altered but not fundamentally changed ... where novelty was total, it was conceived as an extension of the old rather than as novelty itself'.[3]

---

[3] John Elliott, The *Old World and the New 1492-1650* (Cambridge, 1970), pp. 7, 21, 26. Also D.B. Quinn, 'New Geographical Horizons: Literature', in Fredi Chappelli ed. *First Images of America: The Impact of the New World on the Old* (Los Angeles, 1974), 636. My title however echoes John Elliott's own 'Renaissance Europe and America: a Blunted Impact?', in ibid. 11-23, where he re-asserts the principle that 'it is reasonable to talk about the blunted impact of the discovery of America in European consciousness' but also emphasizes the diversity of classical and Christian values and beliefs in Europe, which made it possible for Europeans to respond with flexibility and relative openness. For another perspective on the problem, see Anthony Pagden, 'The impact of the new World on the Old: the history of and idea', *Renaissance and Modern Studies*, 30 (1986): 1-11, who is less concerned with measuring impact than with showing how succeeding generations of Europeans, from Erasmus to Humboldt, constructed the issue according to changing intellectual projects. Pagden is himself skeptical that modern historiography can meaningfully continue to discuss 'impact', on the grounds that none of these earlier constructions has been driven by a rigorous historical analysis.

These generalizations sometimes fail to survive closer scrutiny of the primary sources in their contexts of production and reception. Of course it was natural for Columbus to, at least initially, imagine that he was in the Eastern parts of India and Cathay, but the issue is whether this kind of assumption was unreasonably maintained against empirical evidence due to some kind of reluctance to accept novelty and challenge tradition.[4] Arguably, Columbus' case can be read contextually in the light of a combination of reasonable expectation and political motivations, rather than as some kind of psychological aberration, let alone one shared by all sixteenth century Europeans (as others were quicker to express scepticism about his geographical assumptions). The general adoption of the image of a new world (with titles like *Mundus Novus* or *De Orbe Novo*) in the writings of widely-read authors like Vespucci and Anghiera, together with the principle stated at an early stage by writers like Gonzalo Fernández de Oviedo and Giovanni Ramusio that the authority of modern experience could correct classical learning, or the emphasis placed on the unique historical importance of the discovery and conquest of America by influential humanist historians like Francisco López de Gómara, all seem to militate against the idea that there was a widespread European reluctance to embrace the discoveries in their novelty and "otherness".

But of course all this largely depends on where we look. If we leave the interpretations of those writers directly involved with travel and conquest and consider the response of the learned world to the news of the discoveries, there are some significant examples which seem to support the view that the impact was uncertain and slow. We need only consider here the ethnological and cosmographical syntheses by Johannes Boemus and Sebastian Münster. Boemus's *Omnium gentes mores, ritus et leges* (Augsburg, 1520) was a popular ethnographic synthesis, often reissued and translated, which relied on classical and humanist (or medieval Latin) sources about exotic peoples, ignoring all the evidence from the recent Spanish and Portuguese discoveries.[5] Indeed, the author, a humanist cleric who was canon at Ulm Cathedral, went to some lengths to deny the trustworthiness of modern travellers like the Italian adventurer

---

[4] On Columbus' perceptions of native Americans, and the literature that informed them, see Peter Hulme, 'Columbus and the Cannibals', in *Colonial Encounters: Europe and the Native Caribbean 1492-1797* (London, 1986), 13-43; B.W. Ife (ed.) Columbus, *Journal of the First Voyage* (Warminster, 1990), pp. xxii-xxv; Valerie Flint, *The Imaginative Landscape of Christopher Columbus* (Princeton, 1992).

[5] These even failed to emerge in his expanded edition of 1536.

Ludovico de Varthema, openly refusing to draw from his highly popular *Itinerario* of 1510, which described a recent journey to Arabia and
India, because this probably contained many lies. Only educated men
writing in Latin were fit for an authoritative synthesis, and—we may
add—those men had not yet written about the newly-discovered lands.
It did not help, of course, that Boemus' interpretation of cultural diversity was also reactionary, as he rejected a utilitarian (Ciceronian) account
of the origins of civil society for a Christian Biblical perspective in which
the cultural fragmentation of mankind was the consequence of a process
of corruption from a single moral core given by God; hence, even
though there could be civil progress, alternative (gentile) religions and
customs were deviant.[6] As for Münster's influential *Kosmographia* (1544),
a vast compilation which went through various revisions until it reached
its definitive form in 1550, it was mainly designed as a commentary on
geographical maps and plates. Although it made use of modern travel
accounts, its flaw was that there was no attempt to discriminate between
ancient and modern sources in order to create a sense of anachronism.
Nor did it attempt to identify and eliminate instances of fabulation: all
sources were included as equally authoritative.[7]

However, I would suggest that Germany in the first half of the sixteenth century is not the best point from which to assess the impact.[8]
As I have written elsewhere, those cosmographical works produced in
countries with little direct experience of colonial enterprises tended to

---

[6] Klaus Vogel offers the important qualification that Boemus did not reject modern
travellers out of ignorance, but because they fell outside his criteria for the selection of
authorities. See K. Vogel, 'Cultural Variety in a Renaissance Perspective: Johannes
Boemus on the "manners, laws and customs of all peoples" (1520)', in H. Bugge and
J.P. Rubiés (eds.) *Shifting Cultures: Interaction and Discourse in the Expansion of Europe* (Münster,
1995), 17-34. On the importance of Varthema as a new kind of traveller see Rubiés,
Travel and Ethnology in the Renaissance: South India through European Eyes, 1250-1625 (Cambridge,
2000), ch. 4.

[7] The cultural reasons for Münster's incongruities are dissected by Anthony Grafton,
New Worlds, Ancient Texts. The Power of Tradition and the Shock of Discovery (Cambridge Mass.,
1992), 97-111.

[8] This is not to deny the importance of number of individual narrative accounts published in German, in particular those by conquerors and mercenaries in South America
such as Hans Staden (Marburg, 1557) and Ulrich Schmidel (Frankfurt, 1567). Although
these two narratives were printed with some delay in the second half of the century (as
was Nicholas Federman's account of a German expedition to Venezuela organised by
the Welsers), there was an earlier tradition of reception of newsletters concerning the
Spanish and Portuguese voyages amongst the financial and humanist circles of a number
of Southern German cities, and (for example) the Latin version of some of the letters
of Cortés was first printed in Nüremberg.

be traditional not only in the general theological conception, but also in the primacy given to authoritative classical sources as against new observations.[9] By contrast, consider the case of the Venetian Giovanni Ramusio, working together with the mapmaker Jacopo Gastaldi so as to make new accounts correct ancient ones, and new maps supersede Ptolemy. Through the application of humanist philological methods of manuscript collation and faithful reproduction to the new literature of travel, by ordering his materials logically according to a practical geography, and by subjecting them to some sort of contextual reasoning, Ramusio was formulating the critical method of systematic verification which had eluded his contemporary Münster.[10] Consider also the case of Francisco de Thámara, Ciceronian humanist and professor of rhetoric at the university of Cádiz, obviously a good vantage-point from which to assess the new discoveries. In 1555 he issued a translation of Boemus's work, *Livro de las costumbres de todas las gentes del mundo, y de las Indias*, with substantial additions relating to the New World based on the key historical sources by Oviedo and Gómara (he also described India and the East, but more briefly). Was Thámara's highly competent 'Suma y breve relación de todas las Indias y tierras nuevamente descubiertas por gente de España assí por la parte de Poniente como de Levant' less significant than the original omission of recent reports by the rather reactionary Boemus, especially when those were, in many parts of Germany, still difficult to verify? This is not to say that there was an automatic intellectual response to the discoveries simply based on the physical proximity of humanist scholars to primary reports. Obviously there was a geography (as well as a chronology) of reception and impact. In the context of fierce religious and political controversy within Europe, there was also a dynamic tension between rival centres of cultural activity which affected both the reception and the elaboration of the new literature of travel. Metropolitan cities like Seville, Lisbon, Antwerp, Florence and Venice, for example, not only enjoyed privileged access to new sources of information throughout much of the sixteenth century,

---

[9] J.P. Rubiés, 'New Worlds and Renaissance Ethnology', *History and Anthropology*, 6 (1993): 157-97, 180.

[10] On Ramusio's editorial methods see G.B. Parks, 'The Contents and Sources of Ramusio's Navigationi', *Bulletin of the New York Public Library* 59, 6 (1955): 279-313; For the importance of Gastaldi's maps for Ramusio's overall strategy see Marica Milanesi, 'Tra testo e carta. Relazioni di viaggi, cosmografia e cartografia nel XVI secolo: Ramusio, Gastaldi, Postel', paper presented at the workshop on *Travel, Travellers and Travel Writing in the Late Medieval and Early Modern World*, European University Institute (April, 2002).

but also suffered the peculiar constraints which conditioned intellectual life under the emerging Counter Reformation.

One additional point of great importance is that there is no reason why sixteenth-century scholars should have regarded the American discoveries as something essentially separate from the new accounts of Africa and Asia brought about by the Portuguese and those who followed them, or from any other accounts of exotic peoples in the Levant, Russia or Central Asia. For Simon Grynaeus and Sebastian Münster, humanist editors of a retrospective collection of voyages titled *Novus Orbis* published in Basel in 1532 (and which became the 'modern' source for Münster's own cosmography), this 'new world' included most of Asia no less than America, given that much of the East had been equally 'newly found' by European navigators beyond what had been known by the ancients.[11] Similarly, when Ramusio published his epoch-making collection of voyages in mid-sixteenth century Venice he included all routes and all peoples, and divided them not according to the three continents of classical antiquity, but rather around the three new areas of commercial and colonial expansion—the Portuguese sea route from the Atlantic to India and the Spice Islands, the Spanish discoveries in the Americas, and finally those countries which surrounded central Asia along the medieval land route to Cathay once described by Marco Polo (a Venetian whom Ramusio accordingly hailed as a 'modern').[12] This Renaissance perspective on the discoveries is often overlooked by modern historians all too often concerned with one area of expansion alone. It suggests that to oppose the large numbers of books published in sixteenth-century France devoted to the Turks and Asia to the smaller number of titles relating to America in order to emphasize a 'blunted impact' in relation to the New World can be rather misleading. We should in

---

[11] The *Novus Orbis* was collected by Johann Huttich and Sebastian Münster, and published with a preface by Simon Grynaeus, a leading Protestant humanist. There was a German translation in 1534, and expanded editions appeared in 1537 and 1555. For much of the sixteenth century this was the key northern-Protestant travel collection, published with an erudite readership in mind. For details see Max Böhme, *Die grossen reisesammlungen des 16. ahrhun derts* (Strassburg, 1904).

[12] Ramusio's praise of Marco Polo as an accurate recorder of what he saw despite belonging to a period where 'few men were intelligent of that doctrine', and despite spending so many years surrounded by the 'unpolished Tartar nation', was not devoid of Venetian patriotism, but also responded to the humanist concern for establishing continuities between old and new observations. It was now finally possible to read him as an accurate observer rather than a writer of fables. Ramusio, *Navigazione e viaggi*, ed. by Marica Milanesi, VI vols. (Turin, 1978-88), vol. III, p. 22.

fact be adding up all these accounts into our estimate of the extent to which Europeans wrote about, published about, and read about exotic lands and peoples throughout the Renaissance.[13] When we do this, what emerges is the picture of a civilization with an extraordinary and indeed unprecedented capacity to cast its gaze across the whole world with curiosity and passion for learning. The ethnographic impulse of early modern Europe is historically unique. Obviously few people read as much travel literature as Ramusio, or shared his wide-ranging vision, but it increasingly mattered that some of the most creative late humanist thinkers were able to do so.

That the historiographical paradigm has been changing was already apparent in 1991, when in the context of an important conference on 'America in European consciousness' John Elliott, revisiting his older views in the light of new research, asserted that he had perhaps over-emphasized 'the degree of indifference shown by early modern Europeans to the new discoveries'.[14] He also rightly noted that when assessing impact the issue of degree of interest was separate from questions of assimilation and cultural transformation.[15] In a previous book I have in fact tackled the issues of assimilation, or cultural translation, at great length, challenging the paradigm (still dominant in the 1991 conference) by which European observers were keener to 'neutralize' novelty than to understand difference.[16] What from a post-Enlightenment perspective often looks like a European 'defensive strategy', for example concerning the complexity and power of non-Christian civilizations, is, I argued, best understood as the kind of interpretation which made sense in a set

---

[13] European publications for America are relatively well researched. For an essential guide see *European Americana: a Chronological Guide to Works Printed in Europe Relating to the Americas, 1493-1750*, edited by John Alden and Dennis C. Landis, 6 vols. (New York, 1980-1988). The question of early reception was analyzed by Rudolf Hirsch, 'Printed reports on the early discoveries and their reception' in F. Chiappelli (ed.) *First Images*, 537-52, who concluded that 'a definite and broadly based interest in early discoveries did exist' (549). Estimates for Asia and Africa are more difficult to come by. See however the important work by Donald F. Lach and Edwin van Kley, *Asia in the Making of Europe*, 3 vols. in 9 books (Chicago, 1965-1993), especially vol. 1 'The Century of Discovery' (Chicago, 1965), 154-217. Comparative works are still sadly insufficient, despite the classic account (for France only) by Geoffroy Atkinson, *Les nouveaux horizons de la Renaissance française* (Paris, 1935). For material on the Spanish colonies, Francisco Esteve Barba, *Historiografía Indiana* (Madrid, 1964) is a thorough survey of the narratives which were produced, rather than an analysis of their publication and impact.

[14] J.H. Elliott, 'Final Reflections: the Old World and the New Revisited', in Karen O. Kupperman (ed.) *America in European Consciousness 1493-1750* (Chapel Hill, 1995), 395.

[15] Ibid.

[16] In my *Travel and Ethnology in the Renaissance*.

of cultural contexts with distinct assumptions and political agendas.[17] For my case-study I then used the often neglected material relating to India rather than the New World, not only on the grounds that the fundamental issues of perception of 'the other' are the same, but also in order to argue that the literature of encounter in the early modern period needs to be looked at in a comparative fashion. The next logical step is, therefore, to take account of a variety of 'areas of encounters' overseas, and 'contexts of reception' in Europe, in order to address the issue of the actual impact of travel writing on the transformation of intellectual culture, rather than pursuing what is perhaps an illusory measurement of impact according to relative numbers of authors responding directly to new discoveries, and rapidity of response. As Rosario Romeo wrote in his now classic and still remarkably valid *Le scoperte americane nelá coscienza italiana del Cinquecento* (1954; 1971), by the end of the sixteenth century the American peoples were no longer the object of abstract myths or radical condemnations, but constituted a concrete element in a wider European vision of the natural and moral world.[18] In his work of 1970 Elliott himself observed that 'the qualitative changes introduced into European thought by accounts of the New World and its peoples far outweigh the quantity of information at the disposal of the reader'.[19] One could go further and insist that there is some anachronism in the expectation that early sixteenth-century scholars should have singled out the American discoveries for their importance. Erasmus perhaps did not react to the news of the Spanish and Portuese discoveries, but why should he be more concerned with that topic than with

---

[17] My starting point is that evidence *per se* does not lead to cultural and intellectual change, but is crucially mediated by existing cultural assumptions and dynamics. By contrast, Elliott's comment that the 'explosive potentialities' raised by the discovery of America were extremely slow to have an effect—for example a sustained attack on the historical and chronological accuracy of the Bible, or the possibilities of relativism as a weapon for challenging long-established assumptions—takes for granted that the libertine Enlightenment was to a significant extent an inevitable outcome of the encounter (*The Old World and the New*, p. 29). If we emphasize the principle that evidence and its interpretation are culturally constructed, what needs explaining is not the 'slowness' of the impact—Elliott's accurate observation that the dramatic debates *only* happened after 1650—but the fact that after 1650 the impact was able to take this particularly radical form. At this point our two arguments tend to converge, as Elliott emphasizes the importance of the 'work being undertaken behind the stockade' before 'any sustained break-out' could take place. Before 1650, however, the post-Enlightenment interpretation of what the battle was about was entirely missing.

[18] Rosario Romeo, *Le scoperte americane nella coscienza italiana del Cinquecento* (Riccardi: 1954; 2nd ed. 1971; reprinted by Laterza: Bari, 1989), 120.

[19] Elliott, *The Old World*, 13.

bringing peace to Europe, educating Christians, or positioning himself
vis-à-vis Luther? Surely it is for us more interesting to reflect upon the
fact that André Thévet, Jean de Léry and especially Michel de Montaigne
did write about Brazilian Indians in a way that created a new intellectual agenda for those still concerned with furthering the Erasmian
ideals of a truly learned and Christian Europe.[20] Surely an essay like
Montaigne's *On Cannibals*, and the way it was read, casts a longer shadow
than a mere reckoning of the many decades that it took some German
or English humanists to acknowledge that cosmography could no longer
be built around what Pliny, Diodorus and Strabo had written.[21]

What I propose here is a history of the genre of travel writing in
relation to the evolution of humanist culture: or, in other words, what
travellers did for humanists, and humanists for travellers. This question
touches upon the crucial relationship between popular culture and elite
culture. Many of the writers identified by Rousseau as 'uneducated'—
sailors, merchants and soldier-conquerors, for example—had been collected by Ramusio for their 'scientific' value, but were primarily concerned
with practical aims. Obviously a variety of colonial contexts produced a
variety of needs for information, and some of the most empirical and
detailed writers described lands and peoples, sometimes rather systematically, mainly in order to understand which trade to conduct, or (when
contemplating settlement and perhaps conquest) how to identify and
communicate with potential allies and enemies. For leaders of expeditions, men like Cortés and Pizarro and their close associates, another
important issue was political justification. Even missionaries, arguably
the most 'educated' of those primary travel writers identified by Rousseau,
were of course motivated by a utilitarian desire to understand the peoples they sought to convert, a desire often combined with elements of
religious propaganda and theological debate. On the other hand, it is
never possible to separate entirely utilitarian aims from ideological
assumptions and from a certain amount of self-fashioning, as it is never
possible to rule out an element of curiosity, however culturally constructed,
from these descriptions.

---

[20] For the importance of the French literature on the Brazilian Indians see the various works of Frank Lestringant, in particular his *Le Huguenot et le sauvage. L'Amérique et la
controverse coloniale en France au temps des guerres de religion 1555-1589* (Paris, 1990).

[21] Or, as Anthony Grafton neatly put it, the discovery of the New World was of great
importance in sustaining that cultural revolution by which 'between 1550 and 1650
Western thinkers ceased to believe that they could find all important truths in ancient
books'. Grafton, *New Worlds, Ancient Texts*, 1 ff.

It will be my argument that 'popular' writers (or the authors of oral reports who dictated to someone else) were often subtly influenced by the concepts and strategies formulated by intellectual elites, and, to that extent, there is never a purely 'popular' discourse; many of the writers who were also observers, and quite a few who acted as editors or compilers, men like Columbus, Vespucci, Varthema, Pigafetta and Cortés, for example, albeit not having the full-blown humanistic education that a traveller like the imperial ambassador Ogier de Busbecq could claim, in fact operated at the crossroads between popular and elite discourses. That is, they had a limited access to formal education and especially to Latin and Greek, but nevertheless were capable of reading and interested in vernacular literature, including vernacular translations of classical authors. I believe that a concept we can use here is that of 'popular humanism', many of whose expressions can be linked to urban culture and sometimes also to court culture. Furthermore, I will also argue that not only were these 'popular' writers engaged by humanist editors and scholars, so that, for example, the conqueror Cortés could act as informant to the historian Gómara, his chaplain, or the merchant Nicolò Conti could inform Poggio Bracciolini during a remarkable Florentine encounter: but, indeed, that in the course of this interaction the humanists themselves, by reading and editing and through sheer debate and conversation, were often influenced in crucial ways by the narrative weight of the testimony of the more popular writers.[22] Some historians claiming a humanist understanding of their task, like Gonzalo Fernández de Oviedo or Francesco Sansovino, let the primary narratives speak for themselves to a remarkable extent, sacrificing order and style to authenticity.[23] In some other cases, men like Giovanni Ramusio and Richard Hakluyt contributed decisively to the emergence of a new scholarly pursuit based on translating and editing primary travel accounts in vernacular languages. Often acting in communication with many others, they operated as a think-tank for geographical lore, since they sought to make their works serve a political or ideological agenda.[24] In these various

---

[22] For an extensive analysis of the encounter between Conti and Poggio see Rubiés, *Travel and Ethnology*, ch. 3. See also the brief article by Ingrid Baumgärtner in *The Literature of Travel and Exploration: An Encyclopedia*, vol. I, 277-9.

[23] Oviedo's reliance on primary sources was related in a complex way to his notion of autopsy. On the latter see now Jesús Carrillo, 'Taming the Visible: Word and Image in Oviedo's *Historia General y Natural de las Indias*', *Viator*, 31 (2000): 399-431. On Sansovino, see Paul Grendler, "Francesco Sansovino and Italian popular history 1560-1600", *Studies in the Renaissance* 16 (1969): 138-80.

[24] For Ramusio, a Venetian civil servant who corresponded with Gonzalo Fernández

ways a 'popular' genre largely motivated by more immediate practical
concerns, and often conditioned by the rhetorical strategies which served
those concerns, gained authority and entered the mainstream of elite
culture.[25] This made it possible for the humanist scholar or philosophical
dilettante himself to attempt to become a travel writer, and for La
Popelinière and Rousseau to claim that, indeed, the ideal traveller was
a philosopher.

This discussion carries implicit a broad definition of humanism, and
indeed, appreciating the pervasiveness and flexibility of humanistic culture is the key to my argument about the way travel writing was able
to inform the origins of the Enlightenment. In other words, for our
understanding of the transformation of European intellectual culture in
this period the continuity in classical rhetorical education is more
significant than the well-known ideological discontinuities between lay
and clerical, Protestant and Catholic, and devout and libertine.[26] Obviously
there would never have been a powerful humanism if education had
not escaped the strict confines of the traditional universities dominated
by the religious orders and the Church, but by the time we meet the
Jesuits it is clear that scholastic traditions and religious concerns were
not incompatible with a classical training, even if thoroughly pruned

---

de Oviedo, support for his own city's commercial imperialism was significant but,
I would argue, secondary to his intellectual enterprise of reforming geography and replac-
ing the imperfections found in Ptolemy, Pliny and Strabo; although he was keen to make
available the Iberian discoveries in Italian (rather than, interestingly, in Latin), Venetian
agendas alone would not have made the publication necessary, as a well-established commercial power ruled by a narrow elite could use the materials with discretion, and foreign competition made it sensible to restrict the circulation of information. Ramusio
published his collection because he believed that travel accounts deserved to be read
systematically by an Italian-centered but ultimately cosmopolitan republic of letters committed to 'modern' learning and practical knowledge. Hence, as he explained in the dedication of the first volume to his friend the humanist doctor and scientist Ieronimo
Fracastoro, the book was written for the 'doti e studiosi' as well as for 'signori e principi'
(Ramusio, *Navigazioni*, I, p. 5). For Hakluyt, on the other hand, the publication of his
materials was central to an ideological program of national mobilization for empire, in
an effort to catch up with Southern Catholic powers. Hence in his case scholarship was
more crudely tied up with imperialism.

[25] I elaborate this point in J.P. Rubiés. 'Travel Writing and Ethnography', in Peter
Hulme and Tim Youngs (eds.) *The Cambridge Companion to Travel Writing* (2002), 242-60.

[26] We can adopt a conventional definition by which a classical education—but not
necessarily the primary use of Latin and Greek, or the slavish imitation of classical examples, or any particular ideological stance deriving from Cicero, Seneca or Plato—is the
key to humanistic culture. Training in philological criticism, combined with the sense of
historical anachronism which resulted from contrasting the classical past with the present, gave humanist scholars and tutors a critical edge with independence from the
espousal of any particular philosophy or theology.

from heretical teachings. It then becomes necessary to rely on a number of adjectives in order to introduce distinctions within this common
educational background: we can talk about Ciceronian humanism,
Christian (or Erasmian) humanism, civic and courtly (or chivalric) humanisms, skeptical (or libertine) humanism, post-skeptical (Neo-Stoic, Tacitist
and 'modern scientific') humanisms, Calvinist and Arminian humanisms
if you may, and of course Counter-Reformation humanism (mainly
Jesuit). Authors from all those sometimes contradictory backgrounds
shared an educational tradition and a number of disciplinary practices
largely derived from classical antiquity, pointing towards a common cultural horizon which we can describe as a nascent 'republic of letters'.
It was indeed the pervasive influence of this humanistic culture, consisting not only of enthusiasm for the knowledge derived from Latin
and Greek sources, duly edited and printed, but (perhaps more importantly) also the increasing reliance on vernacular translations of modern
works, on educational travel, and on the international use of languages
like Italian, Spanish or French, which made the emergence of an all-
European republic of letters possible across deep national and confessional
divides. In these circumstances, elite culture was bound to be committed
to some kind of cosmopolitan ideal—not only for ideological reasons
(which there were), but also for practical ones. Perhaps, then, the most
important distinction was not ideological but methodological: the true
humanists were not those merely competent in Latin and possibly Greek,
but those also capable of approaching classical learning critically, through
a sense of historical discontinuity, and hence in a position to further
their moral concerns through an idea of educational improvement.
Humanism may be very Christian, or not, but it always involved a
dynamic idea of civilization.[27]

Even if we grant the value of a broad understanding of humanistic
culture, we must also consider the issue of its chronological limits. Can

---

[27] A recent study by David Lupher, *Romans in a New World: Classical Models in Sixteenth-
Century America* (Ann Arbor, 2004) offers a systematic illustration of the deeply dynamic
nature of the interaction between humanist learning and writings about (in this case)
Spanish America. In this comprehensive analysis of the uses of Rome as model for both
imperial and anti-imperial discourses, 'debate about the nature of Roman civilization
and especially over the way Rome acquired and maintained an empire provided a stim-
ulating and productive framework for assessments of Spain's presence in the Indies and
of the native societies the Spaniards encountered there'. Moreover, 'the largely unprecedented ethical and cultural challenges raised by the Spanish encounter with the New
World precipitated a powerful and sustained reevaluation of Europe's Greco-Roman
heritage' (7).

we talk about a coherent intellectual tradition between 1550 and 1750 as basis for what is otherwise, and rather obviously, a dramatic process of cultural change? When does the humanist stop being a late humanist to become a scientist or a *philosophe*? According to certain criteria, Grotius, writing in Latin about law, history and theology in an innovative manner, is still a humanist inspired by Erasmus, but Voltaire is perhaps not. Montaigne, alone in his study surrounded by Latin and Greek quotations, is clearly a humanist writer, even though he uses French rather than Latin for his own essays; and Gibbon surely is a direct heir to Tacitus, even though he is also in many ways a innovator whose work is impossible to imagine in any earlier intellectual context.[28] The key issue is the fundamental continuity of European intellectual culture from the Renaissance to the Enlightenment, by which humanists eventually become antiquarians and then *philosophes*. This humanistic education permeated the cultural horizons and disciplinary training of the European intellectual elites whether they were religious or lay, Catholic, Protestant or libertine. Indeed the culture produced by a classical education made it possible for Europeans to share certain intellectual horizons despite important ideological and national variations. Hence Catholic missionaries like the Dominican Las Casas or, even more clearly, the Jesuit Acosta, must be seen as both humanists and late-scholastic writers.[29] The historians of

---

[28] Or, as John Pocock recently put it, 'Gibbon as humanist was necessitated to become Gibbon as historian and as philosopher'. Pocock, *Barbarism and Religion*, II 'Narratives of Civil Government' (Cambridge, 1999), p. 376.

[29] Whilst the Jesuits incorporated a solid training in the humanities as part of their educational system, eventually defined in the *ratio studiorum*, the case of the anti-imperialist Las Casas can be more controversial. Perhaps the key to this complexity lies in the fact that he was originally a settler in Hispaniola and Cuba, and only years later improvised his intellectual training as a friar, that is, when already an activist for a cause. His primary education in Spain at the Cathedral School of Seville had been managed by Christian humanist teachers. Las Casas was obviously not a typical humanist, because so much of his classical world is derived from Augustine, and his anti-imperial arguments are scholastic (however radicalized). Nevertheless, his appeal to the ancient world in the *Apologética Historia* in order to equate the achievements of ancient pagans with those of modern ones has something of a humanistic flair, and led him to use a very wide range of classical authorities, albeit not very critically (Jesús-Angel Barreda, 'Documentación bibliográfica de la Apologética', in Las Casas, *Obras Completas*, VI, 213-33). It is also interesting to note that for his account of the origins of civilization he turned from Aquinas to Cicero (Anthony Pagden, *The Fall of Natural Man: The American Indian and the Origins of Comparative Ethnology* (Cambridge, 1982), 140-5; see also Jaime González, *La idea de Roma en la historiografía Indiana* (Madrid, 1981), which deals with Las Casas's rhetorical uses of Rome). Besides these intrinsic issues, Las Casas is also important because much of the more 'humanist' imperial historiography of the Spanish conquest was ideologically conditioned—if often negatively—by his work.

empire Gonzalo Fernández de Oviedo and João de Barros were both writers of chivalric romances in a medieval tradition and imitators of Pliny and Livy. Bodin was both a humanist jurist and a *politique*, La Mothe le Vayer was both a humanist and a philosophical libertine. The *querelle* of the ancients and the moderns might serve as an indicator of a change of attitude towards the classical inheritance in the seventeenth century, but the dispute in reality was largely rhetorical, as many *savants* and *philosophes* writing in either camp shared much of their erudition and may be defined as both 'late humanist' and 'modern' within a cosmopolitan republic of letters.[30] Montaigne, defender of the ancients, also became one of the most influential writers in a republic of letters which increasingly relied on the French language (rather than Latin) to learn about modern scientific and moral ideas. It would certainly be wrong to suggest that whilst the generation of Charron, Botero, Grotius, Peiresc, Galileo and Bacon, or their immediate followers Gassendi, Descartes and Hobbes, is still 'late humanist', the subsequent generation of Huet, Fontenelle, Locke, Bayle and Vico is already 'modern'. In reality, obviously humanist writers of the sixteenth century from Vives to Bodin are in many ways 'moderns', whilst prominent eighteenth-century writers like Montesquieu and Gibbon are still, to a large extent, crucially engaged with the classical example of Rome and its writers.

For my purposes, the issue of defining a particular influence as 'humanist' is perhaps most fruitfully solved not by adopting a highly restrictive definition or an artificial chronology, but by considering the existence of a number of 'national' paradigms for the reception and impact of travel writing according to the key political, religious and hence intellectual conditions which operated in each significant cultural area within Europe. The contrast between the English and the Spanish cultural models is, for example, very striking, and can be used to illustrate the role of these local conditions.

In Spain, the opportunities to create and consume travel literature were soon vast and unique, as the Catholic monarchy claimed overlordship not only over many key commercial centres across Europe (including city-ports like Seville, Antwerp, Barcelona, and Naples), but also over vast territories overseas, from the Canary Islands, through the

---

[30] For a classic account of the querelle's significance see Paul Hazard, *La crise de la conscience européenne 1680-1715* (Paris, 1935), ch. 2. For a recent assesment see Marc Fumaroli, 'Les abeilles et les araignées', *La querelle des anciens et des modernes* (Gallimard: 2001), 7-218.

Americas, to the Philippines. However, much of what was written about non-European peoples was mediated by missionary concerns, and a lay historiography about empire informed by humanist models was often severely limited in its public expression by Crown patronage and censorship. Administrative concerns generated a great deal of geography and ethnography, but, with the exception of some historical works, very little was destined for publication, or allowed to flourish once published. This is also true of the juridical and theological debates undertaken by defenders and attackers of the rights and wrongs of the conquest: these debates were considered perfectly legitimate, but they took place within particular institutional channels which led from the University to the Royal Council whilst generally avoiding a wider reading public. The nature of the Spanish reception of Italian humanism mirrored these constraints. Despite the existence of a strong political connection to Italy, the process of cultural reception was highly selective both in terms of the genres that received institutional support, and in terms of the ideological positions which were considered legitimate. In particular, an incipient Erasmian culture at the court of Charles V was soon marginalized under the pressure of the Inquisition, and eventually, under Philip II, subjected to a powerful Counter-Reformation censorship. Although classical culture was generally received, and there was a great deal of creativity through the adaptation of literary genres (many of Italian origin) in the vernacular, historical, scientific and geographical erudition soon lagged behind, and philosophical discourse was generally conservative. Even Stoic rational cosmopolitanism, and Platonic mysticism, both of which appealed to many Spanish humanists as eirenicist in spirit but generally compatible with the Catholic tradition, were suspect. Important humanists like Fadrique Furió Ceriol, an original political thinker who had planned a universal history of the New World, were put under pressure to abandon contentious (because too liberal, we might say) views and stopped publishing; others like the Biblical scholar Benito Arias Montano and his Ciceronian disciple Pedro de Valencia (who was employed by the Council of Indies as compiler of geographical relations) were watched closely and became extremely circumspect, and still others like the doctor Francisco Hernández, commissioned by Philip II to undertake an important botanical expedition in America, saw their work—including an antiquarian account of the Mexican past—almost buried in the royal Library of Escorial.[31] The interesting views about

---

[31] This is not the place to review the curious debate on whether a genuine humanistic

Turkish customs expressed in a humanist dialogue like the anonymous *Viaje de Turquía* were never available to the reading public.[32] Interestingly, none of the major travel collections of the sixteenth and seventeenth centuries was published in Spain. It is true that, despite the prominence of missionaries in the study of American Indian traditions (as well as the gentile civilizations of Asia), writers like Oviedo, Gómara, Zárate, Sepúlveda and Herrera did create a tradition of imperial historiography with an important ethnographic and natural-historical component.[33] Yet even they, nationalist propagandists par excellence, often saw their work censored for political reasons, or failed to continue to publish (some prominent humanists active in America, like Pedro Sarmiento de Gamboa who worked for the viceroy of Peru, or Francisco Cervantes de Salazar who had the patronage of the city of Mexico, failed to publish their

---

movement existed in sixteenth-century Spain, where genuine 'classical philologists' were replaced by 'lawyers and theologians who had a training in humanist Latin and classical literature' (Jeremy Lawrence, 'Humanism in the Iberian Peninsula', in A. Goodman and A. MacKay [eds.] *The impact of Humanism in Western Europe* [London, 1990], 249). On the nature of Spanish humanism in general see José-Luis Abellán, *El Erasmismo Español* (Madrid, 1976); Luis Gil Fernández, *Panorama Social del Humanismo Español 1500-1800* (Madrid, 1981) and José Antonio Maravall, 'La diversificación de modelos de Renacimiento. El Renacimiento Español y el Renacimiento Francés', in *Estudios de Historia del Pensamiento Español*, vol. II 'La época del Renacimiento' (Madrid, 1984), 123-92. On Furió Ceriol and his project see Ronald Truman, *Spanish Treatises on Government, Society and Religion in the Time of Philip II* (Leiden, 1999), 89-114, and the still relevant Henri Méchoulan, *Raison et alterité chez Fadrique Furió Ceriol* (Paris and The Hague, 1973). Montano is discussed by B. Rekers, *Benito Arias Montano* (London and Leiden, 1972), and Pedro de Valencia has recently attracted the attention of Gaspar Morocho and Jesús Paniagua, who are publishing an ambitious series of *Obras Completas* (León, 1993-). For an overview see Jesús Paniagua, 'El Humanismo Español y la Crónica Oficial de Indias de Pedro de Valencia', *Caravelle* 76-77 (2001): 223-34. For a recent discussion of why the botanical work by Francisco Hernández could not be published without further adaptation to European cultural assumptions see Jesús Bustamante, 'Francisco Hernández, Plinio del Nuevo Mundo: Tradición Clásica, Teoría Nominal y Sistema Terminológico Indígena en una Obra Renacentista', in Berta Ares and Serge Gruzinski (eds.) *Entre Dos Mundos. Fronteras Culturales y Agentes Mediadores* (Seville, 1997), 243-68. Despite the hesitations of Philip II, eventually a summary and partial edition appeared in Rome (1648).

[32] Famously attributed to Andrés Laguna by Bataillon, but still controversial. See Marcel Bataillon, *Erasmo y España. Estudios sobre la historia espiritual del siglo XVI* 2nd ed. in Spanish (Madrid, 1966), pp. 669-92, but for a different view F.G. Salinero (ed.) *Viaje de Turquía* (Madrid, 1980). At this stage, perhaps more interesting than establishing authorship is discussing further the dialogue's rhetorical aims.

[33] These writers of course relied on being able to use a wide range of sources, including some produced by the friars whose political views to a large extent they opposed. Hence Gómara was able to give some depth to his account to Mesoamerican culture by using materials collected by the Franciscan missionary Toribio de Motolinía, who albeit less radical than Las Casas, would not have enjoyed Gómara's overall denigration of native customs and political organisation.

major historical works despite enjoying such high connections).[34] Generally speaking, within the Hispanic Renaissance, the humanist *letrado* was conditioned by service to a Crown which struggled to define a paternalistic justification for empire, and which tended to promote an ideologically restrictive university education largely geared towards limited practical ends.

The Jesuits' model of a methodical training in the humanities purified of heterodox religious or philosophical opinions expressed well both the selective nature of Counter-Reformation humanism, and the leading role of the religious orders in the Spanish historiography of human diversity. However, missionary writers like the Franciscan Bernardino de Sahagún also suffered from royal censorship. Because they documented idolatry so extensively, in fact it became quite rare for these authors to see their histories published. The ambitious political cosmography by the Augustinian Jerónimo Román, *Repúblicas del Mundo* (Medina del Campo, 1575) was quite unique in that the author actually overcame the obstacles of inquisitorial censorship, to produce a second revised version in 1595 which still included a substantial amount of materials from Las Casas' apologetic analysis of the civilizations of Mexico and Peru. Most of the missionary ethnography and antiquarianism exercised its influence through a number of complex manuscript transmissions and influences. It is, for example, interesting to note that some of the main *letrado* specialists on Indian law—writers like Alonso de Zorita or Juan Polo de Ondegardo—often relied on missionary sources and contacts, and responded to the terms of the debate about Indian capacities and rights set by those religious writers (and, in fact, it was almost

---

[34] Cervantes de Salazar however was doing little more than following Gómara, who had succeeded more than others cared to admit. Another interesting example is Fernán Pérez de Oliva, humanist orator and moral philosopher who is best known for his *Dialogue on the Dignity of Man* (posthumously published in 1546 by Cervantes de Salazar and by Oliva' nephew Ambrosio de Morales). In the 1520s, before joining the University of Salamanca, Oliva had sought the patronage of both Hernando Colón [Ferdinand Columbus] and Hernán Cortés by producing two heroic accounts of discovery and conquest in the vernacular, the first based on translating material from Peter Martyr of Anghiera, the second by re-writing Cortés' own second letter. See J.J. Arrom (ed.) *Historia de la Invención de las Yndias* (Bogotá, 1965) and William Atkinson, 'Hernán Pérez de Oliva. A biographical and critical Study', *Revue Hispanique* 72 (1927): 309-484 (which includes Oliva's incomplete narrative of the conquest of New Spain). Possibly the patronage was too weak and nothing was published, but essentially these humanist rhetorical projects were taken up by Ferdinand Columbus himself, who produced the apologetic biography of his father (it eventually appeared, but only in Italian) and by Gómara, by far the most successful of these writers.

impossible to avoid having to define a position for, or against, the radically pro-Indian theses of Bartolomé de Las Casas).[35] Despite these constraints, by the first decade of the seventeenth century occasional
publications, like the account of the Philippines by the royal judge
Antonio de Morga, demonstrate the continual potential for a lay ethnography, whilst the more ambitious historical works by Inca Garcilaso and
Bartolomé Leonardo de Argensola exemplify the survival of a humanist
historiography with Stoic and Platonic themes which was alternative not
only to a religious monopoly of exotic historiography, but also to the
dominant, Castilian-centered imperialist school represented by Gómara
and Herrera.[36]

It has often been remarked that English interest in travel writing was
closely associated with the growth of an imperialist ideology in the second half of the sixteenth century, and can be studied as one aspect of
the relatively late but extremely wide-ranging reception of continental
Renaissance culture in the island, beginning with the publication of
Iberian materials by Richard Eden and Richard Willes in their pioneering
collections. In a recent work, Andrew Fitzmaurice provides an account
of the role of humanism in shaping an English imperial discourse, based
on the analysis of promotional literature for the early colonial ventures.
In particular, he emphasizes the presence of 'deliberative rhetoric' as
crucial to the development of a humanist (and ultimately Ciceronian
and Machiavellian) moral discourse concerning 'good government', exploring in some detail the tension between virtue and profit.[37] The significance
of this promotional genre, and indeed of the Machiavellian moral idiom,
was as we have seen rather minimal in the Iberian empires, where, on
the other hand, the existence of an 'imperial' historiography inspired
by humanist rhetorical strategies and Ciceronian themes would seem
rather crucial.[38] This prompts the question of whether there were different

---

[35] Neither Zorita nor Polo de Ondegardo published their works.

[36] It is safe to say that in general in Spain the humanist tradition was imperialist
rather than humanitarian, and used a hierarchical concept of civilization to deny rights
to the natives. However, it would be wrong to reduce the anti-imperialist emphasis on
native innocence and Christian corruption to a scholastic discourse monopolized by missionary friars and neo-Thomist theologians.

[37] Andrew Fitzmaurice, *Humanism and America: An Intellectual History of English Colonization
1500-1625* (Cambridge, 2003).

[38] The boundary between Machiavellian and Ciceronian views is sometimes very subtle, especially as Cicero's views moved between Stoic or Platonic rational idealism and
academic skepticism. In particular, whilst it was possible to adopt a secular and relativist
Machiavellian reading of the *De officiis* concerning the relation between *utile* and *honestum*,

strands of humanism, with the possibility for radically different ideological manifestations, or whether only northern-English—but not southern and Iberian—humanism was 'true' humanism, because it was more
clearly civic and more radically Machiavellian. More sensibly, we may
query whether any definition of humanism, in England or elsewhere,
which takes the moral issue of profit and virtue in a civic context as
its central concern, or which circumscribes the impact of deliberative
rhetoric to 'an argument for profit and possession', is perhaps reductionist
(and I would certainly disagree with the contention that it was in England
alone that 'the humanist imagination dominated colonising projects').
My argument would be, rather, that any analysis of this issue must be
properly comparative, as not only was humanism at root an international
influence, but indeed the issues which crystallized the humanists' use of
travel writing—issues of moral philosophy, science and empire—were
also largely international in scope and impact. Hence the existence of
national paradigms, analyzed through their mutual interaction rather
than in isolation, not only provides us with the basis for a geography
of reception but, more interesting, with the basis also for a general
chronology of intellectual transformation.

We could argue that, roughly speaking, there were three main phases
in the history of the humanist appropriation of travel writing. The first,
between 1450 and the 1550s, was dominated by the Iberian colonial
experience, but was also closely connected to Italian humanist models
and reception (and in fact the most important travel collections were
published in, or near, Venice). It was marked by the humanist reception and elaboration of a variety of narratives of exploration and conquest largely written for practical aims, although not without an element
of curiosity. From the 1550's to the 1640's this tradition was superseded
by a 'Counter-Reformation' model, largely formulated by Philip II as
ruler of a vast colonial system, and by the Jesuits as the most intellec-
tually innovative missionary order within the Catholic world. This model
maintained on the one hand a traditional emphasis on Providentialism
combined with a classical education, strengthened by a strong belief in
scientific empiricism. On the other hand, the Crown and the Church
also exercised a strong control of information, and in particular censored
any works describing native idolatry, or espousing the rights of conquerors and settlers over those of the king, or questioning the overall

---

amongst Spanish humanists predominated a Christian Ciceronianism which was philosophically closer to moral realism.

legitimacy of empire. That the Counter Reformation model was subject to important tensions was in part due to national and sectarian rivalries (for example those pitting Dominicans against Jesuits), and in part a consequence of the emergence of the counter-discourse of international Protestantism. This was largely created by French Huguenots, and later developed by English imperialists, or by Dutch and German publicists. Although this Protestant counter-discourse initially seemed dominated by an anti-Spanish Black Legend, and was therefore marked by the rhetorical use of the savage as innocent victim of Catholic falsehood and cruelty, it also produced an independent tradition of humanist claims to imperial dominion which combined rights to trade with gentile nations with rights to punish and dispossess them.[39]

From 1610 to the 1720s we can talk about a transfer of leaderships. On the one hand, after precipitating the collapse of the Spanish system, France took over the Catholic imperialist discourse, only to witness a number of antiquarian and philosophical debates which exposed fatal internal divisions within the missionary movement (especially when Gallicans, Dominicans and Jansenists combined to attack the Jesuits), as well as a growing vulnerability to sceptical and anti-religious arguments. On the other hand, leadership in compiling and publishing travel narratives and cosmographies moved to the Netherlands, although important texts and collections were also published in France and England. There was also a general shift in the genre of travel writing, as the traditional control of the ethnographic discourses by practical explorers, missionaries and armchair cosmographers was challenged by independent lay travellers and by antiquarian scholars often pursuing contradictory strategies. Although many of these travellers and antiquarians were still by training and ideology late humanists, and relied on classical lore and philological skill for much of their thinking, others increasingly espoused new post-sceptical philosophies, and often came to challenge the genres, methods and assumptions which had characterized the humanists' elaboration of Europe's New Worlds.[40]

---

[39] This tradition is traced by Richard Tuck in *The Rights of War and Peace: Political Thought and the International Order from Grotius to Kant* (Oxford, 1999). For a comparative account of imperial claims, Anthony Pagden, *Lords of All the World: Ideologies of Empire in Spain, Britain and France c. 1500–c. 1800* (New Haven, Conn., 1995). Benjamin Schmidt, *Innocence Abroad: The Dutch Imagination and the New World* (Cambridge, 2001) offers a detailed account of the rhetorical uses of the American Indian in Dutch culture.

[40] Philosophical historians also in many ways came to challenge the humanist 'art of reading' of primary sources, for example (as Jorge Cañizares-Esguerra has shown) by denying the authority of Amerindian sources and of insufficiently skeptical Renaissance

II

For the purposes of this article, I will focus on the first phase. We can distinguish three key roles adopted by humanists in relation to travel writing: as editors and travel collectors, as historians and philosophers, and as travellers themselves. Each of these roles merits careful analysis. Although my more detailed examples concern the role of humanists as editors, I shall also seek to argue generally that the whole genre was conditioned by humanistic culture, both in terms of production and consumption.[41]

Many humanists influenced the development of the genre of travel writing by acting as editors, translators and travel collectors. From Poggio Braccioloni, who in the mid-fifteenth century wrote up a Latin version of the oriental travels of Nicolò Conti, to Samuel Purchas, who early in the seventeenth century commissioned William Methwold to write up a relation of the South Indian kingdom of Golconda, many examples of the genre of travel writing were shaped by the dialogue between men educated in the humanities and observers who lacked the skills and motivation to write or at least publish on their own initiative. Merchants like Conti and Methwold, soldiers like Hans Staden, or (well into the seventeenth century) sailors like Robert Knox, not only were stimulated to record their observations, but often subjected their spontaneous ethnographies to the methods and interests of their more educated editors (and suffered amplifications and excisions as a result). It was this intervention which produced well-ordered narratives with a scientific, non-fabulous status. It was also as editors that many humanists showed their appreciation for the value of medieval travel narratives—from Marco

---

observers (*How to Write the History of the New World* (Stanford, 2001) 11-129). Paradoxically, this attempt to de-familiarize the 'native other', challenging (for example) the basic humanist equation by which Mexicans and Incas were comparable to Greeks and Romans, only led to a new kind of dogmatism, one which tended to denigrate native achievements—often sounding like a new version of the imperialist thesis first presented by humanist historians of the conquest. In effect, one could argue that the seeds for Enlightenment debates about the reliability of native sources or (conversely) about the validity of philosophical interpretations produced in Europe, can be traced back to the far from homogeneous reception of primary ethnographies and native records by sixteenth-century writers with a humanist educational horizon.

[41] Constraints of space require that in this article, originally destined for a conference on 'The Early Modern Travel Narrative: Production and Consumption', I limit any detailed analysis to the role of humanists as editors. However, as I shall argue more extensively elsewhere, there is a basic continuity of issues between this editorial role and the way humanist historians used primary materials or even (as philosophical travelers) developed their own techniques of observation and interpretation.

Polo's widely read account, printed in Portuguese by the Moravian printer Valentim Fernandes, in Spanish by Rodrigo de Santaella, and in Italian by Ramusio, to the more obscure account of an early-fifteenth century Castilian embassy to Timur, first published in Seville by the erudite antiquarian Argote de Molina in 1582.

When considering the logic of editorial interventions and its impact, we encounter again the need to distinguish different degrees of humanistic training and vocation. We must begin by acknowledging the role of many clerics with knowledge of classical literature. For example Rodrigo de Santaella, who translated Marco Polo into Castilian in 1503, was a canon of the cathedral of Seville best known for his religious works, but he had also travelled in Italy, acquired a knowledge of Greek uncommon in Spain, and on his return acted as a prominent patron of higher education, incorporating the liberal arts. He can be considered as a Christian humanist.[42] Similarly, Hans Staden's German account of his captivity with the cannibals (Marburg, 1557) was corrected, 'authenticated' and offered as example of Protestant piety by the professor of Medicine and astronomer Johannes Dryander, whilst Robert Knox's account of his captivity in Ceylon was methodically organised by John Strype, an Anglican vicar but also an antiquarian. What is surprising about this case is not only its lateness, but also that Knox could write perfectly well, as he had indeed been to boarding school. What was at stake was not just the capacity to write, but access to the cultural codes, scientific and ideological, controlled by those with a humanistic education.[43] That

---

[42] On Santaella as Christian Humanist see Bataillon, *Erasmo*, 84-5. For a comparison of his translation of Marco Polo with that by Valentim Fernandes, see Francis M. Rogers, 'Valentim Fernandes, Rodrigo de Santaella, and the recognition of the Antilles as opposite-India', *Boletim da sociedade de geografia de Lisboa* 75 (1957): 279-309.

[43] On Staden's self-presentation and his relation to Dryander see Hans Staden, *La mia prigionia fra i cannibali 1553-1555*, edited in Italian by Amerigo Guadagnin (Torino, 1991), xxvii-xxxiv and (for Dryander's preface) 5-11. See also Neil Whitehead, 'Hans Staden and the cultural politics of cannibalism' in *Hispanic American Historical Review* (2000): 721-51, which refers to a new critical edition in preparation with Michael Harbsmeier. Dryander also subjected the author to questioning and compiled an ethnological section. Staden's account saw various German editions, and in 1592 it appeared in Latin in Theodor de Bry's collection. Ulrich Schmidel's narrative of American adventures provides another important German example of the mediation exercised by metropolitan humanist elites in authorizing, editing and publishing primary accounts. First published by Sebastian Franck in 1567, it was included by de Bry in his collection in 1597, and appeared again in both German and Latin (with engravings) as edited and annotated by Levinus Hulsius in Nuremberg in 1599. On Robert Knox and Strype, see S.D. Saparadamu, 'Introduction' to Robert Knox, *A Historical Relation of Ceylon*, in *Ceylon Historical Journal*, V (1958), vii-lv. Knox was also stimulated by the scientific interests of Robert Hooke, who wrote the preface.

the practice persisted in the seventeenth century despite the parallel proliferation of 'educated travellers' is also illustrated by the case of François Pyrard de Laval, whose *Voyage aux Indes orientales* was thoroughly edited and revised by canon Pierre Bergeron in a succession of editions (1611, 1615, 1619).[44] Of course, many humanist travel collectors were also clerics, notably in the Protestant tradition—both Richard Hakluyt and Samuel Purchas fall into this category. In all these cases, the issue is defining the degree of methodological rigour and historical criticism in the actual editorial work.

One important question is the degree of transformation of the primary material determined by the outlook of editors whose erudition was rooted in the classical world. The appeal to ancient models was of course crucial in the representation and interpretation of newly observed religious beliefs and practices which, from a Christian perspective, could only be described as 'gentile'. This tendency also affected the conceptualization of 'gentile' forms of barbarism and civilization. Although these comparisons, analogies and false identifications have sometimes been used to denounce European ethnocentrism, and to emphasize the 'bluntedness' of the impact of the New World, in reality they followed a powerful cultural logic and need not be seen in stark opposition to the development of an empirically-informed and increasingly sophisticated ethnography.

We can use *De insulis nuper inventis*, a letter published in Pavia by the doctor-humanist Nicolaus Scyllacus in 1497 (but written c. 1494) describing the second expedition of Columbus, as an example worth discussing in some detail, as it allows us to investigate the degree of intervention practiced by early Italian humanists upon travel narratives which represented a novelty, and to which they responded within months. Although he had made his career at the University of Pavia, Scyllacus was of Sicilian origin and had been to Spain, where he maintained contacts and (apparently) also wished to return. His letter, translated from a lost account by a certain Guillermo Coma, is marked by an element of pro-Spanish propaganda politically significant at a time when Ferdinand of Aragon's policies were leading towards a sustained clash with French plans for intervention in Italy. Scyllacus can in this respect be compared to Peter Martyr of Anghiera, a Milanese humanist tutor established at the court of the Catholic kings whose famous Latin epistles, eventually

---

[44] On Pyrard de Laval, see Geneviève Bouchon's preface to *Voyage de Pyrard de Laval aux Indes Orientales (1601-1611)*, edited by Xavier de Castro (Paris, 1998).

published as *De Orbe Novo Decades* (in various versions in 1511, 1516, 1521, 1530), were to constitute the first sustained historical narrative concerning the discovery of the New World.[45] Read together, Scyllacus and Martyr allow us to assess the role of humanistic assumptions in the translation and literary elaboration of the Columbian material.

One striking theme which Scyllacus and Anghiera share, and which I shall take as point of departure for a more extended discussion, is their reference of the mythical Golden Age of primitive mankind—the age of Saturn—in relation to the Indians of the western islands. This classical myth, originally part of Hesiod's *Works and Days*, was well known through the works of many Latin poets of the Augustan age, most clearly Ovid, but also Virgil, Horace and others.[46] Not only were these poets widely read throughout the Latin Middle Ages, but the theme was also 'Christianized' by Lactantius, an influential apologete of the early fourth century widely read by Christian humanists. Lactantius in effect gave the theme a new utopian, millenarian direction by making the messianic theme of the second coming the equivalent of the return of the Golden Age, distinguished by the return of justice and plenty to earth.[47] Many humanists were therefore imbued with this classical image, which had, to some extent, entered the popular literary imagination. From this perspective, it makes sense to ask whether the appearance of the image of the Golden Age in the islands discovered by Columbus and his companions through the writings of Scyllacus and Anghiera represented a humanist distortion of the primary material they handled.[48]

---

[45] Anghiera's work was influential throughout educated Europe (beginning with Italy), and indeed the key historical work on the subject until the 1550's. For a partial recent edition in English and Latin, with an elaborate commentary, see Geoffrey Eatough, (ed. and trans.), *Selections from Peter Martyr*, in 'Repertorium Columbianum', V (Turnhout, 1990). I quote according to decade, chapter and paragraph, but also give references to Eatough's translation, which after comparison with the Latin I have used as basis for quotations.

[46] Besides the better-known writers, we may also note the importance of Latin translations of the cosmological poem by Aratus.

[47] Lactantius, *The Divine Institutes*, translated with an introduction and notes by Anthony Bowen and Peter Garnsey (Liverpool, 2003), Books V.5 and VII.24. However, like many early Christians, Lactantius thought that the second coming was about to happen, to coincide with what he believed was the imminent collapse of the Roman Empire.

[48] This is at least Rosario Romeo's view: 'passando nelle mani di umanisti a giorno delle formule e dei moduli della cultura classica, il quadro viene assumendo i caratteri sempre più specifici della classica "età dell'oro", nella quale il motivo comunistico della assenza di tuo e di mio ha rilievo assai maggiore che nei miti medievali, dei quali soprattutto Colombo aveva subito l'influsso' (*Le scoperte americane*, 16).

Scyllacus' most far-reaching passage in relation to the classical myth of the golden age concerns the Indians of Hispaniola:

> Their customs are peaceful [*mores illis placabiles*]. All things are held in common; there is no indication of avarice, none of that shameful "this is mine, this is yours"; no desire for other people's property, no lust for possessions. Envy has been chased away and everyone has the same sentiments: mutual benevolence, equal fidelity and respect [*observantia*].[49]

Elsewhere these Indians are described as healthy, good-looking, clean, simple in their needs, pleasure-loving, naked and playful but ultimately modest, and eager to imitate the Europeans. Scyllacus, in agreement with the majority of sources for the first Columbian expeditions, echoes the distinction between these 'innocent' Indians and the fiercer Caribs they are said to be prey to. These Cannibals are described somewhat differently: strong, clever and skilful; it is interesting to note that these aptitudes will allow them to learn civilized behavior quickly—they are not therefore excluded from an ideal of integration within Christendom.

Where does the image of peaceful and benevolent natives come from? And what does it mean? We should, in particular, beware of jumping to conclusions about a 'noble savage', as the theme was in fact formulated in a variety of forms and only emerges clearly (but not definitely) later in the sixteenth century, in the works of French writers like Jean the Léry and Montaigne. It is however obvious that in this passage an idea of innocence is being proposed which does contain a potential for criticism of European civilization, in the sense that these Indians are exempt from many of the ills associated with vanity and greed— the kinds of ills denounced by Thomas More in his Christian humanist Utopia a few years later. As for the source of Scyllacus' inspiration, it is tempting to believe that the humanist doctor was alone responsible for elaborating the image of the Caribbean Indians with echoes from the Golden Age described by Ovid, that is, the primitive age when men 'unconstrained, with heart and soul, obedient to no law, gave honor to good faith and righteousness', so that they were secure without judges, needed no arms, and 'the world, untroubled, lived in leisured

---

[49] Nicolaus Syllacius *De insulis meridiani atque Indicii Maris nuper inventis*, ed. and trans. by J. Mulligan (New York, 1859), 82-4. I have used this edition as it offers both the Latin text and an English translation face-to-face. I have also consulted the annotated edition by Luciano Formisano with facing Italian translation, in Gabriella Airaldi and Luciano Formisano (eds.), *La Scoperta nelle Relazioni Sincrone degli Italiani* 'Nuova Raccolta Colombiana' (Rome, 1996), 107-67.

ease'.[50] We can certainly see how elsewhere Scyllacus fills his pompous Latin version with references to Pliny and borrowings from Strabo: despite his declaration to the contrary, when translating his source Scyllacus was obviously tempted to add his own geographical specula-tions and to display his classical erudition (this led him to an interest-ing mistake concerning the route followed by the expedition, imagining that Columbus had travelled around Africa and towards the Indian Ocean, rather than across the Atlantic). However, against this evidence of erudite intervention, which tends to complement (rather than make up) the key descriptive passages, I believe it to be very likely that behind Scyllacus' image of the Golden Age there was an empirical observation already present in Coma's Spanish letter. That would be a statement to the effect that the people of Hispaniola do not value possessions, a statement inspired by evidence of their relative contempt for gold, and supported by their nakedness, timidity and apparent innocence, all of which other observers, including Columbus, had noted. The key issue is therefore clarifying the relationship between the humanist writer and his empirical source.

The source for Scyllacus, the 'illustrious Spaniard' called Guillermo Coma, possibly Aragonese or Catalan, remains a bit of a mystery (some, rather foolishly, have even denied his existence). In fact the issue of authorship raises interesting points about the way humanists received and used primary reports. Coma probably did not travel with Columbus, not only because his name has not appeared in any of the records of the expedition, but also because this would have made it difficult for him to write to Scyllacus in Pavia quickly enough, unless we assume that he left with some of the returning ships which captain Antonio Torres (as planned) took to Spain in February 1494. This in turn would make little sense, as it is in fact obvious from the contents of the *De insulis*, which offer a detailed narrative of the expedition up until February 1494, that the source letter was sent precisely with these ships—and whoever sent it must have stayed behind. Coma, on the other hand, refers to one authority by name, Pedro Margarit, a nobleman of the household of King Ferdinand who had joined Columbus' second expe-dition. Margarit stayed in Hispaniola in February and exercised a position of responsibility as Columbus' military right hand until he left, together with fellow-Aragonese friar Bernat Boil, in September 1494, disillusioned

---

[50] Ovid, *Metamorphoses*, I.88 ff; I have used A.D. Melville's translation (Oxford, 1986), 3-4.

with the local conditions and with Columbus' rule, in this way inaugurating the succession of desertions and complaints to the court which would plague Columbus' colonial governorship.[51]

Scyllacus explains that he translated the letter into Latin as soon as he received it from Coma. Scyllacus' Latin version was written by December 1494, the date of the two dedications, although only published later, probably in 1497. Hence it is likely that Guillermo Coma received, or had access to, a letter sent in February 1494 by Pedro Margarit (or someone close to him).[52] Coma then sent a version to Scyllacus, whom he may have met either at University in Italy, or when Scyllacus was still in Spain. I am inclined to believe that, in turn, Coma transmitted rather faithfully the contents of the letter he had copied or been sent, one similar in structure and narrative strategy to the better known letter of the same expedition written for the town council of Seville by the Andalusian royal physician Diego Álvarez Chanca.[53] It also seems likely that Coma interviewed one or more of the members of the expedition to ask for corroboration or clarification—this at least is suggested by a comment he inserts concerning the finding of gold.[54] Coma, whether the Catalan doctor suggested by Spanish editor Juan Gil, or another friend of Margarit, wrote in the vernacular, leaving Scyllacus ample room to make the Latin version more erudite and more confusing.[55]

---

[51] Margarit came from a Catalan noble family, although he had settled in Aragon. Friar Bernat (or Bernardo) Boil was probably of Aragonese origin, although he had made his ecclesiastical career mainly in Catalonia. Both were close servants to the Trastamatra king of the Crown of Aragon. For details of Margarit's background and career see Manuel Serrano y Sanz, *Orígenes de la dominación española en América* I (Madrid, 1918) ch. 7.

[52] An intriguing possibility is that Boil, a Minim friar (but formerly Benedictine) in charge of organising the evangelisation of the Indians, was the author of the letter copied (possibly only in part) by Coma. Boil is known to have sent a letter to the Catholic kings with Torres in February 1494. Boil might have sent a copy to Coma. He could also have easily communicated some of Margarit's observations.

[53] Chanca's letter is published in *Cartas de particulares a Colón y relaciones coetáneas*, edited by Juan Gil and Consuelo Varela (Madrid, 1984), 152-77. It contains no reference to a Golden Age. Instead, Chanca is emphatic that the natives are idolaters and that their apparel is such that it would suit madmen in Spain.

[54] 'illud pulcherrimum, quod scribere puduisset me, nisi ex fide fuisset acceptum, percusso clava saxo, quod monti adiacet, prosiliisse magnam auri quantitatem . . .' Scyllacus, *De insulis* (1859), pp. 78-80.

[55] Juan Gil, in the commentary to his Spanish version of Scyllacus' letter, suggests Coma's identification with a Barcelona doctor. See *Cartas de particulares*, 177. Gil's edition offers alternative readings and is a useful complement to Mulligan's. Many of his findings, including the identification of Coma with the Catalan doctor, are taken up by Formisano, *La Scoperta* (1996).

We do not have Coma's original letter to test the hypothesis that the humanist's Golden Age theme was actually based on original material, but we can be more decisive with a similar, and more famous, report by Anghiera relating to Cuba. This appeared in the third book of his first decade, addressed to Cardinal Luis of Aragón (and to King Federico, of the Neapolitan branch of the Aragonse Trastamara family). It was signed as written in 1501, but from materials relating to the second voyage (February 1494 to February 1495). This six-year perspective, for example, allowed Anghiera to write about Cuba as 'the land which Columbus thought was a continent'.[56]

This is how Anghiera introduced his more explicit theme of the Golden Age:

> It has been discovered that with them the land, like the sun and water, is common, nor do "mine and yours", the seeds of all evils, fall among them. They are content with so little that in that vast earth there is an excess of land to farm rather than lack of anything. Theirs is a Golden Age [*aetas est illis aurea*]: they do not hedge their estates with ditches, walls or hedges; they live with open gardens; without laws, without books, without judges, of their own nature they cultivate what is right. They judge he is evil and wicked who takes pleasure in inflicting injury on anyone. Nonetheless, they cultivate maize, yuca and *ajes*...[57]

Is this, again, the humanist's fanciful invention? Here the reference to the 'Golden Age' points directly to the classical poets. On the other hand, the whole tenor of the letter assumes that Anghiera, based in the Spanish Court, is reporting on the basis of written and oral accounts received from the newly discovered lands. The passage can not be read in isolation from the general narrative, which is empirically informed and in part was based on Columbus' own writings. Anghiera, for example, when relating Columbus' exploration of Cuba (which concludes with this passage) used material contained in the recently published *libro copiador* (in particular, Columbus' letter of 26.2.1495). Columbus' letter offers the following passage at this point of the narrative:

> Ya yo dixe cómo estos caciques no tienen bienes propios, y que ansí me lo avían dicho, porque la tierra es tan grande y tan fértil que sobrara aunque ubiese cien veces otros tantos.[58]

---

[56] Anghiera was in fact always doubtful of Columbus' geographical notions (Edmundo O'Gorman, 'Pedro Mártir y el proceso de América', *Cuatro Historiadores de Indias*, Mexico 1972, 13-37).

[57] Anghiera, 1.3.24. See Eatough, *Selections*, 69 (155 for the Latin).

[58] 'I already said that these *caciques* have no private goods, and that this had been reported to me, because the land is so large and fertile that there would be an excess even if there were one hundred times as many [people]'. I quote the letter from the

For Columbus this lack of private property was a problem, as he was concerned with confirming that Cuba was the same Cathay described by Marco Polo, as he makes clear in the following lines when he declares his hope that the interior will resemble better the urbanized and wealthy Cathay described in the 'histories about this province'. It seems clear that Anghiera has been prompted by this passage about lack of private property (we can follow the textual link), but he has also totally transformed the emphasis by elaborating extensively the image of the Golden Age.[59] Interestingly, with this Columbian source now published, it is easier to be precise about the amount of fictionalization created by Anghiera, far too often exaggerated.

Let us also note that the image of the Caribbean Indians offered by Anghiera is not always positive: for example, these people of Cuba are also 'idle', since they do not work the abundant cotton to make themselves clothes as protection from the cold of the mountains. The whole passage is written after 'cannibals' have been described, and after the tragedy of the town of Navidad has cast a shadow over the peoples of Hispaniola. Quite clearly, *the idea of the Golden Age targets a specific set of features of the native way of life*, rather than seeking to confer upon them an idealized mythical status. The literary elaboration is however Anghiera's work: he needed little more than what Columbus or another observer could have said in order to be transported to the Golden Age of the classical poets, as many primary descriptions already suggested natural innocence. (In Columbus' first letter to Santángel, these Indians are naked, timid, innocent, good-looking, without idolatry, and in sum, 'sin engaño y liberales de lo que tienen', without malice and free with their possessions). Elsewhere Anghiera states (as later pro-native writers like Las Casas, Pedro Cieza and Inca Garcilaso would often concede) that these people are ignorant of the Christian revelation, and indeed in this

---

libro copiador as edited by Juan Gil in Cristóbal Colón, *Textos y documentos completos*, ed. by Consuelo Varela, and *Nuevas cartas*, ed. by Juan Gil (Madrid, 1992) [document XIII, pp. 286-315], p. 307. Hence Rosario Romeo was mistaken in suggesting that the theme of lack of private property was purely humanist, and not Columbian (see n. 48 above).

[59] Columbus never refers to the Golden Age (whilst he talks a great deal about Paradise), although there is evidence that he had read Ovid's *Metamorphoses*, and in particular the first book, since he copied some verses on the end flyleaves of his copy of the *Historia Rerum Ubique Gestarum* of Pius II, following Toscanelli's famous letter and some other extracts. However, these verses only dealt with the formation of the Universe and of the four elements out of chaos (Flint, *Imaginative Landscape*, 63). It seems that Columbus, with his Providentialist beliefs, was far more interested in cosmology than in the image of the Golden Age of mankind.

passage Columbus is made to equate 'the state of nature' with such ignorance.[60]

More intriguing is the preceding speech by an old chief, naked but full of gravitas, offering Columbus a moral warning which has been 'translated' into Christian terms:

> News has been brought us that, trusting in your powerful hand, you have travelled through these lands until now unknown to you, and have brought no ordinary fear to the people living there; I warn you then to be aware that when they leave the body souls have two paths, one gloomy and hideous, prepared for those who cause trouble and are the enemies of the human race, the other delightful and pleasant, appointed for those who in their lives have loved peace and quiet among nations. If, therefore, you remember that you are mortal, and that rewards will be duly assigned to each in accordance to his present actions, you will attack no one.[61]

This need not be entirely fictional either, as Ferdinand Columbus related the same encounter and even dated it. More decisively, it is contained in the letter by Columbus of 26.2.1495, which must have been the basis for the other versions. In Columbus' own account we also find an elaborate speech by the 'very old man' (presumably the *cacique*'s father), and although communication was rudimentary, the gist is the same. Columbus' letter reads:

> él avía sabido cómo yo avía corrido todas las islas y tierra firme, la cual era aquella en que nosotros estávamos [incidentally, a strong indication of authenticity for the *libro copiador*, as only Columbus could have made the old cacique identify Cuba with the mainland!], y que yo no tomase banagloria puesto que todo el mundo oviese miedo, porque yo hera mortal como todos los otros: y de aquí començó con palabras y señas afigurando en su persona cómo nos naçimos y teníamos ánima, y mostrando el humor [Rubiés correcting Gil's 'amor'] que tenía con el cuerpo, y que del mal de cada cuerpo ella era la que se dolía, y al tiempo de la

---

[60] 'until then he [Columbus] had thought that such things were unknown to him [the old man] and the other inhabitants of those regions, as they lived happily in their natural state' (Anghiera 1.3.21). I can not find an equivalent expression in Columbus' writings. On the other hand, I am very reluctant to agree with modern English editor Geoffrey Eatough's statement that Anghiera is actually claiming that the natives, because they live in a Golden Age and have a moral idiom, do not actually need any Christian faith to be saved—that good actions (natural ethics) are sufficient for salvation (*Selections*, 303). This is reading a late-seventeenth century libertine position (or a controversial sixteenth-century theological definition of implicit faith, or *fides in voto*) back on a markedly pious Renaissance humanist whose enthusiasm for the Spain of Ferdinand and Isabella was inspired by its war against Muslim 'infidels' and by the expulsion of the Jews.

[61] Anghiera, 1.3.21. See Eatough, *Selections*, 68 (154 for the Latin). In his commentary Eatough acknowledges, but also underplays, Martyr's possible dependence upon Columbus as source.

muerte al despedimiento d'él sentía gran pena, y qu'esta ánima iba al rey del çielo
o en el avismo de la tierra, según el bien o el mal que avía obrado en el mundo.[62]

It is very clear that Anghiera followed Columbus for his version—
suggesting that even the most apparently fictionalized of the humanist's
paragraphs are prompted by an 'authentic' source. All he needed to do
when adapting the material for his Latin epistle was to recast this speech
rhetorically—there was no need to consult classical sources describing
(for example) the encounter between Alexander and the Indian brahmins
in order to give the speech the tone and dignity of a classical oration.
In fact, we may add, the encounter described in these passages makes
sense: surely the distinction between two kinds of behavior, 'good' and
'bad', would have concerned the chief, who was aware of what was
happening in Hispaniola and was afraid for his own people. Whatever
his beliefs concerning the path of the human soul (we will never know,
although we may want to consider Ramon Pané's account of the religious
mythology of the Indians of Hispanola), the speech would have been
'translated' by Columbus himself in terms of rewards and punishments
in an afterlife. The linguistic context gave Columbus a great deal of
flexibility. An Indian baptized (according to Anghiera) as Diego Columbus
acted as interpreter, and Columbus emphasized that this Indian, whom
he had taken to Spain after the first expedition, now understood Castilian
well.

---

[62] 'He had learnt how I had travelled through all the islands and mainland, which
was the one where we were at that moment, but that I should not grow vain just because
everybody was afraid of us, because I was mortal like all the others; and from here, he
began with words and signs to show on his own person how we all are born and have a
soul, and showing her humour with the body, and how it was the soul which suffered
when any member was hurt, and that at the time of death, when relinquishing it [the
body], she [the soul] felt very sad; and that this soul went to the king of heaven or to
the depths of the earth, depending on the good or ill works which she had done whilst
in the world'. Colón, *Textos y documentos*, p. 306. As Gil notes, the *libro copiador* contains
many scribal errors and requires a number of editorial interpretations. For a facsimile
(and first transcription) see Antonio Rumeu de Armas, *Manuscrito del libro copiador de
Cristóbal Colón* (Madrid, 1989), 2 vols. (see facs. F. 19r; transcription p. 509). Here I have
altered the reading commonly given 'amor' for 'humor', because the sentence otherwise
makes no sense; an alternative would be to replace 'con' for 'por', translating 'showing
the love she [the soul] had *for* the body'. The parish priest and chronicler Andrés
Bernáldec, who had access to a copy of this Columbian document in 1496, paraphrases
the caciques' speech with some interesting variants but omits this one sentence (*Memorias
del Reinado de los Reyes Católicos*, eds. M. Gómez Moreno and J. de Mata Carriazo [Madrid,
1962], 326). There is a further version of the speech reported by Las Casas who, as is
well known, had access to some of Columbus' personal papers. However, in this case
Las Casas seems to follow Anghiera, not Columbus.

One conclusion we can reach from these examples is that humanist editors—or humanist historians, as in Anghiera's case the two roles blur—had an important role in re-casting the primary material in terms that spoke to the moral, scientific and philosophical themes of classical culture. However, they did not simply impose classical assumptions to the point of inventing a new ethnography: more often they showed a great respect for empirical details contained in the primary narratives produced by the less educated observers.

This respect for the 'raw sources' becomes especially clear if we consider the standards of textual transmission which humanist editors applied to the collections of travel which were published throughout the sixteenth century, from the early examples of Valentim Fernandes (Lisbon, 1502) and Françanzano da Montalboddo (Vicenza, 1507), through the more ambitious *Novus Orbis ac insularum veteribus incognitarum* (Basel 1532, 1537, 1555), and, most important, the three volumes of Giovanni Ramusio's highly influential *Navigationi et Viaggi* (Venice, 1550-59), leading to to the English and German publications by Eden and Willes (1555, 1577), Richard Hakluyt (1589-90; 1590-1600) and Theodor de Bry (1591-1634). All the northern collections relied on Ramusio as a model. Notwithstanding some important variations in editorial practice, these humanist collectors not only made available a vast number of narratives in original or translation, but also came to define the scientific and ideological pretensions of the genre as central to the cosmographical culture of the Renaissance.

Whilst as editors humanists decisively shaped the genre of travel writing in its published form, they also played a crucial role in the transmission and elaboration of primary accounts of exotic encounters as historians, cosmographers, and (often within those genres) philosophical commentators. Some of these writers we may consider as exponents of a lay historiography of the Iberian colonial ventures or, increasingly from the seventeenth century (but still more rarely), those by the French, English and Dutch. Natural histories and cosmographies, however, were far more than an ideological expression of colonial agendas: they also expressed serious scientific and religious concerns. It would be impossible to attempt a comprehensive discussion here, and I shall simply mention some of the historiographical tendencies that from the middle of the sixteenth century were to transform the European perspective on world history. In particular, the historiography of conquest published in this period offers us a platform from which to assess the application of humanist standards to the literature of encounter produced in the previous sixty years. It also illustrates what was available to the educated reader within each national context at a crucial moment in the history of the evolution of humanist culture, as the Christian confessional divide was strengthened along national lines, and the Erasmian tradition of Christian Ciceronianism became marginalized.

The works by Anghiera and Oviedo first represented the history of the New World according to humanist models, in Latin and in vernacular. However, we can consider the decade of the 1550s as crucial in the publication of key works of what we may call the imperial historiography of the Hispanic Renaissance, both in Spain in Portugal, with titles of international resonance like Francisco López de Gómara's *Historia de las Indias y Conquista de Mexico* (1552), Pedro Cieza de León's *Parte primera de la chrónica del Perú* (1553), and Agustín de Zárate's *Historia del descubrimiento y conquista del Perú* (1555), but also the bulk of Fernão Lopes de Castanheda's *História do descobrimento et conquista da Índia pelos Portugueses* (1551-1561) and of João de Barros' *Decadas da Ásia* (1552-1563). All of these works were translated, in part or whole, into at least another European language. It was also in this decade that many of the key accounts of overseas colonization were published in Italy, France, and England, including Ramusio's already mentioned *Delle Navigationi et Viaggi* (1550-59), which made available in Italian and with remarkably modern editorial criteria a great deal of material (old and recent, Iberian or other) about all the parts of the world; André Thévet's *Les Singularitez de la France Antarctique* (1557), extremely influential for its iconography of the Brazilian Indians; and Richard Eden's *The decades of the Newe Worlde of West India* (1555), which largely relied on Spanish and Italian material and inaugurated the belated but, within decades, fundamental tradition of English travel collections. It was also in these years, finally, that the debate in Spain and the Spanish colonies about the rights and wrongs of the conquest came to a head in the dispute at Valladolid between the Dominican missionary Las Casas and the humanist Juan Ginés de Sepúlveda (1550). This was largely an internal debate within the Monarchy of Castile and the Catholic Church, but Las Casas' fatal decision to publish some of his writings in 1552-3 denouncing the Spanish mistreatment of Indians, including the famous *Very brief account of the destruction of the Indies*, also offered readers all over Europe the seeds for what was soon to become the Black Legend, just as Philip II succeeded Charles V to his Spanish, Italian and Flemish dominions.

If the 1550s appear as a crucial decade for the dissemination of the imperial historiography of Spain and Portugal, eventually united after

1580 under the same monarch, the end of the century also represents a watershed, as it saw the crystallization of what we might call a counter-offensive of International Protestantism (soon to break down into a number of distinct national projects in France, England and the Netherlands) which had been building up since the 1560s, from the publication of Girolamo Benzoni's *Historia del Mondo Nuovo* (Venice, 1565), through the works by Léry and Chauveton, up to the massive collections by Hakluyt and Theodor De Bry. There was at the same time, running in parallel we could say, a very assertive Counter Reformation claim to historiographical universalism which was largely dominated by the Jesuits, and which led to the essential works by Maffei, Acosta, Botero and Trigault. It is in fact remarkable the extent to which the shift in the international political landscape was reflected by the historiography of travel and conquest.

These historians of missions constituted one further tradition of production and reception of exotic travel writing, distinct from the lay imperial (and occasionally anti-imperial) historiography. In this case religious concerns dominated, but often by also including political and scientific aims. There was, arguably, a tension between the traditional scholastic training of some religious orders and the increasing reliance on humanistic culture by the Jesuits, although in very few cases can this distinction support a clear-cut opposition. In most of Asia the missionary genre, mainly (but by no means exclusively) represented by Jesuit accounts of India, Japan and China, functioned with independence of any immediate political framework, given the superficial, or otherwise remote, nature of the Portuguese and Dutch imperial systems. By contrast, in the case of America one might be tempted to distinguish sharply two historiographical traditions, one secular, humanist and imperial (even if some of the writers were actually clerics), the other religious and rooted on scholastic theology, clashing around the issue of the justification for conquest and the treatment of the Indians. These two positions, one represented by Oviedo, Gómara and Sepúlveda in Spain, or Barros in Portugal, the other by Las Casas but also influenced by the Dominican neo-Thomist School of Salamanca, would clash philosophically about the interpretation of classical sources for natural law. Hence the scholastic natural law that gave natives a right to private property and political autonomy in civil affairs was opposed to the Ciceronian natural law that made it imperative to conquer and subjugate those otherwise in breach of it (images of sodomy, cannibalism and human sacrifice were routinely invoked to support the latter kind of argument). The two traditions would cast a long shadow towards later historiographies, with for example Antonio de Herrera culminating the elegant Castilian imperial tradition in his Livian *Historia general de los hechos de los castellanos en las islas i tierra firme del mar océano* (1601-15), whilst the contemporary Franciscan Juan de Torquemada with his *Monarquía Indiana* (1615) brought to fruition the chaotic, rhetorically inferior but in some ways well-informed pro-native missionary approach, which he indeed set against Herrera.[63]

We may qualify the opposition of humanist imperialists and scholastic missionaries by noting that the dispute between Las Casas and Sepúlveda in Valladolid only represented the most extreme views within each camp, as writers like Oviedo and Gómara, for example, are not above criticizing Spanish greed and cruelty, and Sepúlveda came later to qualify his denigration of the Indians to some extent. However, the duality must be rejected as simplistic at a deeper level. There were, to begin with, important divisions within the tradition of missionary writings, with for example the Jesuit José de Acosta, whilst in part still an heir to the School of Salamanca, in many ways adopting a much more skeptical view than Las Casas about the moral capacities of the Indians. No less significant is the existence of a current of lay historiography which is best defined as 'Christian humanist' rather than merely imperial, and which sought to integrate a positive view of the providential meaning of the conquest with a profound criticism of its civilizing mission in the light of native accomplishments and Spanish destructiveness.[64] This tradition would be forcefully represented by influential historians of Peru from Pedro Cieza de León, writing at the time of Las Casas and Gómara, to Inca Garcilaso, who was a contemporary of Herrera and Torquemada. Hence whilst it is often true that the more humanistic court writers were less humanitarian than those authors working from a 'medieval' scholastic perspective, there also was an important middle position, ultimately Erasmian and Platonic, struggling to make itself heard, and sometimes succeeding.[65] One could argue that it was the

---

[63] David Brading, *The first America. The Spanish Monarchy, Creole Patriots and the Liberal State* (Cambridge, 1991), 275-92.

[64] These writers emphasized the universality of human nature and the comparability of European and non-European civilizations, often as basis for a softer form of imperial overlordship. Their opponents emphasized a hierarchical view of civilization and questioned the degree of native accomplishments, and even capacities: hence one needed to enforce European civilization in order to spread Christianity.

[65] Here I depart from Richard Tuck's emphatic opposition of the scholastic and humanist traditions in his *The Rights of War and Peace*.

Platonic Garcilaso, rather than Herrera or Torquemada, who would more deeply influence Enlightenment writers.

To these imperial and missionary strands we might want to add cosmographies and political geographies, and the tradition of world history that grew around them, developing with increasing clarity the twin projects of a history of religions and a history of civilization. In the creation of all of these humanistic culture played a crucial role. From the geographical works of Thévet, Botero and Purchas, to the historical ones of Bodin, Le Roy and La Popelinière, there was a little distance. They all led towards the dramatic antiquarian debates of the seventeenth centuries—about primitive religion, the history of idolatry, the history of languages, the history of myths and fables, Biblical and gentile chronologies, the origin of the American Indians, the use of comparative methods, natural religion, and atheism. In these debates the various positions often became tactical moves in a complex struggle between rival orthodoxies (Catholic and Protestant), eirenicist alternatives (Erasmian, Platonic and Stoic, whether Catholic or Protestant), and various forms of libertine thought (Deist or Phyrronian)—with the added complication that many devout Christian writers adopted a methodological scepticism in order to combat atheism from a fideist position, with mixed results.

If philological training and access to the classical tradition made humanists capable editors and influential historians, their active knowledge of the new literature of travel and their participation in the creation of new geographical and historical horizons made it inevitable that men with a humanistic education and a vocation to participate in the republic of letters—men with intellectual projects and cosmopolitan ideals akin to Sieur de la Popelinière's—would eventually become themselves travel writers. There was of course a growing tradition of educational travel within Europe, which was originally mediated by humanists and would lead to the aristocratic Grand Tour. However, in parallel to this we also find from the second half of the sixteenth century a growing number of educated travellers in exotic settings who made writing up their curious observations a central part of their identity as travellers. Although many Jesuit missionaries could be counted within this category, I am here referring specifically to the lay travel writers who operated independently from any strong institutional constraints (even though some, like O'gier de Busbecq, may have been ambassadors), and whose remit went beyond a practical desire for information. From the popularized humanistic culture which informed Vespucci and Pigafetta, to the more thorough formation of writers like Jean de Léry, or of natural historians like Oviedo, Thévet and Hernández, the educated traveller of the sixteenth and seventeenth centuries was essentially a humanistically educated traveller. The process led to those erudite, philosophical and antiquarian observers with whom I began, men like Ogier de Busbecq, George Sandys, Pietro della Valle, François Bernier, Jean Chardin, Paul Rycaut or Gemelli Careri, and finally to the academic travellers of the Enlightenment who emerged in the latter part of the eighteenth century as if responding to Rousseau's call for a truly philosophical traveller—men like Joseph Banks, Anquetil Duperron or Pierre Sonnerat.

It has been my argument that these various generations of philosophical travellers did not in fact emerge out of the Enlightenment, but rather out of a humanistic tradition which preceded the Enlightenment, and which made it possible. I have also suggested (although only a more detailed treatment will allow me to substantiate this fully) that it is incorrect to assume that the inevitable comparisons between the newly described civilizations of America and Asia, and those of the ancient world retrieved by humanist antiquarians, did not lead European scholars to any fundamental change of perception either of their new worlds, or of the ancient world.[66] Instead, I would argue, there was an intricate cross-fertilization of themes, often leading to a subtle intellectual challenge to European assumptions about religion, history and politics. This process was largely fuelled by the crucial role of men imbued with a humanistic culture in the production and consumption of the new literature of travel. From an early stage, humanistic culture permeated the production and elaboration of primary narratives. Late humanist culture defined its new horizons through the consumption of travel narratives. Eventually, the humanist became an antiquarian and a *philosophe* through reading travel, and through writing it.

---

[66] My conclusions are therefore different from those reached by Sabine MacCormack in her otherwise illuminating 'Limits of understanding: perceptions of Greco-Roman and Amerindian Paganism in Early-Modern Europe', in Kupperman (ed.) *America in European Consciousness*, 79-129.